Part 1

'An Incredible Journy'

The life of Grandparents Karl and Idla Noreen

"An incredible journey of remarkable proportion of a courageous couple, from the top of the mountains of Norrland Sweden, to the untamed shores of South East Alaska."

TURIST KLASSE

Norén, Gøte, herr
Norén, Ida, fru
Norén, Karin, frk.
Norén, Ruth, frk.
Norén, Sune, herr
Norén, Karl, herr

Funäsdalen, Sverige

NORWEGIAN SEA
NORWAY
SWEDEN
LAPLAND
GULF OF BOTHNIA
BALTIC SEA
SKAGERRAK
KATTEGAT
DENMARK
JUTLAND
GOTLAND
ÖLAND
BORNHOLM
FYN
SJÆLLAND
ÅLAND (AHVENANMAA)
LITHUAN
LATVI
ESTO
Gulf of Riga
GULF OF
Vesterålen
Lofoten
Harstad
Narvik
Abisko
Kiruna
Vittangi
Malmberget
Gällivare
Jokkmokk
Bodø
Rognan
Kvikkjokk
Mo i Rana
Mosjøen
Brønnøysund
Namsos
Steinkjer
Levanger
Trondheim
Orkanger
Kristiansund
Molde
Ålesund
Åndalsnes
Oppdal
Røros
Dombås
Otta
Lom
Jotunheimen
Lillehammer
Elverum
Hamar
Gjøvik
Fagernes
Bergen
Voss
Odda
Haugesund
Stavanger
Egersund
Flekkefjord
Farsund
Mandal
Kristiansand
Lillesand
Grimstad
Arendal
Larvik
Tønsberg
Horten
Drammen
Oslo
Drøbak
Moss
Sarpsborg
Halden
Kongsberg
Hønefoss
Kongsvinger
Östersund
Åre
Strömsund
Vilhelmina
Lycksele
Umeå
Skellefteå
Piteå
Luleå
Boden
Haparanda
Arvidsjaur
Sorsele
Storuman
Sundsvall
Härnösand
Kramfors
Örnsköldsvik
Hudiksvall
Söderhamn
Gävle
Falun
Borlänge
Mora
Karlstad
Uppsala
Norrtälje
Stockholm
Södertälje
Västerås
Örebro
Nyköping
Norrköping
Linköping
Motala
Jönköping
Vänern
Vättern
Trollhättan
Uddevalla
Göteborg
Borås
Varberg
Halmstad
Helsingborg
Malmö
Lund
Trelleborg
Kristianstad
Karlskrona
Kalmar
Växjö
Västervik
Visby
Skagen
Frederikshavn
Hjørring
Ålborg
Randers
Århus
Silkeborg
Viborg
Esbjerg
Vejle
Horsens
Fredericia
Kolding
Odense
Nyborg
Svendborg
Copenhagen
Roskilde
Køge
Næstved
Rønne
Nexø
Flensburg
Kiel
Lübeck
Hamburg
Rostock
Stralsund
Rügen
Frisian Is.
Helgoländer Bucht
Tornio (Torneå)
Kemi
Oulu
Raahe
Kokkola
Jakobstad (Pietarsaari)
Vaasa
Seinäjoki
Kristinestad
Pori
Rauma
Turku (Åbo)
Tampere
Helsinki (Helsingfors)
Espoo (Esbo)
Hanko (Hangö)
Mariehamn (Maarianhamina)
Saaremaa (Ösel)
Hiiumaa (Dagö)
Kuressaare
Pärnu
Haapsalu
Paldiski
Ventspils
Liepāja
Klaipėda
Riga
Jelgava
Kaunas
Kaliningrad
Gulf of Gdańsk
Gdańsk
Thistle
Brent
Statfjord
Oseberg
Balder
Ekofisk
Dan
Draugen

An incredible journey of remarkable proportion of a courageous couple, from the top of the mountains of Norrland Sweden, to the untamed shores of South East Alaska.

"AS WE THOUGHT ABOUT BEGING THIS JOURNEY TO A NEW LAND AT OUR AGE, AND NOT EVEN KNOWING THE LANGUAGE AND HAVING FOUR YOUNG CHILDREN DEPENDING ON US, OUR THOUGHTS WERE, WE MUST HAVE WORK TO SURVIVE, WILL WE REALLY MAKE IT THERE or WILL WE HAVE TO RETURN TO OUR HOMELAND OF SWEDEN???" These were their thoughts and memories as they began their plans towards their adventure!

Here begins the memories in their own words of their individual growing up years, each individually from different yet very humble beginnings and later we will move forward to the combined lives of Karl and Ida Nore'n as they begin their lives together, and later still take their journey towards the unknown with their four young children, leaving the security of their homeland and struggle forward towards a new beginning in a strange land, feeling lost not knowing the language nor the customs.......

So the record begins with papa Karl Gote's early life in Sweden.

Karl Gote Noren born on 10 October 1903 in Kroppa, Dalarna, Sweden, and this oral history was gotten by recording interviews starting June 21, 1983 and continued for 3 different summers at pappa's home 313 C street Douglas, Alaska. The recordings were completed during 3 of mamma's trips to see her sisters and their families in Sweden and Norway. Because pappa was home alone at this time, it became a good time for visiting and remembrances, on his part he spoke all in Swedish. These interview visits and recordings were completed I believe in the year 1989.

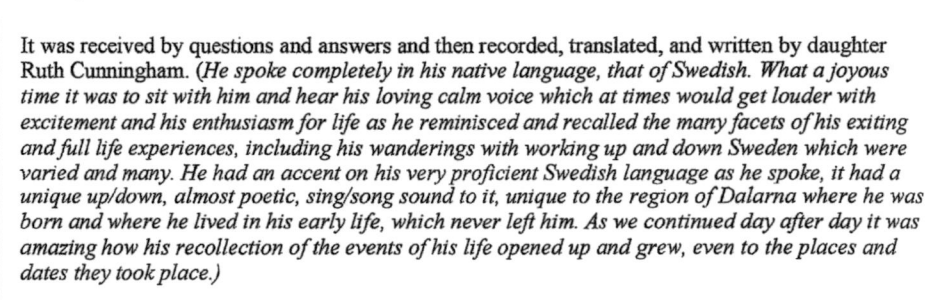

It was received by questions and answers and then recorded, translated, and written by daughter Ruth Cunningham. *(He spoke completely in his native language, that of Swedish. What a joyous time it was to sit with him and hear his loving calm voice which at times would get louder with excitement and his enthusiasm for life as he reminisced and recalled the many facets of his exiting and full life experiences, including his wanderings with working up and down Sweden which were varied and many. He had an accent on his very proficient Swedish language as he spoke, it had a unique up/down, almost poetic, sing/song sound to it, unique to the region of Dalarna where he was born and where he lived in his early life, which never left him. As we continued day after day it was amazing how his recollection of the events of his life opened up and grew, even to the places and dates they took place.)*

The hope is to complete this for a great remembrance for all of us, his children and grandchildren and their children's enjoyment and that it might become a learning experience to us from his wholesome example in living his life, one of honesty and integrity and hard work and for sticking with it even in difficult times, never being afraid of a new challenge or experience. The hope is that all his posterity will get to know their grandfather Noreen for many generations to come; we are so glad that he was willing to share and that this will now be available for all who will read it.

As Pappa and I began our visits together at my request, he said that his feeling was something like: "I really don't like to talk into this recorder and talk about myself, but as you explained that this was the only way that those who come after me, my family, my children and grandchildren would ever know about me and that maybe there might be something that someone could learn from my life and experiences, I will tell you what I remember, because I do care about all my family". As we began and continued through many visits he really got into our project, and became very excited for out next visit together.

My Early Childhood (picture above taken at about 10 years old)

I was born in Kroppa, Dalarna, Sweden on October 10th 1903. My father's name is Karl Svenson Noren and my mother's name is Johanna Tellberg Jonasson. I have many brothers and sisters older and younger than myself and we live out in the countryside. My father had a first wife Sofia she gave birth to 6 children and died within about 6 month of the last one's birth. He then remarried, my mother, she raised the first 6 children and had 4 of her own; I was the only boy of my mother. Many years later after my mother had died my father had one more son, Karl Ivar.

My earliest memories are, let me think...... well, I think they are of going to school, times were very tough than, these were very hard times in Sweden during the early years of my life. First there were local strikes, than there was a general strike. No trains, no nothing, no work for anyone, everything came to a total stop, for that matter all of Sweden was totally stopped, not just where we lived. And at this time there were no cars seen on the roads, there was hardly a bike it seems as I try to remember, there were hardly any machinery found anywhere. There was such a big difference from now (1983) that you would hardly believe it.

But anyway the first that I seem to remember, was of this difficult time of no work, no money, that the people shopped on credit such as barrowed on the value of their house for example, this is what we did so we used our house as credit for all our needs especially for food, and our neighbors did the same. But we could use this as credit for only so long and in 1913 our life became more difficult for this is when they (the creditors) took the house away from my father. Our neighbor Aronson, also lost his house and thousands of thousands of others throughout Sweden lost their properties and there began a flood of thousands of people, countless numbers of whole families, children, began begging for the necessities of life, for they had nothing at all, this was a very difficult time and I was about ten years old.

There were many that lived in company housing and worked for Domarnas Jarnvag (the railroad) they too had to leave their work and homes for everything closed down. Everyone just went around and around and around and how they survived I have no idea, but I know they went and begged, many came even to our house before we lost it, and they could usually get a piece of bread because we did have bread, homemade bread that my mom made, and we always had a pig so we had bacon (fläsk) too.

We got our grain from the neighboring farmers (bondarna) who had grain fields, my father was out of work too, so he worked for and helped some of the farmers and got the flour we needed, he also worked for and got a male calf in the spring and then brought it home and fed it, it would graze all summer and then in the fall we had meat. This is the way it happened, we also got milk from the farmers, they knew that they could count on and call on my father (gubben) any time and he would be there to help. So this was the reason that we survived at first.

So anyway in 1913 when I was 10 years old, people from (myndigheterna) the law officers in the community came by and placed a notices on our house and also on Aronson's house our neighbor, both on the same day and then they locked the doors and this was done because we owed the store and could not pay for the goods we had receive, and they had to have their payment, so that is how it was. Later it seems that the store owner also, his name was Erik Herdine that he also lost his business. This condition or situation I remember lasted at least through 1913 and 1914 especially. After this time I don't remember very much, but we had to move away from there anyway.

After some time the strikes were over and my father took a job with (domarnas järnvag) the railroad company. He came home and said, than we got to move into the railroad barrack housing (darrackarna) so our lifestyle began to be somewhat normal again. At this time I was in the first middle school, this was the 3rd grade. Now during 1st and 2nd grade I went to school at home in the small school there, there were only two grades in that school in (Kjälla) which was in Islingsby, this was where I was born at home at our house. This was located just outside of Borlange in Dalarna. This was where our first home was before we had to move, it was where our house was located that was taken away from us. So than we moved in 1913 when our house was confiscated for the outstanding debts, and then we had to go to another school that was (på Bruket) that was the name of the place. About this time some people were starting and able to find work again. That was when we had work again too; Pappas work was close to where we lived.

I lived at home at that time, so I lived there close to Borlange during World War One. The ruler (sjäisaren) of Russia and Wilhelm (of Germany) became angry with each other (osams) and Austria and Germany were partners and relatives also.

I remember when it (the war) began, it was in 1914 I have a picture from that time, because *I got a new suit*, there was a Jew that came and sold material and clothes. He came every year; mamma would invite him in for coffee, it didn't matter to Mamma who they were, Jews or none Jews, she would invite them in. Many walked around selling all kinds of things. But mamma bought some material from him that would be enough for a suit. I remember how they measured so there would be enough, yes, I remember that. So than we took pictures (at the beginning) we always had short pants there during that time period. Men or women also wore short pants. When we went before the priest and read before him (a study for a few weeks before confirmation in the Lutheran church around age 12-13) than I got my first long pants I think there was two boys that had long pants that I knew, so you could have them than when they got a bit older around 18-19 years old. Anyway I had those pants for a long time, I couldn't wear them out they were made with some sort of wool.

During the general strike my father worked for the farmers round about doing all kinds of physical labors. But otherwise he did contract work; at this particular time he worked as a (kalare) (making coal to heat houses) he was a coal miller, so that is what he did before the strike. There was a saw-mill close by, well somewhat close. This was just before the breakout of World War One. At this time everything was sold to Germany, they needed coal and they needed (jarn) steel also but my father worked to make the coal, he set everything up (kålmilare) the process to make the coal. He put fire to wood and burned it down and made coal out of it. (For more information on how coal was made look it up on line.)

Mom was at home taking care of everything there at our home and of course the kids, I remember every week Pappa would come home totally black and we had a big barrel, a Norwegian herring barrel, with warm water ready, he would crawl down into it. When he was gone working he would be gone for a whole week at the time because it was quite a distance to walk and of course he had to take care of the fires in the presses of making the coal so he had to stay there during the week. At this time Ester and Hanna and me, Gote and Anna were the only kids at home. The older kids from the first marriage were already gone. During the bad times of the depression around 1909 when it was at its worst, my brother Algot, who thereafter lived in Norway, he actually walked all the way to Norway. He went through Funasdalen (where we lived after I married mamma) and over to Röros into Norway. And Georg one of my other brothers who was younger he also went the same way that Algot had gone just a year or so later. Thousands of people went over to Norway in search of work during this time for things were better there and it was open for work.

In trying to remember about my grandparents, my grandfather's nick name was (Shene Sven i Vägen). My father and my mother both came from Värmland, as did my grandparents. The only thing I really remember about my grandfather is that he was very quick, he never walked, he always ran wherever he went, that is how he got his nickname, he was a little dry up old man. (His nickname is something like, (Sven Quicksilver on the road) He was at home with us and he chopped the wood, I remember he lived in our house and he was to be awakened every morning a 9 a.m. then he would eat (välling) a milky hot soupy cereal and a hard bread sandwich. So I remember especially when I would wake him up, mother would call me, for this was my job, she would look for me, this was probably before I started school and as a kid would do, I would open the door I would run in and holler "it is time to get up" run out again, and would than go back to my play. But this one time he didn't get up, so my mom asked me, "did he wake up?" so anyway I went and looked and my mom too, but the old man was dead. This happened when I was small, before I started school. (Note: He died 12 Sept.1908 in Kroppa Varmland, Sweden; pappa was just 5 years old.)

We had to walk when we went to school, but the beginning school was very close to where we lived, we could run across the field and it only took us a few minutes, it was not far away at all. It was very cold one year in the fall; I remember mamma gave us each a blanket to wrap in, to cover us and our faces. Mamma had a blanket around her too; these were simple and hard times. Mamma sewed all the clothes we wore, during those times nothing was bought. There were no stores that could be found that such things could be bought in, but everyone made everything themselves usually out of (vadmall) a wool type material. Our shoes were bought at first from a shoemaker, but after that, than my father would keep them up, he had a bench with everything on it, he sowed and he hammered, he had all the material to fix the shoes as they would wear out and need fixing, he was really good at that.

Our life was plain and simple we took care of all our own needs as did everyone else, it was not like now, we really didn't have any happy times that I can remember. Everyone was too busy taking care of themselves. It was not anything like now; there are really no comparisons of life now and then. Life was serious and hard. You didn't go to the neighbors too visit or anything, everyone took care of themselves and their needs, there was not time for anything else, just that was a full-time job. We would speak at a distance with our neighbors but no going to each other houses. There were no doctors or midwives, there would be an old lady in the neighborhood that took care of those kinds of things, especially birth of children, if you got sick or if you got constipated you got raisin oil, and that is the only medicine we had.

I don't have many memories of my older brothers and sister, for they had already moved out very quickly, as soon as they could work. The only one I can remember about is Milda, she was the youngest from my father's first marriage, when she was a teenager she had gone to a dance I remember that (gubben) the old man was out and chased her boyfriend off. Our first home gubben built himself, he might have had some help, but it was a good big house but just a couple of rooms though, a big kitchen which was a big multipurpose room and the upstairs was open where the wind would come through the rafters so you could not sleep up there in the winter, only in the summer could we and did we sleep up there. In the winter there was only one room for the four kids to sleep in, there was a bed that would pull out, and in the day you would push it in just like an accordion, but it was very wide so we all slept in it (skakafoot) foot to foot, it was the way it was because there was no money to buy more, this was the way people lived.

We did play with the neighbor kids then, I can't really remember the things we played, there were mostly girls except one boy Gunnar Aaronson but he was so sickly, he had earaches all the time, so there was not much or many to play with or about.

I was born in Islingsby. When I was a little boy in our home it was very strict, if a thing was said, it was done, there was not a maybe or later, if a thing was said then that is the way it was, and so it was always, and sometimes when you are small you would forget, than we would get in trouble, we got an awakening, (ear pull or slap?) (vi fick oss en dagsedel) but he never really mistreated us. Because of this, I too feel strongly about certain things, and I also am set and strict when it comes to certain things of importance. (Note: I don't remember pappa ever being physical in any way when he would discipline us, but his voice could roar when he got excited).

But when I was little there in Islingsby I remember that we played football (soccer) with a homemade ball made out of old clothes rolled up. I also had a dog that I played with sometimes, he lived under the stairs there were four stairs going up, my father (gubben = the old man) cut out a round hole so that is where the dog lived, but this was a very special dog, I have never seen a dog like that again, he looked like a tiger, he had stripes and they were green and black. Let me think for a moment, no, I can't remember his name and I guess it doesn't matter. But I remember when the first car came past our house though, we lived on a small road where mostly horses and horse dawned wagons would go past, but this black car came past and don't you know, the dog jumped on the car and he fell and the car ran over the him, and I remember how I felt that, that was too bad, for then we had to shoot the dog, because he was hurt too badly.

Where we lived was in the country side, there were only three families that lived out there. We had bought the property from a neighbor; Iceberg lived in the first house than our house was in the middle and then Aaronson on the other side, and these were beautiful lots. My father (gubben) (his picture to the side) he planted and made it beautiful, he planted fruit trees and bushed and vegetables, he was kind of a specialist on this and wanted to plant things that no one else had. He had a fruit tree that was called a glass apple tree, when it was ripe you could see the black seeds through it and count the seeds inside the apple, and God help us if we were to touch this tree. I was there a few years ago and the tree still stands, Gunnar was with me and I took a few of the apples the tree but it was old now and it wasn't at all the same apples anymore, but they tasted kind of good although they were hard and they had not been taken care of course over all these years. I thought I would bring some home, but Anna Lisa (my brother Karl-Theodor's daughter) said you can't bring them in to America, so I can't remember but I think I threw them away.

Back then we ate very plain food, we did not have very much, we ate things from the garden potatoes, carrots etc. bread and (välling) hot milky serial, meat from a pig, we didn't have all the fancy stuff that is available now, you just couldn't find things like that back then.

Our first move: It was when we moved into a barracks, that was when our house was taken from us during the general strike I told about earlier, we lived there until 1916. Our life during this time was very interesting, the war broke out 1913 so I remember in the fall 1914 there was a lady that had a newspaper and she read that the war had broken out between Germany and Serbia and the crown prince of Germany was killed by a sniper while out visiting with the people like they used to do, this was the son of the kingdom's leader his name was (tjäisare) France Joseph, anyway someone shot him and he did die.

Serbia belonged to Germany at this time and several other countries as we now know them now also did, it was a big kingdom at this time. But this did not help the war efforts between these two, they had their eyes on taking England and France they plotted together with another country's leader (tjäisare) Wilheilm. The sister to this (tjäisare) Wilheim in Germany his dotter or maybe it was his sister, I can't remember which but she was married to the Swedish King Gustaf the 5th so in this way we in Sweden where we were located were locked in, even Norway the only one we could do any business with was controlled by Germany. And we didn't get out to anyone else, because England was also at war and had their boats and were also shooting. So at this time we were not able to get goods from any other place. These were hard times, there was no work except as my father would help at the farm. But we had it good anyway because we did have potatoes, and (gubben) the old man saw to it that we had some (fläsk) bacon and milk that we could get from the farm, they knew they could call on him over there anytime they needed extra help. So we had it pretty good during this time anyway, better than most.

After the general strike was over, but the war was still going on, this is when we moved, the war lasted until the fall of 1918. Difficult times continued during this time too. In Borlänge where we were, this is a bit further away, but there in the restaurant they served roots such as rutabagas and turnips they would cut them in slices and cook them and it stunk so bad that they had to open the doors, and then they had Norwegian Salt Sill (fish) they shipped loads of Salted (sill) herring in to Sweden, that the people had to lay the fish in water to soak to get some of the salt out of the fish otherwise you couldn't eat them because it would just be too salty, but then after that they would be cooked, and there was plenty of herring, because they shipped it in by the barrels from Norway. But anyway this is what the people ate year in and year out, there was nothing to be found, even butter, there just wasn't any. People would be out looking for food items like that, walking and searching. 'Oj joj joj!!' (An expression like 'oh my golly!' indicating it was tough!) It was amazing even with all these problems people stayed pretty healthy.

In 1918 a new illness came, the "Spanish flue" and everyone got sick in our family also except my mom, even I too got sick. We lived in Grängshammar at this time we had moved there in 1916. This is the year I began to work; I got 10 öre an hour. (That is about a penny in U.S. money) I worked 10 hours a day, 6 days each week, I wasn't even thirteen yet, I was twelve years old at this time, I would turn thirteen in October. I would take a team of horses and lead them in the field and go round and round plowing and planting. Than life became very busy! By this time we had a better situation with food, we got land to plant potatoes and my father he planted and yielded so many potatoes that we got enough to feed the pigs too. He would buy 2 or 3 small three week old pigs and raised them throughout the summer; farmers would come from further south, from another state like Smaland and other places south of us, and sold these small pigs than we would feed them throughout the summer and then have plenty of foods in the fall and winter.

There in (Grängshammar) we could get grain from the neighbor farmers cheap; my sister Hanna got a job out at a neighboring farm (herr gård). She was a young girl, she probably did cleaning and other things that needed to get done, I really don't know but she worked out there, but while out there she got the Spanish flu too, but she then got better. At this time Anna and Ester was in bed at home with the same illness, father and I was out chopping wood and we could hear the church bells ringing continually all day long, continually, continually all day long, all day long, all day long, we became used to the ringing of the church bells.

We became so used to the ringing of the church bells because we lived so close to the church, we could see the church from home because it was just across the river from us, outside the church there were casket after casket after casket laying in a row, so the bells would ring as each of these people were taken into the church for their service, than the bells would again ring for the next, and so it went all day long. I went over there to look, all the caskets were black in those days, but one day there was a small white casket, in those days we could feel this was real special when we saw this small white casket, this was so new for us to see that it left a real mark on us, this was something new for us, we felt it was fantastic that someone would make and have a small white casket. That was the only white casket that I ever saw. The people died like flies. My father (min far) and I while we were out chopping wood also got sick, yes, as I remember we were out chopping wood for the house, we did a lot of that, it was a beautiful sunny day (gubben) father drove the ax hard into the stump and said, "Dear God, I think I am getting the Spanish flue too" he was always so healthy and I also said "Yes, I think I am getting it too" because I didn't feel very well either. So at that we both went into the house and we didn't even take any wood in with us either, we just went in. He said to mother "now I think I am getting the Spanish flu too".

Ester and Anna was lying in the other room sick too, they were not so very sick, but enough that they needed to be in bed. So I stayed in and mamma said its best that you go and lay down. Mamma didn't get the flue, or maybe she did and was up taking care of us anyway, because she was real stubborn and she was a really strong person, she was not big and bulky but she was strong in all ways. Gubben took a big (sup) swig (of alcohol used as medicine back then) and went and lay down on the kitchen cot that was made out of wood, it pulled out into a bed, my father and mother slept on that cot. I can't remember what I laid on but the next day I felt better and I wanted to get up and go out, at that age one could not lay down if you felt somewhat ok, not unless you were really sick. I think I was about 14-15 years old at this time, gubben he got up too and would spit and put in some snuff, he put on his shoes and said now that was enough, now it's not going to be any more Spanish flue.

But then there came a message to my mom (min mor) and she said that Norrbergs Stina had not been down for a long time, everyone was talking about the Spanish flue and how people were dying here and there, and she and her boy Victor had not been down. This was an old lady and her son who lived up in (Norrberg) the northeren mountain, it wasn't so far but there was no road up other than a trail where a horse drawn wooden buckboard that they would load up and drag up to their house with supplies could go, you could not go there with wheels because it was to rocky.

She had a couple of cows it seems and she had a calf. Norrberg Stina as she was called, she was a bit simple minded. When she came down she would always come in to our house to my mom, mor would always give her coffee and something else if we had it, by then there was a bit better with food stuff. My mom said to gubben we haven't seen them for a long time, so he said "well, I better make a trip up there" it probably only took a half an hour to get up there, so I went along too and we were maybe about half the way up there, when we heard the cows calling, mooing loudly, and he said now, now, now, listen, there is something really wrong up there, with the cows sounded so bad in the middle of the day. They sounded so bad and of course normally they would not, he understood that there was something really wrong; they must not have had either food or water. So the first thing he did was to go directly to the barn. They ran directly to the well for water, and my father dropped the bucket down into the well and wound it back up and watered the cows.

Then he went to the door, it was open, people never locked anything up in those days, and they were both dead. There was nothing we could do, the cows had grass outside so they could eat and there was a fence around to keep them from wandering off. We went down and spoke with those who were in authority, but there really wasn't anyone in authority in these days but there was someone who had horses, we didn't, so they went up there with some sort of flatbed (trog) and brought them down. And the black smith and carpenter he did both of those jobs but they called him (sme'en) anyway he built a caskets for each them. I didn't go to the funeral, but the two of them did die. And I can't really remember what happened to the cows, but most likely they slathered them, anyway that was the end of those folks up in the Norrberg.

Countless number of people died all around us even as far as Norway, this illness came from Spain so it covered all of Europe. That is why it was called the 'Spanish flue' because it began there, it came after the war, bodies was laying around rotting after the war, in massive numbers down in France and Germany and all around, this brought this illness and others. There was not enough time and ability to take care of all that needed to be done, to burry bodies and such. This flue even came over to America quite a bit later. The dieses were just in the air and people caught it, it was a terrible time.

Hanna my sister she caught it too and we thought she was better, but she was working on that farm (Herrgård) that I mentioned earlier and she laid there on the farm ill, she and many others, because almost every other person had it. Anyway we got the news that she was better from a person that did the milk deliveries back and forth from the farm, she had sent news. She had a nice boyfriend he was a very nice boy, I saw him because he came down to her funeral, he said she had gone out to early, she had been outside and caught a cold and got pneumonia, and so she died along with many others, but this happened after she was starting to get better, all because she went out to early. This was 1918; she was two years older than me so she was only 17 years old. She was a strong and sturdy girl, red hair and beautiful, I can't remember anything else than numbness in general, there was so many people that died that feelings were gone. She was the only one that died in our family everyone else survived. It was a sad time, everyone was just numb, whole families died in some cases 5 and 6 kids in a family, farther up north in Sweden it was even worse. Even the farm animals sometimes died from not getting water and being cared for. There was so much trouble during this time it is really hard to believe that things could truly become this bad. This was a very difficult time for everyone.

We went of course by horse and buggy wherever we went or walked and that is what we in our family did most all the time. The first time I really saw a car was very exciting, I also got to ride in that car. It was probably before I even started to go to school. It was the first car that was there in our town of Borlange. The people that owned the car wanted to show the car and then to let people go for rides to earn some money. So they would drive around just for a short way, but the car didn't go any faster that the small boys could run, I was so small than that I got to sit up on my father's lap. I later asked what kind or make of car this was, I was told it was from France someplace. I remember that I sat on my father's lap, gubben picked me up, and he paid for the ride, I think it was 10 öre for him and 5 ore for me, the child. They made it a big thing, and talked up a storm, the worst I thought, was the chauffeur he was a site, he had leather gloves and they reached up on his arms and I remember his big chauffeurs hat, he was dressed up for a big show including a leather jacket and he sat there in his open car, there was no top and he had glasses or goggles too, as I looked at him, he almost looked dangerous out. Then they stopped and turned around at the town square, it probably took 15 minutes. Even the men and women all ran alongside of the car, it was a big thing. And everyone held their nose because of the smoke that it made, and that is about all I remember about the first car that I saw.

Several years later when I saw my second car, this was probably an American car; it came on the main road that the horses drove on. It drove past our house and the dog jumped up and ran out the gate and was chasing the car and tried to bite the tires, it happened so fast I really can't remember exactly but the dog went under the car and was hurt really bad and gubben he had to get the gun, I can't remember it all, but I think he had to finish him off, in those days we could have guns, I think he had a 22 pistol. Now you can't have personal weapons in Sweden, but then you could and I think he had to shot the dog, than I do remember that he took him on his back and got a shovel and went and buried him.

The first airplane that I saw was long, long time after this, it was when I was in the army, and I don't think there were any planes before this there where I lived. But the Swedish army built some long time after this. And the first plane I saw was an army plane. But after that they seemed to come more and more quickly with the war on, so they even began to build the army planes in Sweden.

I do remember the first time I saw and heard a radio, I was in Grängshammar where we lived, and my father came home with a small box. You couldn't hear it normally, but you had to have headphones on over your ears. He came home from Borlange with the box and put it up on the shelve, they took down some things my mom had up on the shelve, and then he turned it on, my mom was going the get to listen to it first so, it was so funny he sat the thing on her ears, she was almost scared and my father turned the dial to tune something in and it screeched so loudly we all of us who were in the kitchen could hear it, she threw it off and she said oh, (huva) what an awful thing. We all laughed and laughed☺!! I can't remember who was next, maybe it was Ester turn, but we all tried it. Than (gubben) the old man tried to tune in to the station, because it kept screeching, he wasn't able to get it in either so he was disappointed, but a couple of days later he took it up in the upstairs loft and he did finally tune in to something and we did hear some talk but it was never very clear. At this time period you could only hear through a headset, there was no sound other than that; you had to have it over your ears.

One very serious time that I remember was when the Titanic went down. When I was really small I remember I got to go with my father on a tourist trip, on a boat named the "Dalalven" it just traveled up and down the river named (Dalälven) the Dalariver. We went to Onis, it was an old house, it was there that Gustav Erikson who later became King in Sweden and his name changed and became Gustav Vasa, this was where and when he hid from the Danes when they were chasing him and trying to kill him. This was an old house and the Danish troops came here to look for him, Danish troops were occupying Sweden back then. Anyway, when we came there to Onis to sightsee, there stood a clown of sorts and he had a monkey and for 5 ore the monkey would give you a love note in an envelope to tell you you're fortune like, "you would have good luck or something like that" and he had a music box that would play some fun music, but at this particular time it was playing "Nearer my God to thee". And this was really the first time for me that it sank into my mind the seriousness of the ship Titanic going down. This was probably when we lived on Bäckebacken (translated Hillstream) we had just moved there it was probably in 1913 that this happened. But the boat (Titanic) went down 1912 however back than it took time for news to travel with no radios or anything else.

But I remember he was playing that hymn "nearer my God to thee" I can sing that melody still to this day; it became so implanted in my mind. This made a real and deep impression in my mind of people on that ship that had gone down and that so many had died. I had read something about this in a paper that our neighbor had earlier, we didn't have a paper but this one neighbor did and I remember a picture of a boat standing on

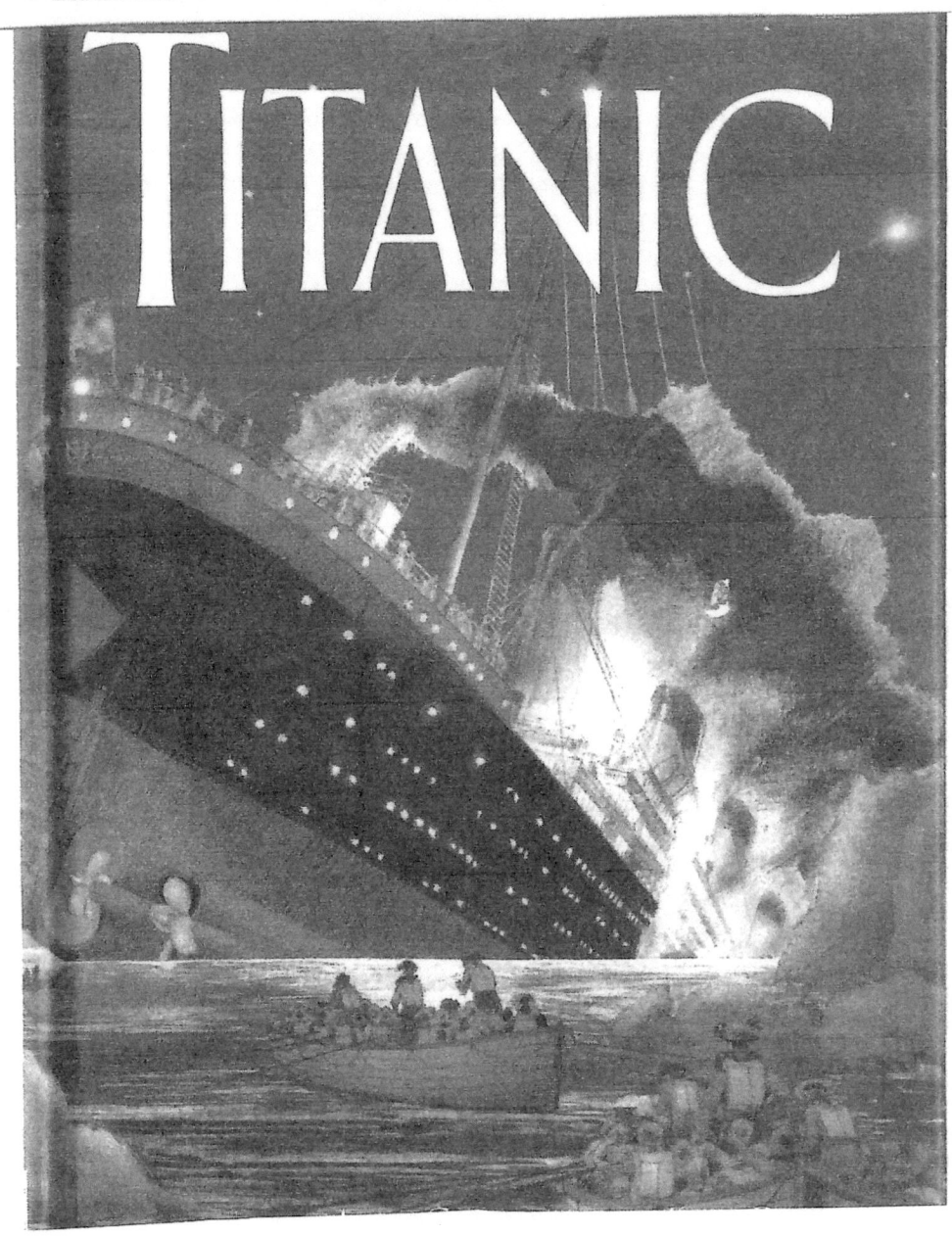

This illustration shows how the *Titanic* scraped along the side of the iceberg.

Underwater, the iceberg gouged holes through the *Titanic*'s metal hull.

TITANIC

April 14 1912

TITANIC DISASTER GREAT LOSS OF LIFE
EVENING NEWS

• Pappa Göte was 9 years old in 1912, aprox. age in this picture!

end with a big iceberg beside it, I can't remember if it was drawn or if it was a photo but it made a lasting impression. It probably was not like that in reality, but it was of the big ship standing on end and a huge iceberg in front, it was probably a drawing but it showed how it might have been. This was a very sad memory and time.

Remembering back to when I was a little boy in school, the teachers were very strict, my beginning school teachers name was, let me think, her name was (Fru) Mrs. Vake, she was married and her husband died in the years that we were in school. We were going the go to the funeral to see what was going on, so we walked across the field that we always walked across when we went to school, it was sunny and nice on this day. There we saw a horse drawn carriage with the casket on the back, this was a special experience because Ester my sister came with us and when we came home later, they asked us what it was like and what we had seen, there was a man who sat up high on the front driving the carriage and the casket was on the flat part, so they asked and I of course remembered and could tell but when they asked Ester, did you see anything? "Yes, I saw Vake, he was sitting up on top driving" she thought it was the man who had died and that 'he' was the driver. We teased her about that for a long time and she was so very angry with us about that.

Ester was special, she had meningitis when she was small and was never the same after that, and she was always slow of mind thereafter. In those days there were no doctors so when we were sick we laid at home until we were well, she had a high fervor and there was no help. The only medicine I can remember as a small child was raisin oil and (sabadil etika) some sort of vinegar for head lice that they put your head into. These are the only things that I can remember. Ester was probably just one or two years old when this happened, as she never had a normal life, she lived out her whole life this way, she is still alive today, she is 85 years old and has lived in a nursing home now for many years. (This was 1983) She didn't go to regular school, but I remember that she did write some letters and she drew. It was really hard on my mom, but so is life it seems, we must learn to endure hard things.

We went to school for six years and learned reading, writing and arithmetic, just the main subjects so as to be able to function in life and take care of ourselves. At this time period there were no higher schools of learning anywhere, not even many in America. After we were finished with six years of school, than there was work to be done, both at home as well as other places earning money that needed to be done. In the early 1900 it was a ten hour work day, we worker from seven till nine a.m. than we had breakfast for a half an hour, than we worked till twelve noon and had a one hour lunch 12 to 1 was lunch (middags mål), there was a coffee break in between lunch and dinner. Than we worked till six p.m. it was a ten hour day. This was from Monday morning at seven a.m. until Saturday at six p.m. We worked sixty hour per week, and it was not easy work, the first job I had was when I was twelve years old, thirteen in October, this was August when they began the harvest, it was to cut down the rye, wheat, oats, all kinds of crops and all kinds of grain.

They had come so far as there was a self-binder from Canada or America that would bind the grain together this was the first year they had this help. But they had to have four horses that pulled this whole thing, it would cut the grain down and there was a man who was the driver of the whole thing and as it emptied of course he could not pick it up, unless all the horses pulled evenly so they had to have a small boy like me who walked with a whip, and pick once in a while on the two first horses so that they would not move differently, but all pull together, instead of putting all the work on just one horse. If they didn't draw evenly than one horse had all the work. So someone had to move them evenly, and this was my first job. To walk and walk in that (stub åker) stubby field, it was very difficult, hard and tiring job for a 12 year old, and we got paid 10 ore an hour. Every month I received approximately 22 to 24 kronor for the months' work. I think my father had 50 ore an hour, but he didn't work in the fields that much. He did contract work to make coal, they would chop wood in 3 meter lengths and raised it up and set them around and made a fire in the middle and then they had to watch the logs (we could look up how coal was made in 1915 in Sweden?) It took a week or two until they burned down into coal sometimes if not watched carefully it could burn up so it took around the clock watching but he never had any burn up in his shift, he was a conscientious hard worker.

So anyway he had kind of his own work for himself, he liked that, he was a very private individual, he was able to get a job on a contract, and he received so much for the job. He was very independent and always looking and seeking, he was very proactive and when he was making coal he always had maybe 2 or 3 helpers that worked with him around the clock. He had 16 to 20 of these kinds of mines up there in the woods. After the coal was finished than they had to pull it out of there, there was some kind of (krok) gaff-hook, with a hook on the top to pull the coal out with, by hand, it had a handle on it, than they would chop it into the coal and pull it out from the top. This was a very dirty job, everyone always looked black, and two men would live in a little coalers shack that they built for themselves.

He did this kind of work during World War 1, it was because they needed coal to melt iron and all the iron went to and was sold to Germany. Everything that they could get a hold of including potatoes and butter even the tree sap that they would get off the trees was sent to Germany. Father would buy the tree sap by the bag full and shipped it all by railroad. I remember one time he was weighing in a bags of tree sap and he grabbed the bags and thought the bag weigh to much so he opened it up and there towards the bottom someone had put in big rocks to have it weigh more so they would get played more, they were paid by kilos at that time. He didn't buy any more from those people; he was upset as he was a really honest man.

What about home life?

Christmas memories from home are that we did celebrate and we had a Christmas tree and I remember that we always had hot rice mush (Risgrynsgröt). We only had this at Christmas time, so this was special, otherwise we didn't have rice because it was too expensive to buy, and it just couldn't even be found at any other time of the year even to buy. My father bought 1 kilo for Christmas, but we never had it at any other time of the year.

As I think about my mother, (her picture to the side) she was a hard worker and had order in our home. I really can't remember

Dalarna

DALARNA

May pole celebration in folk dress in Dalarna, Sweden

Karl Svensson Norén
Hösat -82

Karl Svensson Norén

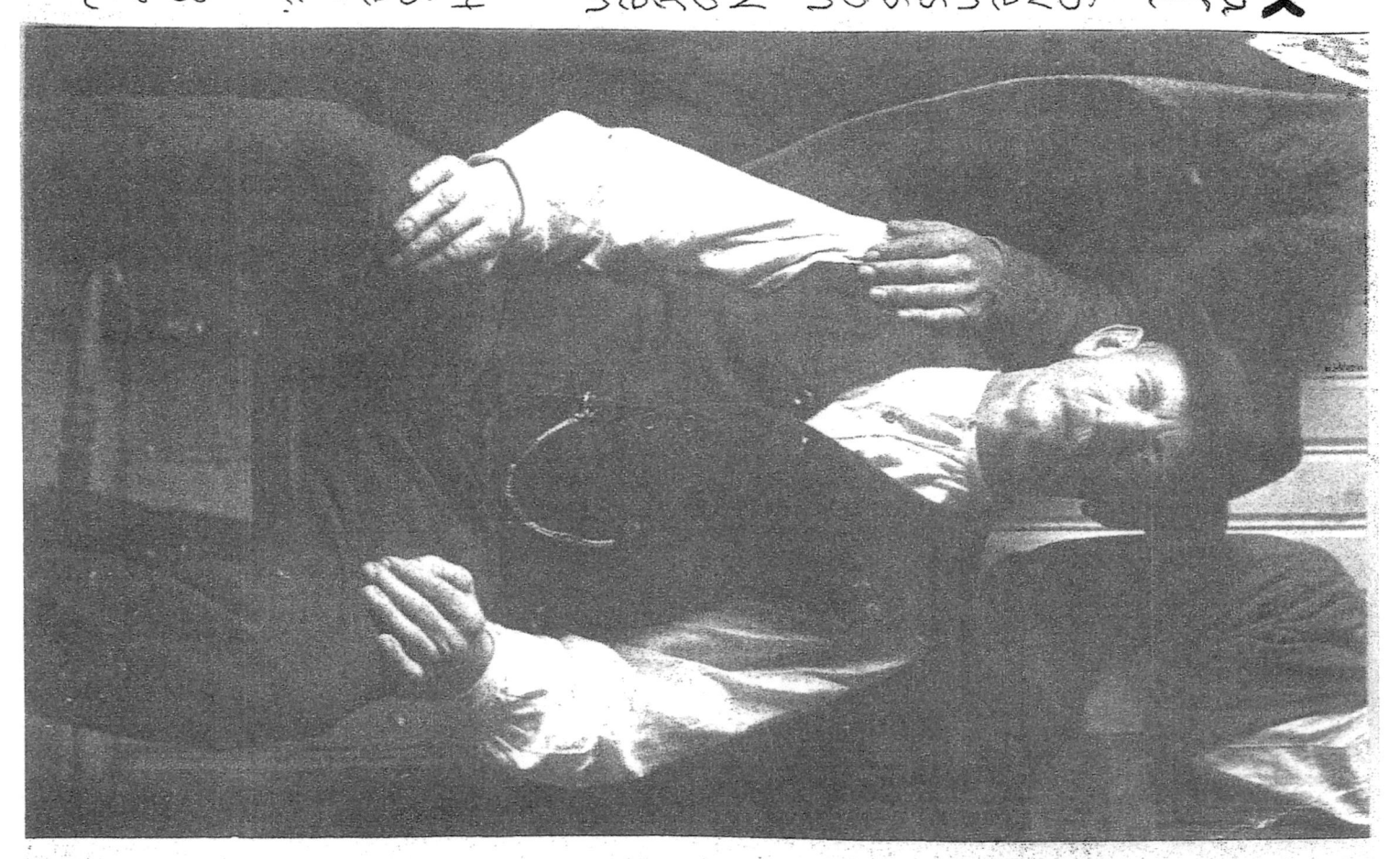

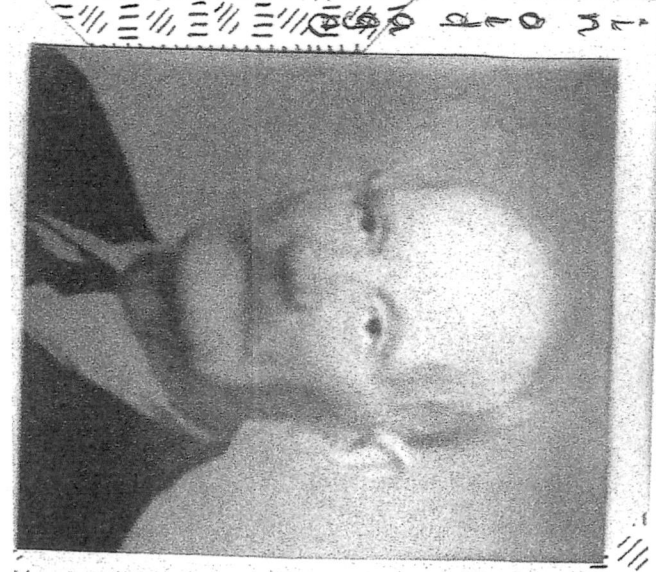

← His father
Karl Svensson Norén ↓

1978 ALASKA

Pappa
Karl Göte Norén
10 Oct. 1903

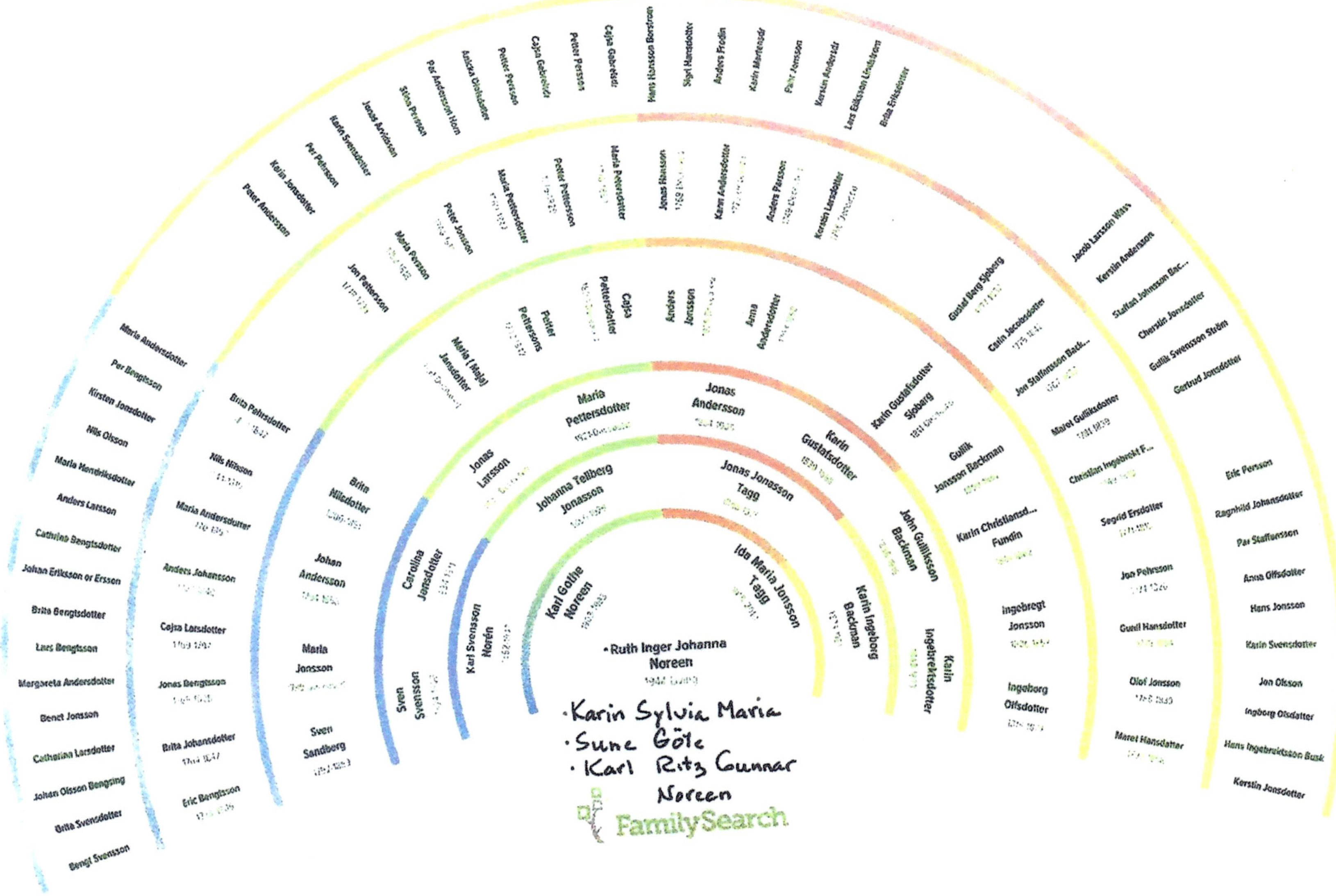
Ruth Inger Johanna Noreen
Karl Gothe Noreen
Ida Maria Jonsson Tagg
Karl Svensson Norén
Johanna Tellberg Jonasson
Jonas Jonasson Tagg
Karin Ingeborg Backman
Sven Svensson
Carolina Jansdotter
Jonas Larsson
Maria Pettersdotter
Jonas Andersson
Karin Gustafsdotter
John Gulliksson Backman
Karin Ingebrektsdotter
Sven Sandberg
Maria Jonsson
Johan Andersson
Brita Nilsdotter
Maria (Maja) Jansdotter
Petter Peterssons
Cajsa Pettersdotter
Anders Jonsson
Anna Andersdotter
Karin Gustafsdotter Sjoberg
Gullik Jonsson Backman
Karin Christiansd... Fundin
Ingebregt Jonsson
Ingeborg Olsdotter
Eric Bengtsson
Brita Johansdotter
Jonas Bengtsson
Cajsa Larsdotter
Anders Johansson
Maria Andersdotter
Nils Nilsson
Brita Pehrsdotter
Jon Pettersson
Maria Persson
Peter Jonsson
Maria Pettersdotter
Petter Pettersson
Maria Petersdotter
Jonas Hansson
Karin Andersdotter
Anders Persson
Kerstin Larsdotter
Gustaf Berg Sjoberg
Catin Jacobsdotter
Jon Staffansson Back...
Maret Gulliksdotter
Christian Ingebrekt F...
Segrid Ersdotter
Jon Pehrsson
Gunil Hansdotter
Olof Jonsson
Maret Hansdatter
Bengt Svensson
Brita Svensdotter
Johan Olsson Bengsing
Catharina Larsdotter
Benct Jonsson
Margareta Andersdotter
Lars Bengtsson
Brita Bengtsdotter
Johan Eriksson or Ersson
Cathrina Bengtsdotter
Anders Larsson
Maria Hendriksdotter
Nils Olsson
Kirsten Jonsdotter
Per Bengtsson
Maria Andersdotter
Peter Andersson
Karin Jonsdotter
Per Pehrsson
Karin Svensdotter
Jonas Arvidsson
Stina Persson
Par Andersson Horn
Anicka Olofsdotter
Petter Persson
Cajsa Gabrielsdr
Petter Persson
Cajsa Gabrielsdr
Hans Hansson Borstrom
Sigri Hansdotter
Anders Frodin
Karin Martensdr
Pehr Jonsson
Kerstin Andersdr
Lars Eriksson Lindstrom
Brita Eriksdotter
Jacob Larsson Wass
Kerstin Andersson
Staffan Johansson Bac...
Cherstin Jonsdotter
Gullik Swensson Strom
Gertrud Jonsdotter
Eric Persson
Ragnhild Johansdotter
Par Staffansson
Anna Olfsdotter
Hans Jonsson
Karin Svensdotter
Jon Olsson
Ingborg Olsdatter
Hans Ingebrektsson Busk
Kerstin Jonsdotter
·Karin Sylvia Maria
·Sune Göte
·Karl Ritz Gunnar Noreen
FamilySearch

Pappa Göte's parents - Karl Svensson Norén and Johanna Tellberg Jonsson Norén

Mormor 45 år Morfar 52
1914
Domnarvet

- Farmor and Farfar to us - because they were our father Göte's parents.

The Children of
Johanna Tellberg Johnson
HAnna, ANNA,
Ester, Göte
aprox. 1914

1915-20
A selfbinding machine
for harvesting

Pappa Göte

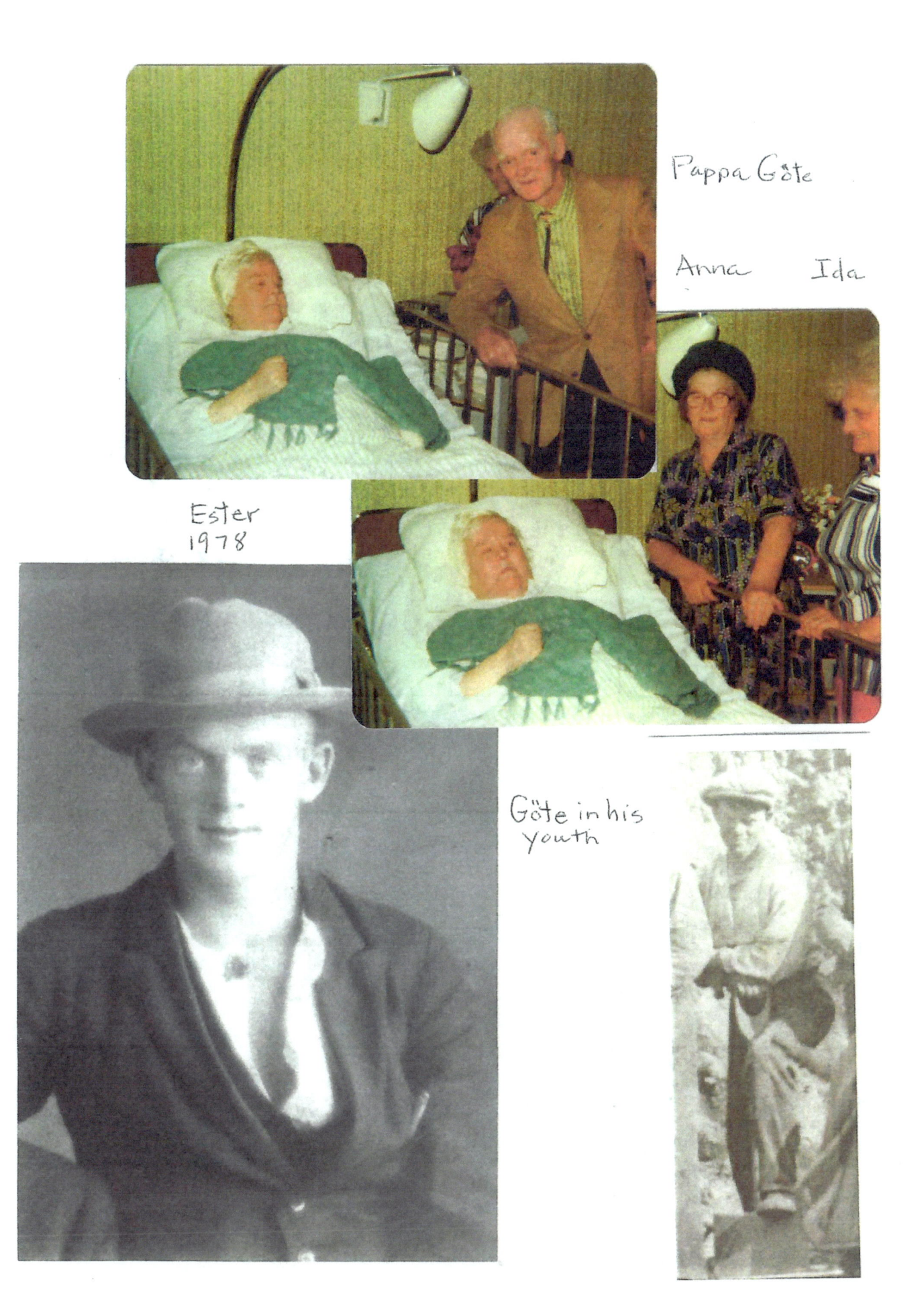

Anna   Ida

Ester
1978

Göte in his
youth

that she openly taught us about the teachings of Jesus at home that much other than by example. That seemed to be the preacher's job, but she was a believer that is for sure because she did read the bible. But she didn't have time to go running off or around to church either, because there just wasn't the time for that in her or our lives, there was always too much to do. And thinking about it in reality there probably just wasn't in her life either the nice looking clothes as the preacher's wife had. Father too probably believed in God because during special occasions such as at Christmas holiday, it seemed that they went to church, when there was a lot of songs and music at that time of the year, and just to get out and mingle with and see other people and such. But mamma she did read the bible often as I remember. And I remember that the transportation to and from anyplace was by horse drawn sleds during this early period of time.

We didn't have doctors or dentist either in those days to go to. Not even in the bigger towns such as Borlänge, there were no doctors or a dentist there either. But there was a doctor in Domnarvet, the railroad company had built a clinic and hospital there, and they had also built a public bathhouse there. If there was a sickness or problem of any kind at home, it was mother that would take care of those problems, such as she was always the one that pulled out our teeth and took care of sickness or whatever situations might arise as needed.

I remember one time when my dad had an awful accident, his big toe was actually chopped off, this happened when the barn door we had a problem with fell as they were working with it, it was uneven when you pulled on it to open it, so as they were trying to fix it, there was a man upstairs in the loft and he was pulling the door up and because it was broken and my dad was downstairs, he was watching at the bottom and it slipped and fell on his toe. It must have been the weekend or holiday because (gubben) the old man had his nice shoes on, not his work shoes when the door came crashing down and it chopped into the shoes and his toe, the old man jumped up and screamed and cussed, my friend Sigrid Eriksson and I we were the same age, he and I we started to laugh at him not realizing the seriousness of the situation and he got really angry at us.

It was then that we understood it was serious. So we ran out into the oat field and hid. Of course I knew I had done wrong by laughing when he got hurt . We weren't all that old we were in grade school. He had to go by horse wagon to the railroad station to take the train to Borlange and the company doctor (his name was Dr. Helsjö) everyone called him the butcher he was a real (rövare) scoundrel, but anyway the doctor came in there where he was, they were going to tie him down, but father wouldn't let them do that, he was stronger than both the doctor and the nurse, so he refused to let them do that. He said to them "just cut the toe off and that is right now!" so it must have still been connected in some way, but the doctor did as he was ordered to do, father he was a real stubborn sort. I heard after that, that he was taken in to a room to lie down after the procedure and he was told not to get up at all, he was to lie down so he could begin to heal, so of course he was given a bedpan to use, but (gubben) the old man he held it until it was a bit quieter in the hall, it was not so far to the outhouse so he went on all his fours and held his foot up in the air and made it, no bedpan for him.

He got a real bawling out by the doctor and they both were very angry as words were flying from one to the other. But gubben wouldn't do what he was told, so he didn't stay there long. They wanted to get rid of him and were glad when he soon did go home. I remember how he would scoot across the floor on his button there at home; it seems there were no crutches back then, I can't remember any at that time anyway. I went there to the small hospital and visited father while he was in there, my mother had an orange that she had gotten for him. I walked the whole way; it was over one Swedish mile (about 7-8 km) we didn't have the money for transportation, but after all that walking he gave me the orange to eat of course. Thereafter I remember Karl Åhs had a horse and a two wheel wagon and went there to the hospital later to pick him up to bring him home. He wasn't there long at all, he would change the dressing on it himself, they put some sort of salve on it and mother would help him too.

At home things were very strict; we kids would not ever even think to played pranks on my mother or father, no never, if we had we would have gotten (en dagsedel) a severe punishment, something not easy to forget. When they said a certain thing, that was that, it was to do exactly that which we had been told. Things at home were very exact and straight, we knew how it was and that was that! But I never would have thought to do anything to get into trouble anyway.

As for myself, this was the only one time that I remember having an accident, I can remember this was the time I almost drowned in the bathhouse, this was when I was a schoolboy, this happened before father's accident. I ended up at that same hospital. There was a (badmastare) lifeguard of sorts at the swimming pool, it started with my friend Gustav Kjällander we were the same age he and I (he was an uncle to Astrid Kjällander our relative in Borlange). The two of us ran on the road all the way from home, all the way up there, it was at least one half Swedish mile (about 4 km) When we got there and came in to the bathhouse there was some kind of rope that you could take hold of and slide out and drop into the water we were very used to water so the two of us of course had a race to see who would be the first one to jump in. I hurried to get undressed and I ran to grab that rope that was hanging there and the rope was slippery and I lost my hold or grip on it and came down to fast into the water.

I remember I could see the window up above, I saw the light but I couldn't swim my arms couldn't move but then Gustav he screamed and called for help and the pool master was close by so he jumped into the pool and got me out. When I woke up I was at the hospital that was right next door to the bath house, he had carried me over there, than I ended up laying in the hospital and guess what, there was an article in the newspaper saying that Göte Noren 9 year old had an accident and then outlining what had happened. Just think, it would be such fun to get a hold of that newspaper, it was there in the Borlänge paper. There was nothing to write about in those days so this was news. It must have been in the year 1912. We kids were always out there swimming and playing having fun we lived close to the water. When we were children we also played the sport of Swedish football (soccer) we started playing that as soon as we could run it is a national game to this day.

The first movie house that I remember was also in Borlänge, the name was (röda kvarn) the red grind. I remember it was cowboy and Indian movies on Saturdays, during the week there was nothing. It probably cost 10 öre to go, I don't remember any other movie other than cowboy movies, but that was what we were interested in any way of course. But there was a lady that sat there playing the piano on the stage as the Indians and cowboys galloped and chased each other across the screen. She was really good she made it very exiting; she would have a bang or crash hard on the piano keyboard at just the right places to make it exiting, we were all really excited and into what was going on, it was very interesting as I remember. Oh ho!! How exiting!! This was when we lived down on Bäckebacken I think.

After that I also sold newspapers for a while, but that didn't last too long, business was not very good; this was while I was in school. We first lived in Islingsby, than we moved to Bäckebacken there in the barracks, and then we moved to Grängshammar which was my last place that I lived at home with the family, from there I left home to go to work.

Some memories of home were that we always had (råggrynsgröt) hot cooked rye cereal with lingon berries and milk in the evening after work. But first for dinner each day we would have (sill) herring and potatoes or (fläsk) bacon and potatoes and then we would have the (raggrynsgrot) wheat or rye mush with lingon berries sometimes we would also have (tjock mjölk) a yogurt milk and oatmeal, sometimes it would be sweet milk this was like our desert after the meal. We always worked until 6 pm and then we were ready to eat our dinner and it was always at that same time. We would get up and work for 2 hours than come in for breakfast it was at 9 am and as I remember we usually ate a sandwich and water and then when lunchtime would come for lunch we were usually close enough to go home so we would eat between 12 and 1 and maybe have pancakes and jam and after that we would work until 6 pm, there were no coffee bottles back then and I wasn't that much for coffee back then anyway. Than the big meal was at night after a long day's work, than there was no more servings after dinner, at that point it was finished for the night. Nothing more was eaten or drunk, not coffee or anything and by 9 pm my father always went to lie down.

When I was home and a small boy, I had a brother named Georg; he was my half-brother, the son of the first wife of my father. He had a button accordion and that he used to play, it was made in Italy, they were the only ones that made accordions back in those days, it had 3 rows, that was as big as they made them back then, he was really good at playing it, he played at the dance (bana) arena outside and down the road there not far from our home, back then the music played was horn or wind instruments. Accordion is a wind instrument too and I snuck it and played it sometimes when I was alone, once in a while I pulled it out and tried and was able to manage a little bit of music. But once mother caught me and she said "now it is enough you cannot do that anymore" she was worried about it, she said that it was expensive and that was the last time I even saw it. I don't know if he took it with when he went to Norway or if he perhaps sold it, but it wasn't there anymore.

Georg was killed in South America later, but he too as I said earlier left home and went to Norway during the depression, and he went out for whale fishing on big ships just like my older brother Algot had done, down to South America. As Georg laid over there one winter in (fifesland ?) in the islands, as they needed two men to be there to check on the machines and things there in that station, all the other men went home, but these two stayed there during the winter and of course they got paid for their time there. Than when the work was done in the spring they left and went to Monte Video by a Norwegian boat, this was of course a Norwegian catch station. Now they had loads of money, they first had what they had earned and then they had the money also they had earned during the extra winter months, so they went then with their pockets full to Monte Video and of course there was a party and celebration. How all this happened exactly we don't know of course, but Georg was robbed and shot, this was 1917 he did not die right away but was in the hospital there for some time. There was a Swedish counsel down there, they had taken pictures every day at the hospital and then sent this home to father along with the papers that he had died at last. My dad didn't take good care of these papers, but I remember it stood that he was shot by a man from Finland. There were many kinds of people that had gone there to South America for many years for work, one after the other. So anyway they caught the man that had shot Georg and had taken him into custody, but he just got a week of sordid job and released. The law down there couldn't do anything and they couldn't feed people like that for extended time either so they chased them out. The place down there was full of this kind of wild (skrat) garbage, seamen, and whale fishermen from all over.

After about 2 years Algot again went to work on a Norwegian whale ship which left from Sandefjord, Norway and that took the whole crew to that same Norwegian holding catch station where Georg had been in South America, they made coal for the ships there too, they fired the ships with coal in those days, because there was no oil at that time, so they went in there to fill up more coal, this was a place that the Norwegians had built down there in South America. The place where they caught the whales or where the fishing place was, it was further south of there that they would bring the fish in to this station for processing, as they did not take the whole fish back but only the oil from them that was taken back to Norway. So at that station was also where they would cut up the whale and cook the oil out of them and processed the fish.

So Algot said than about a year later when he went down whale fishing to South America again that this time he would try to get to the bottom of what had happened to Georg, that he would find the guy that had robbed and killed him, but no luck, he of course was not there, maybe he had been killed too? This was in the year 1917, the year after we moved to Grangshammar. This was such a sad happening that really cut deep! The papers that had been sent home of this happening was there when (gubben) our father died, but they probably burned all of those papers up along with my report cards from school and presents and things that I had saved there. My father he had a drawer, the top drawer in the dresser where he kept all his important papers and things and I was allowed to keep my things in his drawer over in the back corner.

My sister Anna and brother Theodor was home for the funeral, but the (käringen) the woman housekeeper that (gubben) my father lived with probably didn't care and didn't want anything to do with it. Just think if they would have had so much of a thought as to keep the papers, so I could have looked at all the papers that were there. I said to Anna my sister, just think if someone had had the sense to keep that stuff, she said yes, think, think, now we can think about it, back than we didn't think about anything, we just said we didn't want anything. And we wrote to you too, and yes, they did do that, and tell me about our father's death and wanted me to sign the papers, which I did and sent it right back releasing all the belongings, it was all given to the boy (Karl Ivar) he was born from that relationship. I just figured that it was just old furniture and such and couldn't think or remember it was anything important. The only thing that I have seen is the clock that was hanging on the kitchen wall in our home is now hanging on Karl Ivar's wall; I remember how it would chime in our home when I was little.

I remember one time when (landsman) someone in authority came to our house and put a green tag on the clock because we owed money, this meant that it would be confiscated unless the bills were paid. At another time I remember the authority also came to the house and put a green tag on a pig out that was out in the yard that he thought was ours, but it was one of our neighbor pig that had gotten lose, because the gate had come opened into our yard. There was a gate on both of our sides of our yard and in the middle was the winding water well that both families would use. Well, the gates had been left open and our neighbors pig came into our yard and the (landsfiskalen) country authority had someone with to help him. It wasn't hard to get a hold of the pig because he was used to people and they got a hold of the pig and put a green slip on him.

You could not take the slip off once it had been placed on something. I remember Mother stood on the stairs and watched, she knew it was our neighbor's pig (we also did have two piglets that we had bought in the spring just like our neighbor Isberg had, and we would feed them during the summer and use them for food during the winter) but anyway she didn't dear laugh out loud as she stood there watched (Note: Pappa Göte was laughing really hard as he was recalling this funny memory) she had an apron and she held it up in her hand by her face, and she was shaking really hard as she was laughing quietly, but everyone remained quiet, after they left the pig went home again, I wonder what the neighbor who's pig it was thought? He never did say anything!

The beginning of my life away from home

Another place that we would work at times was in the woods, cutting wood for sale, we got so much for each cubic meter. But I was not so old when I left home to find other sort of work. There really seems as though there was a decision already made and in place for you, it was just time to leave home at a certain point, it was the only thing left to do at a certain time or age during that time period. There were not any more positions or work in that area but for one and that of course was our Father who lived there at home. During the depression everyone had to leave and go out to find work, to work for other people. I got a job for the man that was our neighbor they began to build a paper company in Borlänge 1918 that was just when the war was beginning to die out. It was the first day of May 1918 that I remember, for this was the day I left home and I went to Borlänge to work. I remember it was the first day of May demonstration with speeches and the workers would stand with flags, this was a political rally or demonstration day always held on the first of May, so I remember that was going on when I got there.

I remember how Mother would make all kinds of things, homemade things for food, she made a sausage it was called 'Värmlands sausage', she would make the sausage, wrap it in old linen or shirts whatever could be find, she didn't have any coverings for the sausage, everything was homemade she made the sausage long and wrapped it, and then tie lengths off, than she would cook it, and then she would cut it up, it was salted well and I remember I got some of that to take with me as I left to go to Borlänge.

Our neighbor was a (ungkar) single young man and he came over to the house to visit and drink coffee at times, I was at home and didn't have anything to do, my father said, don't you have anything for this one to do, talking about work for me. I was about 15 years old, (jo då) yes, I do, but then he left, I thought it was just a bunch of talk, but the next day he came over and said, if you come to Kvarnsveden you can learn how to become a carpenter. You will have to work and be an apprentice for 3 years before you become a (snikar mästare) receive a master in carpentry and your carpenter license. I said yes, absolutely, so I went there and began learn and I got to sit on a stump for 3 months on that first job. Yes, there was one old stump that was just right to sit on, and another stump I was told was there to straighten the nails on, this was my first job, there was a big 15 liter barrel full of crocked nails and another empty barrel.

So the order was to straighten the nails put them into the empty barrel and so the nails could be used again. I straightened nails there 10 hours a day, day in and day out, I sat there, oj joy joy!!!(An expression of being overwhelmed, like oh, my gosh!!) Than after that I got to help the carpenters by holding on to one end of the boards and light work and things like that. I was there till the next fall about one and a half year; this was in the years 1918-1920. I also did some carpentering on the side there, for there were more people that were building there at that time and by then I could work at carpentry and I did because I had learned a lot, but I had to work in the black, because one had to put in the time and learn the trade, and then once you had the certificate or documented paper to actually work in the open you could go to work for pay.

There was a power station being built and there was also being built a paper company there in Kvaensveden. My sister Milda and her husband and Astrid their daughter was born there and the brothers were all born there and all lived there in Kvarnsveden so I was over there and did visit with that family while I was there. World War one, was still going on at this time. Anyway I finally did get the certificate, he the boss, wrote on it that I had put in the time and was now a full and legal carpenter. But the carpenter jobs were not paying all that much. So I bunked in the same barrack with men who were building a foundation, moving dirt and such things there on some other jobs. I laid there listening to the other men talking about how they were taking off to a place north where workmen were needed for a railroad building job. There they earned so much more money than where we were, so I thought I am going to go and check it out too. But I didn't get that exact job. I came home again a couple of years later in 1923 in the spring, my sister Ester was of course still home but Anna was not home anymore, she must have been working someplace too. There had been a strike in the woods in the timber industry there, and the strike had ended so they now needed a bunch of workers up in Voxna, Hälsingland so I thought I would try that.

The strike ended in the middle of April so there was a real push than of course at that time for timber, timber, everyone wanted and needed timber. We took the train up there; I had never been a timber worker before, this was my first time with this kind of work. We worked through May and pulled the timber by horse over to the Voxnam River the timber was put into the river and moved on the water when the spring flood came. But after that job ended, my friend Dalsten and me, we talked and thought we should go down there where they were building the railroad again, I still had that in my head. They were constructing the (östkustsbanan) East coast railroad, so we did go down there; it was to go from Gävle, Söderhamn up to Härnosand. So we took off to Söderhamn. We were not used to these circumstances; there were old (rallare) wanderers there, mustaches and a bit rough looking. So we took off on the road up to Hudiksvall then and up to Sundsvall, but in Sundsvall Dalsten turned around and went home. He ran out of money. I was broke too, but I went on alone anyway. I was a bit stubborn, anyway there was nothing to do at home, the only thing there was (jordbruket) farming, but I was not interested in that so it was just to keep going, and I wanted to and was determined to take care of myself anyway, because I had it in my head that I wanted to earn my own money and not give in.

Pappa Göte 1925 in Tränö Hälsingland a worker on the Eastcoast Railroad (Östkustbanan Gevle, Härnäsand (järnväg arbet)
(so stated on back of picture)

pappa 2nd from the right. His work crew with picks and shovels.

On the back of the picture, pappa said he is (en Rallare)

Pappa Göte early work and Army Life

Rallare = (wandering from place to place with work. 19 years old working on the Eastcoast railroad - 1922 - 2nd from the right.

Pappa Göte in the army he said (i lumpen) 1923-24

He is identified by the mark over head.
← blown up

During the depression I remember as I was walking along on the road from Hudiksvall and I saw as I walked by a church; this was the town and church that mammas sister Ingeborg's husband Fredrik Fasth came from, the name of the town was Stöde in Hälsingland. It was Christmas Eve as I approached the church; I had no idea where I would stay so I was walking at night. I went down into where I saw the horse stalls, down there where the horses and sleds were kept. The farmers had hay in there, there were two horses in each stall so I scraped together some scattered hay, it was really cold out and I laid down, I was really frozen and it seemed all of a sudden as I was laying there I heard the church bells clanging, it was morning and time for church so I had to get up and move. I shook off the hay and left and went out again on to the country road, maybe I was thinking of jumping on the train for I had done that before, but just then I looked around and I saw lights on in the houses close by, and it was Christmas morning, as this was close to the church, many were going to church but close by there, there was a house all lit up and it looked so light and nice and it was snowy out and cold, so I knocked on the door, and a man opened the door and invited me in. I asked if I could have a cup of coffee, he said yes of course, of course you can have a cup of coffee. During this time period people were all used to others coming to their doors, for there were so many people walking from job to job during the depression, but on Christmas morning it was a little ridicules' to have wanderers come to the door.

But there I was and there was a big table full of food, and he said go ahead and sit down and he got silverware and plates and so on, but I remember thinking it's too bad that I am not really very hungry right now, but I ate anyway and drank coffee, he was so nice, he said everyone but him had all gone to church. He felt a bit sorry for me that I had to go out into the cold again, if there is anything that you want to take with you, He said you are welcome to it and took out a bag for me! "No thanks" was my reply, "I am really full now" I didn't want to have stuff to carry. So I continued on my way down the road, by now it was beginning to get light outside. Down the road a ways, just at the side of the road there was a small house with lights on. I could see in through the window, I saw an old lady sitting there by the window, I could see there was someone else there too, and they did not have any curtains to block the view. I waved and she waved back so I thought, Oh, I think I'll go in and have a cup of coffee and visit for a while. There were two old ladies that lived there together, I did get some more coffee in fact I drank so much coffee so I nearly pied my pants, so I had to go out to the outhouse. But we visited, they wanted to talk, they too had some boys who were out there doing what I was doing. I sat there visiting till it got light and then I continued up the road. There were different work crews here and there along the way, but in between them there was nothing but (vildmark) wilderness. So when I just came down from Jusne? there was a town that couldn't be seen from the road, it laid just there where the railroad track was to go, the work was only a day here and there, but as I came down to Sunnasna, this was a little fishing town, and there was a crew there, the boss's name was Kalle Norberg, there were big rough looking guys working down there. But he was very nice and he said "come home with me and you can have the evening meal with us" as it was the end of the workday.

He asked, can you stay and work? There were 7 men on the crew and there should be 8, there were teams of horses that they drove and two by two they would work together and I was pared off with one really strong man (Ja vist) Oh yes of course, I said so I got to come along, I jumped in there and started working and the one that I was pared off with he looked just like an old Indian, he was dark skinned man and everything about him was broad and sturdy, they called him (tosockerskraka) I think his name was Almberg he was from Tosocker. He was the most awesomely strong man I have ever met, and I was so young and weak. He was so strong; he took very large shovelful of dirt and moved huge rocks. There were 8 now on the crew two on each wagon, and our job was to have the wagon full of gravel and when the horses returned with the empty wagon to take the filled one away again. This job was moving the gravel for building the railroad, removing the rocks and dirt getting ready for the railroad.

So at first I didn't even have the strength to go home after work, you can understand this was hard work. So I started asking for 5 minutes to go up into the woods to go to the bathroom (for att skita, jag sade att jag var skitnödig, in pappas words) I ended up doing that a little too often and soon they caught on and began to ask me and say "isn't it time for you to go up into the woods again?" Because it was a few too many times to be (skitnödig) needing to go to the bathroom again. So they made fun of me and realized that I was just a little bit too weak for that heavy job. This was in the year 1922 and I was just 19 years old. I have some pictures of this event; I stand there holding a shovel and by the horses. (Below) →

He was a great and wonderful man for thereafter he worked for two, to make up for me, he said to me that "you will make it, take a break, and you will make it". I worked on that job probably until October when that job was done, than I had traveling money, I had probably made 250 kr. From there I again went back up to (Hälsing skogarna) the woods in Hälsingland where I had come from before and they remembered me up there and I got a job again. I also had my tools up there so I went back up there to work and fall trees, chop wood and work in the forests again. I went up there for several years in a row in the fall, to work and chop for the same farmer. I was also known and friendly with many people there in Voxna, Halsingland. So the next year I also went back down to Ljusne where the railroad the (östkustsbannan) east coast railroad was being built. But then the (insenjör) engineer told me "why don't you take a contract down at Ljusne Broen, the bridge over Ljusnan for the railroad had already been built and was finished, but it now needed to be filled in around the bridge, so there was a big sand hill that we took the sand from. The job was to fill the wagons that were on the rail, and then we would were to move it and dump it.

So I took that job, we were paid so much for (cubiken) for a square meter. This was in the year 1924, there were two half-brothers, their names were Kalle and Olle and then me that worked together and I knew their mother too. Soon there came two other (kolingar) jokesters and started to work there with us also. There was a man that would drive around selling food and he came over to us too and he offered us credit until we were paied, so I was able to get credit too, for I was known as being honest and stood for and would pay for everything, so than soon there came those other two to work. These were some individuals that we did not know before, but there was loads of heavy work and they were needed, so they were hired. So anyway they also got credit, I spoke for them, and each of us was of course responsible for himself, so we could ask for and could get a (ett förskått) draw on the paycheck, I of course got some money to pay my bill. But the other two they had something else in mind that they had to pay, so then it went two more weeks till payday, but then they all of a sudden took off without paying their bill. So I had to pay their bill for them, Olle and Kalle they helped too, we didn't go away from our responsibility that was for sure. But I got so (ilsken) angry about that, that I quit that job. I heard from some old wanderers (rallare) that there was work in Orsa.

In Orsa there was a railroad that had been built years before, but now they needed to make some changes, it had to be made bigger and straighter by cutting some off the curves and also be improved with a stronger bed for the rails. I went to use the telephone and I called the man in charge up there, he said "yes, come an up, there is work", so there were three of us, we scraped together money for the fares. I had a clock and I got 5kr. for it at a pawnshop, I had plans of buying it back but I was never able to, it was a new clock too, too bad. So we got up there, and I knew some people up there too, and I thought that maybe we could sleep there. So I went and talked to him and luckily there was a barrack that we were able to use and move into. The job was to fill in the bed for the rails that had sunk down, and to fill in the curves to just the right height. There was the foreman that showed me how, he would set a mark 20 or 30 grade and then we just kept working mile after mile. There were many different crews on this job; each set had a certain distance to do. I was on that job and worked there until it froze up.

At that point we traveled down to Orsa again because it was the end of that job, I was told there by a man that I knew, he said to me "I have a job in Sveg" so we went to Sveg, it was only 13 miles (Swedish miles 12-13 American miles) "Ja aa, there is work and you can take these boys with you" he said. "We need to have a magazine built there at the train station"! And interestingly they still have it to this day, I have seen it outside there and we also needed to put in a track of rails. The man said "so take the job if you want it" so we all took off and went up there. This was the year 1924 and I am 21 years old, we were there over the Christmas weekend, and stayed there over Christmas with an old man who lived there. Then I took off and went back down to Voxna for I had been down there several winters. By this time I had worked on many jobs, as a carpenter, building roads and working on the railroads and in the woods falling timber.

The next year 1925 I traveled down to Söderhamn, there I ran into the same old boss as before and he knew me so he said "do you see those old shifters sitting out there, they came in and wanted a job, will you take them on as a crew and go up to Torne. I said, well I can go up there and look the job over, it wasn't so far. So I went out and asked the old men if they wanted to work for me, they looked me over, I was much younger than they, but they did go up with me to look the job over. The foreman said he would bring horses and the needed materials up there and he told me how much we would get for this part of the job, so we all took the job.

The old ones said, it was a big heavy job and not much pay, I felt the same too, they should have offered more money so we stayed 2 weeks on the job and then went down to get paid and they were paid 100 kr. to each man but I got 500 kr. At the end of the month we got an increase, they got increased to 150 kr for each man, so they felt that was better.

There was other work that the job also included such as welding (smidde) and drilling (borraing) So we were asked to stay on, the old men were told to go to ask the boy (me) I laughed, so I went and asked if we could have some papers in writing on it if we stayed on, so we did stay until it froze up but we were not able to get all the work out that went along with the contract that was written. I didn't get back up there again either, for it had to be finished the next year. By this time I too had gotten the traveling fever, just like the other wanderers (rallarna), someone who moves around a lot) so at that point I heard about work up in Arvidsjaur up in Lappland, they were going to build a railroad from Sundsvall up to Lappland. So I got that thought, I took the old rails and mostly walked from place to place, there were work companies (lager) all along the way up where one could get a meal and a bed for the night. There was one man that I knew he was the foreman at one place along the way where I had worked before and he said "why don't you stay here and work". He had a (en myra) swamp that had to be dug out and drained there had to be a ditch dug to drain the water out, I stayed for just a week and then continued up to Arvidsjaur. There I met a guy whose name was Moline that I later worked with in Funäsdalen somewhat later in life, mamma knew him too.

There should be a road built up there so we took a shift together, in other words a certain distance that we would work on and finish. I also worked in Värmland on the railroad in 1927, I remember especially they needed a rock splitter, I really didn't know how to do that but why not, they were to lay down large blocks. All this was done by hand and we made holes and placed some black powder in it and blew and broke the rock apart. I was there until just before Christmas, I had many jobs along the way. I had a job building a tap (en kran) took lumber I was even a painter for a short time up in Kiruna up in Lappland. Molin went south but I took the railroad up to Kiruna there was iron (malm) in the mountain up there and they sold that. This was about the 1928-29. I also set up the cabins for the work crews and that is when I painted for a bit. I lived in the polis station in one of the cells, that was something that many did and it was allowed the police told me to stay there. I didn't have any work clothes either for the work, but the foreman said that I will find you some (arbetsbyxor) workpants. I was nicely dressed in a suit with a vest, and I became a painter only for a couple of days, I didn't even get paid for the job, he yelled at me for quitting. I thought I would go back to the job on the road that I had built on before, so I thought about that and I took the (malm) iron train to Narrvik, every wagon there needed to be filled, there were at least 20 wagons, so then I took a job to load one of the wagons.

I hopped on the train and rode along. It was beautiful scenery along the trip, we traveled through bends along a beautiful land with birds and wild looking lands, once in a while we would go through a tunnel, I had heard of them along the tracks, but the dust from the iron was really terrible as it was flying all over. It was not so long but one couldn't almost see thereafter. I began to watch for the tunnels, as I sat up on the iron in the wagons. After a while we came to Narrvik. I jumped down and shook all my clothes off; I even took my pants off and shook them off in front of the people that were there. They asked me how it was to ride up there on the wagon, not too bad after I figured it out was my reply. But I became very thirsty, I was told that "you did such a good job" or something like that. Anyway I was able to go to a restaurant and I got coffee and cake (tårta). It did cost but I still had some money left.

At that point I went to the harbor and took a look at the boats. I knew that there were mail boats along the whole coastline and I could go along all the way down to Bode. Mail was delivered all along the coast. So I went along on one boat it was just a small boat kind of like Ida Maria (that was the name of Pappas fishing boat here in Juneau) He said I could ride along if I would polish the (messing) copper on the boat, the handles and so on, the parts on the boat, there was a lot of copper there on the boat, if you do that you can have food also. I got off at Boden (in the northern part of Sweden) I knew the route I was to travel for I had been there working on the roads before on other jobs. The road I decided to go was to go all the way to the Norwegian border and do a roundtrip even up to Kiruna to see what there was up there. Then I went down on the Norwegian side on the (Hukkiruta) down to Boden, there then was a road from Boden that I could take. It was the most crooked road down through a valley, along the beach up towards the Sunetellmark route, the Norwegians had a (druva) mine there that was just on our border with Norway and there I stayed overnight in a baric, and in the morning I was invited to eat with them. After that there was a Norwegian fellow that came with a paper bag to give to me, I asked what that was for? It was a bag full of money, full of the Norwegian 1 krowns, at this particular time they all had a hole in the middle of the coin.

But they had all taken up a collection for me because I was (på luffen) a wanderer without a destination looking for work during difficult times. They lived in the (vildmarken) wild themselves and knew that I was in need, they were really nice fellows. I wandered down through a path that would take me over the border again, it was many miles but I can't really remember how far this was. I came into a little village up there in Lappland where all who were there were Lapps, only the preacher and wife were white. I heard the church bells ringing. I took some of my clothes off and tied them together and then tie them to my back as I came to a creek or stream that I had to wade over, I went over and then dried myself and thereafter took the train down to Jokkmok. I think I saw only one house and I went in and the lady of the house she was frying pancakes on this Sunday morning, so I was invite in for a meal. And I also was invited to sleep there that night. I told the preacher's wife about all the coins that I had been given and how heavy they were. I couldn't keep them in my pockets, my jacket only had one button on it, I thought if I had a string or rope I could string the money on that and put them around my neck but I didn't have a string either.

I don't think there had ever been a transient person wander through that place before, but even so I was probably better dressed than the people that lived there, but those coins were too heavy for my pockets. The lady said that if I waited and stayed there a while, I was invited to spend some time in a cabin that they had, she would try to get some paper money to exchange with my coins. As I left I even got some pancake with me and part of the money in paper bills. As I left there I wandered all the way down to a little cabin (coya) that we had built on another job shift before, it still stood there. But there was no work there so I continued on to Jokkmokk, I felt at home there, there was a lady her name was Anna, everyone called her just Anna where we stayed. I went out to dance and felt really at home there. This is way up north in Norrbatten; mostly Lapps lived there with some whites taking up tracts of land beginning to move in up there.

After a while I followed the same route that I had followed before. There were no roads really to follow only trails that the Lapps had created and that they traveled on through the woods and swamps. Through the swamps they had laid trees as a path over the bog so they could be walked upon. I have never seen a place that had more (myrbar or jortron) cloudberries or bog berries than this place. We ate so much berries we couldn't leave them alone they were so very good. It was miles and miles of bogs with berries in them. Then I went back to Overange to work on building the railroad, the work was just beginning up there in Arvidsjaur We chopped trees down there but I didn't stay there very long. I saw Melin there, the guy I worked with later with in Funasdalen. From there I heard of a job way down south in Kasseforsh in Halland, they were building a (kraftstatjon) power plant. This was just outside of Laholm. They needed workers down there so if we were willing to go down, they would give us tickets for transportation. This was a state job. On the way we went past my home, so I stopped by to see my father and Karl-Ivar was just a little (pavling) one crawling around on the floor at that time. This was around 1935-36.

My mother had died a few years before that time probably in 1927. (Note: She actually died on January 30 1929) Pappa continued: I did go home for her funeral and I did get home to see her every year as I was coming and going past there from different jobs. Her funeral was in the winter, I remember it was white outside; Anna my sister had my address and notified me.

So from there we came down to Laholm anyway after visiting, this was a beautiful old city down further south, there forgotten by the world along the ocean and I worked there on the power station for the Swedish state. There was need for carpenters and I became a timber man carpenter, the job was to build a (fångdam) it was a retainingdam above the dam, this was built just from timber and wood and cement to pull or keep water for other things, like streams or other needs, also if they needed to drain some water if it got to full it could be averted into this upper dam. This was a big job and I stayed on the job till the next year, almost a year. I didn't stay anywhere very long, I liked to move around and go all over, I was alone and had a good work report in my pocket so there were no problems. I wore them out though in my pockets while traveling, but I was always able to find work because(man skötte sig) I always took care of myself to do a good job and they knew they could trust me, I knew many people from time to the next time as I traveled around. I had such good recommendation from each job that there were never a problem finding a job and work as I moved around. These reports or recommendations came with the paycheck for the job, as one moved to a new job.

It was the same in Funåsdalen too. (this was where our family home was). Also when I worked on the east coast railroad one always received a report for the work we had done as we left the job. I traveled up and down, across and back many, many times in my years. During this time we also (tjyvåkte) sneaked on and rode the trains, it was not difficult to jump on and catch a ride, if the foreman saw you they really didn't care because there were so many doing it everyone was riding looking for work, with little or no money. It was a on the way between Laholm and Göteborg there was Halmstad and many others cities in between as I traveled along. So I came to Göteborg and went down to a place named Lillabommen, and (rulla hat) lived it up for a while, there were loads of seamen down there and the money one had didn't last very long, there was still depression at this time for many. For people like me in construction and building and willing to move around things were pretty good, so I had a job most of the time, but at other times one would beg as one moved along and of course sneak on the train for a free ride. There were no busses or cars that one could sneak on for a ride. While there in Göteborg one day down by the railroad station someone hit me on the shoulder and said "what the devil are you doing down here?" I turned around and it was Karl-Theodor my oldest brother (he is sitting center in this picture above, his wife, daughter Anna-Lisa and her daughter behind him, and papa Gote behind in the back, and other cousin in front.)

I remembered that he worked there the night shift at the central bank. So he wanted me to go home with him, he lived there on Postgatan, so we had a celebration party; we went out to eat and had a good time. I had a bit too much to drink that night, and this was the only time I ever got picked up by the police or spent a few hours in the jail. But after only a few hours in the middle of the night it was very dark outside they woke me up and led me to the back door, I wondered now what, outside the back door there was a motorcycle with a side wagon on it, I was told to get in and off we went through the streets out toward a road that led out of town. We went for about a half an hour and I could see the lights and the sky against the dark trees, all of a sudden in the midst of the darkness on the road out of town he stopped, and ordered me out, he warned me to head up the road and not ever to come back again into town. It was so dark I couldn't even see anything but up ahead, only the tops of the trees against the sky. After only a few minutes of walking I heard some noise up ahead, I thought to myself, in the middle of the night what could that be? There was a curve in the road and as I got up a bit further I could now see a light in the distance. It was a brick factory and there they burned with coal, it was warm and nice in there, there were long, long ovens and on the other side of the road there was some housing.

Certainly the police knew that and when he let me off, they knew and took wanderers like me that far. The man smiled as I came in, in the middle of the night. I was well dressed but he knew then that the police had given me a ride out of town. Yes, I told him the police had given me a

25

ride this far and told me to get going up the road. He said, there is nothing to lie down on here except the bricks, but there was a stack of newspapers from others that had been there before me to lie on. He said there were many others that had come through there before me. This was in the fall, probably in August. So I thought it was probably time to go up to Voxna for the timber season again, I knew many there. So than I had to go up to Trollhettan and I was there a few days. From there I continued north.

There were a few cars at this time but mostly horse and buggy to travel on the roads. But I didn't see even one car all the way from Laholm in Bohuslän all the way to Göteborg and of course no chance to get a ride.

But while in Laholm I didn't find the kind of work I was looking for right away so I took a job in the fields harvesting sugar beets. The pay was 60-90 kr. for the barrel, there were many there working from Småland, and they imported workers from there. This was outside town; it was a small town but loads of work, so needing many workers. First you pulled them out of the ground and then lay them in a pile cut off the greens and filled the barrels. It was a poor way of earning money. It took just a week to harvest this field; it was hard work, the roots were long so it took someone healthy. But it was a job, I than did get other work after that, there in Laholm. But I continued up to Trollhattan in Dalsland. They have a canal there with steps, stairs in it, (maybe a lock) it was a nice town, nice people, and nice girls☺. I was there a week and after that time I got going again up toward Orsa. I stayed there for a while I did not have any timetable to go by. And I did get a job in Orsh.

I knew that I needed to be up in Voxna in December for the time of the year they did the timber falling and chopping, I sat there by the railroad drinking coffee and reading a paper as a foreman at the railroad there began speaking to me, he felt sorry for me it was Christmas Eve. I was going to try to make it up to Voxna. He asked me if I had a place to sleep that night. It was snowing and cold out. He also asked me if I was planning on sneaking a ride on the train, I told him yes, they didn't mind he even told me when the train was due in.

Anyway he lived alone, he asked if I wanted to sleep with him, we ended up at the Salvation Army, he lived and worked there. He had a nice room but there was only one bed? But I thought I would stay anyway because it was late. But we had no sooner lain down, when he began to grab at me; I soon realized that he was one of those men's men, ush ush! I did not expect that, this was the first and only time I have ever met such a person in all my life. So I got up and it was snowing and it was still some hours before the train station opened, so I went out in the hall of the church and found a corner. I lay down but didn't sleep very well; I heard the man and some others men talking out there. They asked about me, he said that it was some fellow without work that he had helped and they thought that he was such a great guy for helping me. It was Christmas Evening so there was a bowl of apples there, I helped myself to one and while they sang hallelujah, I quickly left and went down to the railroad station; it was still dark out and snowing. The train station was not open yet, but there were some guys there and they let me in, out of the cold. So I laid there on a wooden bench. But that was the only time I have ever experienced such a thing, but I had never been in or put myself into such a situation like that either of course.

So I got on the train, I did have money this time so I took it to Furudal it was not too far 60-70 km approximately. Anna my sister lived there. She had a job at a hotel and she was not married yet at that time. I also met there some acquaintances that I had worked with in the woods up in Voxna, and we got together. I borrowed a krona, it didn't cost so much in those days to ride the train, and took the train up to Voxna and in that place I was just like I was at home. I went over to Anna Svensson, I became friends with her husband through the timber cutting that we had done together. I met him down at the railroad station and he invited me to go home with him. I knew everyone there. Nice people! When I left there I left my tools there so I would have them for the next year's timber falling season. Each person worked for themselves, so one had to have one's own tools. I had an ax and a timber tail (timbersvans) they cannot be found here (in America) I also had (kilar) edges (barkjarn) bark irons. Everyone had their own except if brothers worked together such as the Tagg boys (speaking of Ida's brother Par and Kristian) they shared tools. I went up to Voxna many winters; I went up there for work 1923, 24, 25, 26, and 27. I think this probably was the year 1927.

You see all the construction jobs, railroad or road construction that I was on, they froze up in October and by November for sure. One year when I was up in Funasdalen (where mamma's family lived) we froze up in September, that was the worst I ever experienced, that was years later of course. Anyway, any moving of earth or stone could not be done because the ground would freeze up, it would be much too cold to cut stone also, so the only thing to do was to go and cut timber in the winter.

It wasn't always a sure thing that one would go back each year, if I did I did, if not I didn't worry about the tools. When I was alone and moving around I didn't care that much what happened or where I was. But it happened so I did go back each year for those 5 years to Voxna. Some years I was also in Halsingland and working in the woods there also, than I bought new tools as, 25 kronor for a saw it wasn't so expensive.

Many times I would hop on the train, one time I was told by some railroad employee to hop on. I chose a place way back in the end wagon and there I sat in the brake shack. In those days there had to be several brakemen in different positions along the train so they had several of those small places on several wagons for the brakeman to sit in and break as they came to hills along the track or when the loads were really heavy. There was just enough room for one in there and no brakeman in that particular wagon so I sat in there; I had a really nice view from up there. I got off at Vansbro Dalarna, I wanted to stay there for a while and knew some people there and wanted to visit them.

One year I rented a horse and even drove and transported timber. It was always important to get a work record or a report card from each work or employer because there were so many people without work that would come into towns, and if they didn't have a record of or from past work they had done that was a problem. So this would show if they had worked, if they were willing to work, if they had tried to find work before, if not they were kicked out by the police as soon as they got into town. Like me in Göteborg, that was my own fault. Not always would the timber cutting employer write out a report, but I asked him for one anyway after that, so he wrote one out for me. Yes, one year I was so daring that I went down to a farmer and rented a horse for the winter and I also barrowed or rented a sled to pull the timber on, and that winter I transported timber instead of cutting. It was not an easy to hook up the horse to the sled, but I did it. So I did all kinds of jobs, if there was a job I would do it. I was not afraid of any kind of work.

I continued to have many jobs and continued to travel partly the same areas and routes as I have already told of, but in part I also traveled and worked in new places. You see Sweden is long and narrow, so when I began, I came into the area Hälsingland, Gestricksland, Medelpad, Dalarna. I was in north Sweden also, they found gold up in Boliden, Västerbotten it lays between Skellefteå and Jorn, I took the inlands rails up to Jorn and they were building railroad between Jorn and Arvidsjaur. But they had just found gold up in Boliden too and that was pretty close, only a few miles 5-6 Swedish miles between these places.(one Swedish mile is 12-13 American miles) I had to walk of course, but I went down there, there were no cars at all so I looked there for a job. There were only 6-7 men that were there working they had not gone to deep. There wasn't much work at that time, but I really didn't want that job anyway. It was not built up at all, there was just building that they would change in when they came up out of the hole and the water poured down there, there was just a wet swamp. So it was just to go to the next job. I went back 2 years later and by than it was all built up; even the railroad had been built up from the (druvan) site out to the Skelleftea railroad. So they could transport the gold and copper (malm astrek) from the mine.

In the year 1928 at midsummer I was there again with a couple boys but there was some frost on the road and so as we were taking the corner we had to speed up to get out from the side road with the frost and it went to fast and I had my arm out the window and the car tipped over on its side, and I broke my arm. We were on the way to Skelleftea that was where the nearest hospital was and where the boys lived too. I had never been there before, the doctor checked me out and I stayed there for a few days in the hospital.

My arm was very swollen so I got a shot for the pain. He asked me where I lived I told him in the barns, he was used to those kind of answers as there were many out looking for work in those days. But he needed to know where to send the bill, and I was or had my name in the church down where I was a resident, that was where the payment had to come from, so the Swedish government paid for things like that. I think I went into shock though; I was so very tired, I was not sick but it took everything out of me. I wasn't able to work at all, it all happened so fast. So I took the train up to Furudal, Dalarna to my sister Anna's she was married by this time I thought maybe I would go see her, but she told me I had better travel down to Bollnäs to the hospital there. But he gave me a ticket to the hospital where I was written (it seems that they had to get help or service in their own district where they were born or where they were a resident) so he sent me down to Falun, I was told to not eat any salt, and that was about all. There was no casts in those days, but after a while as I just kept going, walking down the roads it just got better. It didn't seem like it took too long.

But everything went well, but it was such a long way to the doctors, most of the time there were just midwives or someone knowledgeable that would help when someone would break a toe or something, or have a scrapes and such. I never had an accident with an ax or anything working all those years in the woods! It was important to follow the rules and then you would stay safe.

Sweden

Sweden
Background Information

Geography
Sweden is a land of green, wooded hills and slopes, of clear lakes and streams, of peaceful pastoral scenes, of busy modern cities, and of well-developed systems of transportation and commerce. Though Sweden lies in the Arctic latitudes, her climate is greatly tempered by the Gulf Stream, and local agriculture can provide most of the country's food needs. Emigrants from Sweden can never quite forget the beauty of the countryside or the long seashore with its rocks and bays and crystal clear water.

Sweden is divided geographically into three regions. Götaland in the south includes some of the chief ports of Sweden. Svealand, just north of the largest lakes, is called "central" Sweden, although it is really within the bottom half of the country. Here Stockholm, the capital, is located. Norrland covers well over half of Sweden, including mountainous Lapland, and borders on Norway, Finland, and the Gulf of Bothnia (bahf-nee-a). Sweden thus presents a widely varied landscape: the fertile plains of the south, the wooded lake country, the extensive forests of the north, and the barren slopes of the Arctic area. In the north, winter lasts for seven cold, dark months. Lakes and harbors freeze over sufficiently for buses and trucks to be driven on the ice. The summer rainfall is more than adequate for farming.

Industry
It is interesting that in Sweden, though many of the industries are privately owned, they are controlled with a fairly strong element of government supervision. The state owns and operates the rail and bus lines, power plants, post office, telephones, and radio and television stations, although some private competition in some of these areas does exist. The rich iron mines in the far north are also state owned, yet free enterprises remains the basis of the system, and relatively few industries have been nationalized.

Vast forests constitute the real wealth of the country, but abundant water resources and high-grade iron ore have also combined to create the basic economy, which is particularly known for the production of crystal, timber, paper, cars, trucks, electrical machinery, matches, stainless steel, razor blades, ball bearings, and textiles.

Holidays
Sweden's national holiday is June 6, called Flag Day, at which time the flag is flown over the entire land. Walpurgis Eve [Wal-pur-gees] ("Valborgsmassoafton") on April 30 and May Day on May 1 welcome the return of Spring. Large bonfires are lit, spring clothing is worn, and spring is greeted with chorus songs and poetry. The Friday and Saturday closest to the summer solstice, which is the end of June, are celebrated as Midsummer Eve and Day. At this time the countryside is at its most beautiful with greenery, flowers, night-long twilight and pleasant temperatures. Maypoles are covered with greenery and flower wreaths and danced around to the music of violin and accordion. Folk costumes are worn by those who have them and youngsters stay up to watch the sun rise. Tradition has it that on Midsummer night a girl will dream of her future husband if she picks seven different types of wildflowers and places them under her pillow. The great religious holidays of Easter, Christmas, and the three-day holiday of Pentecost are also celebrated as in many other parts of the world. Easter is a two-day holiday starting with Good Friday. The Christmas season in Sweden lasts for six weeks, starting with First of Advent, four Sundays before Christmas. On December 13, during the darkest season, St. Lucia Day, the Festival of Light, is celebrated. Christmas itself is a three-day holiday, starting on Christmas Eve, December 24. Christmas season ends on January 13, when the Christmas tree is taken out.

HÄRJEDALEN

FUNÄSDALEN

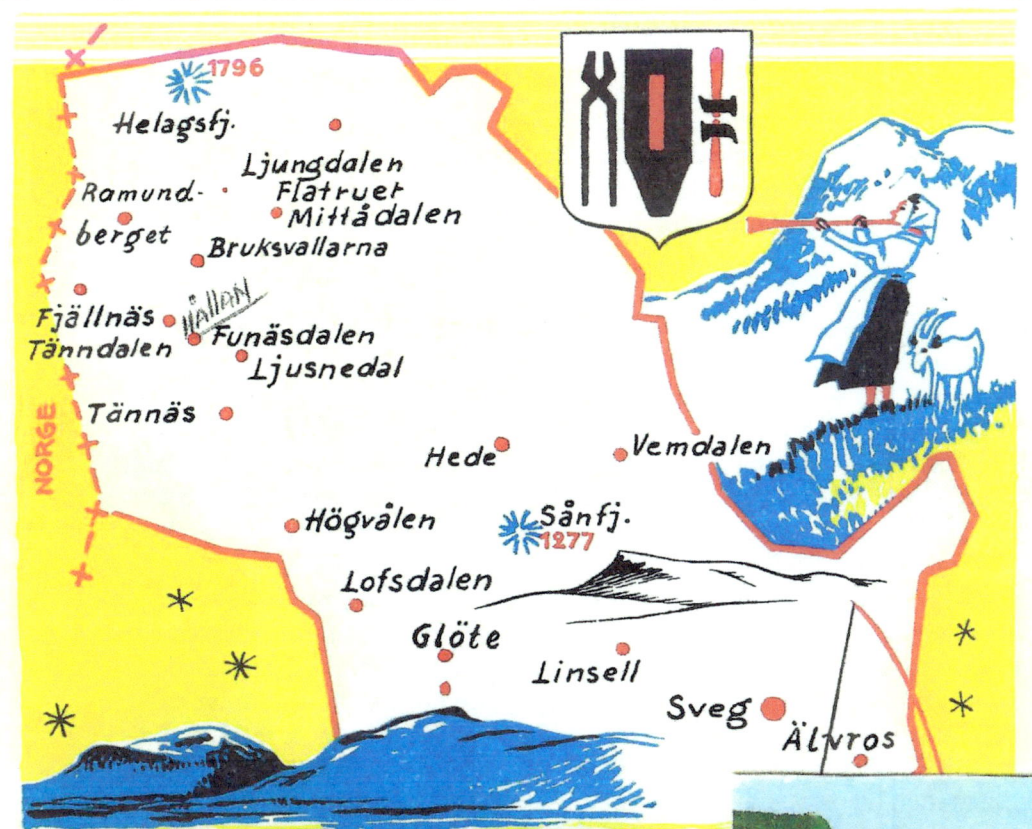

- Helagsfj. 1796
- Ljungdalen
- Ramundberget
- Flatruet
- Mittådalen
- Bruksvallarna
- Fjällnäs
- Vallan
- Funäsdalen
- Tänndalen
- Ljusnedal
- Tännäs
- Hede
- Vemdalen
- Högvålen
- Sånfj. 1277
- Lofsdalen
- Glöte
- Linsell
- Sveg
- Älvros
- Lillhärdal

NORGE

The beginning of my life in Funäsdalen, Härjedalen

I remember being in the hospital on one other occation in Sveg, Harjedalen. I got a red rash that covered my whole body except my head; I got the rash up in Bräkke, Norway at a dance. (Just across the border from Funäsdalen) Ida was there too but I fell down weak, kind of fell apart (capsaisa) I had to have someone drive me to Funäsdalen and to the old midwife nurse there, but she ordered an ambulance that took me to Sveg. I probably looked to terrible. There they wrapped me in white cotton and sowed me into it. I was probably there a couple of weeks because the cook from up there on the job in Funäsdalen by Pär Mhyr in Hållan, her name was Anna she came down to see me, I went out with her a couple of times to dance.

The first time I ever went to Funäsdalen was in 1937 and I ended up staying there thereafter. I had never been there before when I came up there. That was a place (det var ett avhal, en plats någonting på sidan av all förstånd) a hole, even off the map, a place on the side of all understanding, yes not anyone would even dream of going there or want to come to or stay in Funäsdalen permanently.

That year and winter leading up to coming to Funäsdalen I was in Sarna, Dalarna chopping timber. I had been there a couple of winters. From Sarna to Tännas, Härjedalen there is a road over the mountains (#311) it is a dirt road, only those living there really travel on the road. It was a small town and I got really well know there too. I met August Molin there who I worked with in Funäsdalen and many others, one man named Frestrom and they were going to Sveg and then up to Funäsdalen, they were going to build a road up there and it would be a summer job, so I thought I would go along too. This was the first time that we had rented a car to take us up; there were about 4-5 of us that went up there to Funäsdalen. We stayed there at the old café, with rooms for rent, I can't remember the name, maybe it was Gestis that was there, but it wasn't all that special. I took a shift and they did too and then we began to work on the road construction up there through Hållan. (where later on we had a small house that papa built and where we lived) There was a road to where Mattias lived, beyond there, there was forest and mountains up above. We had downhill terrain there, a lean and we got our fill down a ways from Matthias; I had a good shift there and earned good money. I believe I came up to Funäsdalen in the year of 1937 as I said and stayed there all the years after that while there was road construction up there. After that I went down to Sveg to work on the road there, it was the state that was doing the work building and improving the roads in Sweden.

The first time I saw mamma, she was with her cousin Inger Tagg (she was the daughter of mamma's brother Johan, later Lysholm was her married name) they were out walking on the old road that went past Lina Roos house, a little further past Mattias up there in Hållan, there where we were renting their little apartment upstairs. The Roos were actually up in (faboden) an old place in the mountains where they took their cows up to grace during the summers. We had an old kitchen there and we were trying to do some cooking and learning how to make some food. I was kind of the food father, meat I could cook, especially meatballs and of course pancakes I could make those. (Swedish thin or oven puff pancakes) This was the first year that I was up there, so we lived there upstairs at Göns Roos and one Sunday morning there came two girls walking on the old road which took them right past our window, I stood there looking and I said (men nu, men nu, kommer min!) look now, look now, here comes mine! Yes, here come two good looking girls! Johann Parsson who was there, said to us, I know those girls. He was the type who knew everything, had seen everything, and had heard everything, so he looked out the window too and said, yes I know those (tjåjer- slang for) girls. We were new there and had not seen them before, we had been out dancing a few times but these girls had not been there, so we had not seen these two girls before. The other men came to the window too; they had not seen them either. So I ran down to the fence and began to talk to them, we had a nice visit. I asked them if they lived here and they giggled and laughed and in short told me they lived down there below the road.

It was Sunday and a nice day and we had it off, so that evening I took and walked down to Tagg's. I knew Kristian and Pär Tagg, I knew that they lived down there, for I had worked with them on the road crews, so I went down there and **"there they were"** (speaking of the girls, pappa used a louder exited voice) so I got to know what their names were, they joked and kidded "I am from there and there" so that was the first time we met. Actually Ida had just returned from Norway and then Inger, who lived in Trondheim Norway, had also come over with her. So Ida had been gone and that was the reason I had not seen her before. So we got to know each other thereafter. But there were many, many boys there looking for girls, but I too got to dance with them of course! I went out with others too for a while. Ida used to say to me "there is your old girlfriend".

While I was in the Hospital in Sveg the job up in Funåsdalen ended, but I needed to go back up there anyway because my tools were up there. I was really good friends with Pär Myhr so he said to me "that sofa is yours you can sleep there, if you want to stay for a little while". So I lived there with Pär Mhyr and visited at the Tagg's home of course, I was not in any hurry to go anyplace else.

At this time there was the older house that they all lived in, which was torn down later and Kristian and Pär built the house that mormor and Ida later lived in. (the one that never got finished or painted)

At that time mormor (grandma Karin Tagg) and Par, Kristian and Ida lived there but there were many that came and went there, many visitors, Stina of course and Johan and families from Norway and Ingeborg's family from Sveg. Mormor was a hard worker, she was the main one to take care of and run the house. I think she liked me because at times she would go out and chase guys away if she didn't like them.

During that time there were dances to go to on the weekends, down in Funasdalen (approximately 5 km down from Hallan) and also up in Tanndalen (5-6 km up the mountain road towards Norway) mostly inside but also outside in covered areas. We got there mostly by car, Par had an old car that was always breaking down, it took a lot of time for him to keep it going, but when it didn't he would crawl under the car and fix it. He didn't really have the tools but made due and was able to keep it going, and it went and ran pretty well.

(Note: I asked pappa "what was it that made you attracted to mom and decided to choose her and settle down". He simply said)

(Jag tyckte om na,) I liked her, and there were so many other guys that also that liked her and that did a lot towards being interested in her! He laughed.☺ And gammel karinga, (the old woman, meaning Karin Tagg her mother) I liked her more than Ida at the first for she was so full of conversation and made such good sense, she spoke with understanding and was also really fun and would joke and

Swedish Flag

Hållan, Funäsdalen is where we lived in Sweden.

✱ markes the spot Hållan 4 km. from town

Funäsdalens sea where we used to ice skate

FUNÄSDALENS KYRKA

— is where we went to Church —

Baracken Ulvön
Fredagen den 28 de Januari
1941

Älsklingen MIN!!!

Älsklingen Min! Älsklingen Min!

Hur mår du? Hur mår du?
Hur trivs du? Jag trivs gott att
då på inte får vara hos dig
Älskling. Längta då så jag mår
på bara, men på lördag
varit är på hos dig igen
allt samlas. Men i kväll får du
i kväll har jag främst Herr
Perron i säng med brev.
Hur skola Erika och min
eiga lilla älskling. Hälla
Älskling vi ses på lördag kväll
de var Goto i går å karl i
dag. så de orkar sig nog
hemma, hemma på lördag
din egen Göte

The Barracks in Ulvån   Friday the 28th January 1941

MY dearest Love!!!   My dearest Love!   My Dearest Love!

How are you? How do you feel? Are you happy? I am not happy at all when I cannot be with you; I began being lonely the moment I got on the bus, but on Saturday at the latest I will be with you again.   My Golden Friend! thank you for the letter.   Tonight I have written Mr. Person in Sveg a letter, Mr. Able in Grika, and now my little darling in Hållan we will see each other on Saturday evening. It was Göte yesterday and Karl today, so everything will be fine.   Hugs and more hugs on Saturday, Your own Göte

Look

- We went skiing on Skarvarna
- Tänndalen - Pappa - Mamma went dancing there.
- We lived in Hållan - between Tänndalen and Funäsdalen.
- Tännäs - some of Grandma Tagg's family lived there.
- Hede - our cousin & family live there
- Vemdalen - Grandma Tagg lived there in a Nursing Home.
- Sveg - our aunt Ingeborg lived there - we visited there.
- Ytterhogdal - pappa worked there. Mom, Karin, Ruth went along.

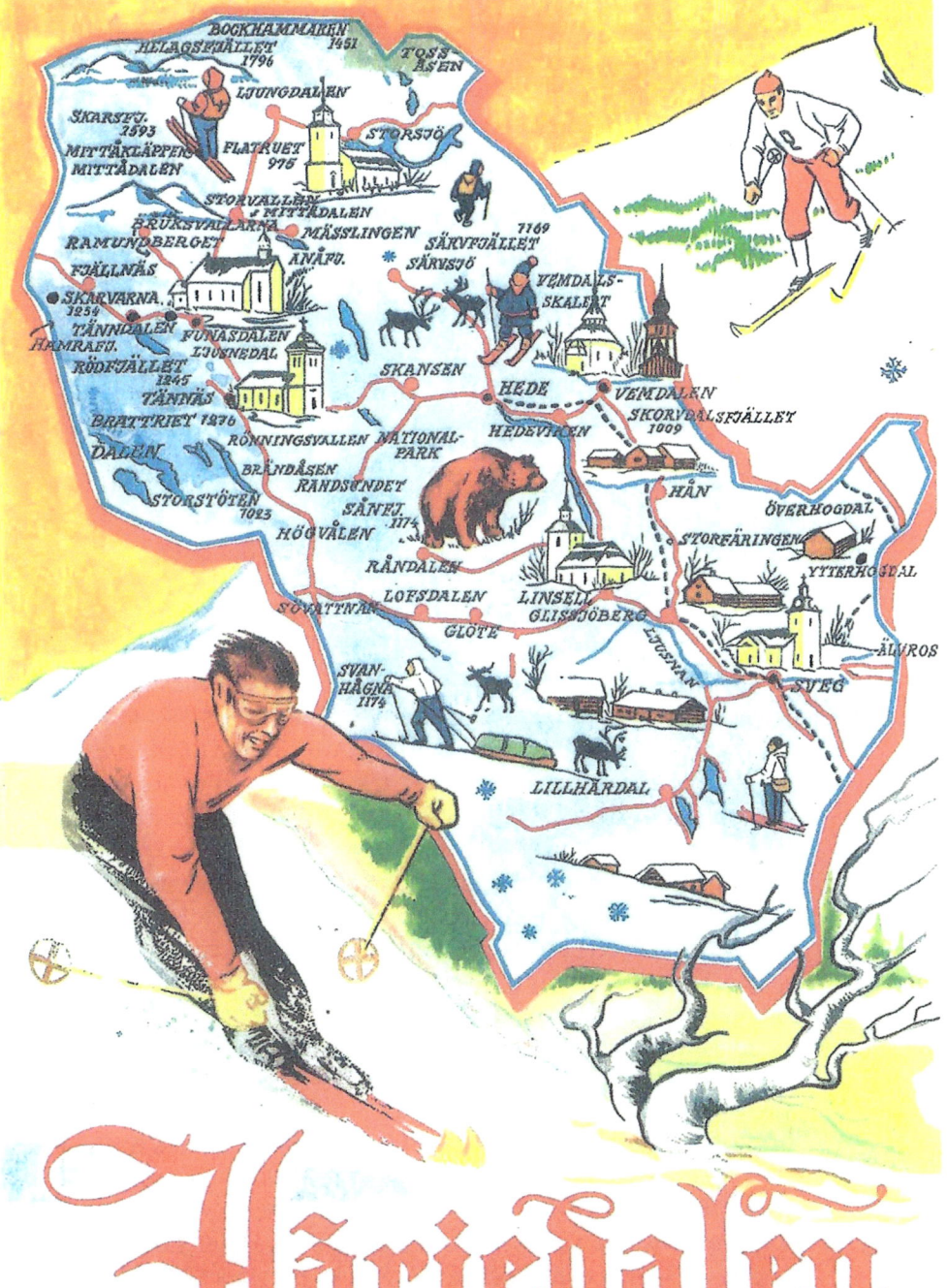

Funäsdalen, Sweden
Hållan - 5 km. North
— 1956 —

Härjedalen

- Our Lutheran Church
- Our school house - red
- Funäsdals sea - where we went ice skating.
- Spring 1956 - grade levels.
  Karin finished 7th
  Ruth finished 5th
  Sune finished 1st

laugh. She was also serious and very orderly in everything. She tried to keep the boys in order and to get them to help, I would help her, this (pigga up henne) lifted her spirits and make her happy and she and I had a lot of good times together. Ida was not home this one time when Pår Mhyr had a birthday, so we were invited to come and celebrate with him and (gamla) the old one and I went to his party, there they had (koka brandvin) made home brew. There were all kinds of people there, the owner of Hedvalls, the general store down town, he came, Ida she also came later. I remember we stood outside at Pår Myhr he had a barn and just in front there was a (stora dyng högen) big manure pile.

They were carrying the home brew out in buckets and some had brought cups others drank out of the buckets. Hedvall a big man, he got drunk and others too and there was a Norwegian lady there and she wanted a drink too so Hedvall tried to give her a hug, but she said something negative to him and gave him a shove and he fell back into the (shit högen) big manure pile. His whole back side was very dirty. Oh, you should have seen (gamla) the old one laugh and of course everyone was laughing, several people reached out their hands and helped him out of there. It was a very funny scene. I stayed there for the whole evening, but I think the old one went home, and it was probably in the morning sometime that I thought of going home. I walked so very weird or strange (kneptigt). And as I was walking home I climbed over the fence (made of long trees the old fashion way) that was on the down side. I remember just like a dream that I went over there, what I went over there for, I don't know, but then I remember tree tops and I walked and walked. What had happened was that I had gone outside the fence the whole way, all the way up to Hållan. Just before I got to Mattias there was a big hole, that had been dug and it was just like a little lake and I walked straight into that pond, I fell down, the water covered me completely including my face. So I was a bit (sanselös sa Norsken) without my senses, said the Norwegian, from partying all night long. But I woke up quickly as I fell into the water.

So anyway I went down to the (till gamla) old one, I was living there at that time. Ida she was gone, she was a (piga) maid in Tännas so I got to live there for a bit. Oh, I was wet but the old one said, now you get undressed and she threw a pair of pants towards me. I don't know if they were mine or someone else's but she said to get undressed and she said, "I will wash your clothes". I did as I was told, and I did barrow the pants from her and she went out to the little stream (bäcken) in front of her house. The sun shone all the daylong so by the evening I was able to get my own clothes on again. But I remember how she laughed when I came down all muddy and wet, it was a white mud that stuck to you. I went out into the middle of the stream and she began to clean the mud off of me. She knew where I had been to fall into that mud for it was only found in one place. And of course this was in the morning about 7 am for there had been that party all night long. Most of the people just laid down there on the ground that night. It was so nice we didn't need to go inside; there was only (mygg) some mosquitoes. But it was nice out.

(Men då gick jag illa, men tänk vad hon tog reda på mig) Wow, I sure did go wrong that time, but my goodness how she took care of me. I still remember it like a dream, my goodness how (shitig) dirty I was. Oh, she was very good at everything that lady, she did not wait until tomorrow but she took care of the problem and did it right away. They were poor of course and didn't have much, there was no fancy stuff to dress up into everyone was very ordinary, and wore the same stuff all the time. The food was ordinary too, I don't think they had much gardening going on, maybe a little but the boys had jobs and they all had a small pension too and

Stina would come over from Norway with provisions and was there to help for some months during the summer. The boys helped during that time at least. But it seemed that there was always coffee and food at all time as far as I was aware of. She was always hospitable and gracious.

Ida worked as a maid (piga) up in Tännas for the shopkeeper up there for a long time. So I barrowed an old heavy cycle and did go up there and visit her, the trip up and back went pretty well. Ida came along with me back to Funäsdalen, getting a ride on the back. It went pretty well as I said until we hit a soft spot with some lose gravel on the road where we almost turned over, Ida was a bit scared I remember but it was kind of funny too, and we did came out of it OK. There were busses that traveled during the day that one could take, but in the evening when I was going there, there were none. But it defiantly was a terrible old motorcycle!

We went out kind of steady for about two years as I worked there on the roads in Funäsdalen and Tännas for most for those two years. We were married in August of 1941. I don't know exactly how we came up with the idea of marriage but it seemed that it was a natural thing, maybe mamma asked me!! (He winked)☺ I can't remember, but her mom also wanted that there should be (ardning pa det) order on things and that it was just time. She was the last child and also a girl and there were a lot of (bus fron runt där) wild seeds around there, so her mom she was concerned about her of course. I understood how she felt, for I had done a lot of traveling and was a bit older, but it made no difference to her or the old one. Maybe she even trusted me more for that.

It must have been planned by Ida and her mom; it was in the fall in the Lutheran church there in Funäsdalen. After the wedding there was a party of course up there in Hållan at their house. There came a whole bunch of workers from the road construction job and one even lost his false teeth at the celebration. Their house was an old red house that was tore down later and another house was built after that, which was the one you kids knew. But during the celebration we were mostly outside. There was home brew and dancing and a big happy party all night long. I had built a little house (barrack) that we lived in at first and we also lived in it as we moved around working on the different road jobs, Ida she was the cook. But on the wedding night everyone partied all night long, just sat around outside, towards morning Ida and I went into our little cabin, but the sun was starting to come up already so there was no sleeping and Stina, Ida's sister came in and sat down on the bottom of the bed and visited into the morning. This little cabin was just temporary, a few men could almost pick it up but this was on grandma's lot at this time. At first after we married we rented a little house from Matthias it was just one room, we rented there from him maybe for one year and then we rented down by Strömen (a good size creek translated 'the stream')

When Karin was born we went to Sweg where Ida's sister Ingeborg lived and we made a bed on the floor and we had not been laying there long, it was very uncomfortable and she said, "no, now I think we must get going," we had to get (sparken) out (the sled with a seat on it) to get mamma there, it was almost Christmas. But in any case we made it to the hospital so Karin was born there the next day 23rd about 11 o'clock I think. And we stayed there for a few days after she got out of the hospital. I think that was when we moved down to Strömen because we needed more room. By the time you Ruth were born we had a midwife in Funäsdalen so we didn't have

Ebba Lagerborg
Funäsdalen Sw.

midwife who helped in the deliveries of Ruth and Sune

Sparkstötting

Pappa Göte in the Army Uniform and Mamma Ida 1943-44

Till mor från Ida Göte
dog 1963   Karin Rut Sune Gunnar

Hållan den dec 1956.

Foto som blev för "America Resan" för
alltid adjö mor bodde hos oss 1 vinter
kan höra henne Alaska Alaska sade Hon
Vi reste juni månad ÅSEN ÄR VI Rotad H○S

Ida Sune Karin Göte Gunnar Ruth
Hållan, Furudalen, Sweden 1956
(Passport Picture)

to leave town for this birth. The midwife's name was Ebba Lagerborg she also delivered Sune. It was lucky that I was home from the Army right at that time.

In Sweden every male had to go into the army, I did my army training in the years 1922- 1923 when I was 20 years old. The army decided where we were to train; it usually would be close to home. The first time they called it recruiting, so first they would give you a doctor exam; check your feet and so on. One would go into the infantry, and another into the cavalry or the artillery, and I was assigned to the artillery. There were big caves inside the mountain where we did most of the training, but we also were training outside. If there should be a war, most of what we were to do would be done inside. But then I was one of 40 chosen out to train to become a (signalist) a communication specialist, person in charge of signaling. We learned how to signal with lamps and with tone and letters a,b,c,d, (the mores code). I still remember most of the signals even after all these years. There were telephone operator duties also to be learned, this training went on for 6 months. There were just 18 of us who made it through the course, and I was one of the 18 that made it. In the day if you could see the next person we used (sharmar) to hold up white and blue signs, but if it was in the dark we used a lamp to blink messages to the next person. So this was the means to send messages back and forth. So this was my work when I was serving in the Army.

When you (Ruth) was born I had just come home from duty during the 2nd World War, this was the war that Hitler had started up. Sweden was neutral and had been for a long time before that, so Hitler dominated Sweden during that time there too. But then they went into and occupied Finland to stage their fight there with the Russians, there they began to get (mothygg) where they fought back against as the Germans began to push their way up through Finland. There was only one way back out for them and only one road to travel on so they got pushed north up into Norway in the North. There is a place up there in the north where the three countries meet, there is a pole there called the three point border. This is where Sweden, Norway and Finland meets, so than to (shydda) guard Norway at that point there laid Borden's fastening, the town there. There were 5 different kinds of people there. So that is where I was stationed and serving at that particular time, I was (inkallad) called and activated at that time into the army because of the war. This particular time was the year 1943 after the outbreak of the Second World War.

Sweden became afraid that Germany might come inside Sweden too, so we had to defend the northern borders, because the Russians chased them out and where were they to go? They had come up their own way up through the Baltic Sea, but then they had been stopped up there. They didn't have enough equipment to press forward. And at that point the Englishmen and the Americans came; they had their boats up there in the Baltic Sea blocking that return passage for the Germans to use. I was up there for some time. The Germans also pressed their way into Norway from the south so that was when the Swedish army began to patrol all the borders with Norway including up in Funäsdalen where we lived, just in case they might try to infiltrate into Sweden. So they choose many of us that would be used on the borders. For some different reason they thought that I was a skier and because I had my residence written in Funäsdalen, Tännas Socken and there was a need up there at that time for loads of soldiers. So equipment and everything imaginable was brought up there, cannons and everything. Most of the soldiers camped out in Ljusnedal, but there in Funäsdalen there were many also. (In på gården) inside in the courtyard where you were born, (speaking to me) in a little house there was an army office too. I had not been able to come home even once from Boden while stationed there on the northern border. But then all of a sudden they asked me if I wanted to be transferred to my home area of Funasdalen and guard and be on the border there by Roros, Norway. I of course said 'Yes'! We were closed in up there in Boden (instangd), so yes, I than got a ticket to leave there and travel down. There were others of my buddies (kompiser) that went to other and different places, but no one else was transferred to Funasdalen. So than I got to be home for a month and I guess it was during that time that you were born (speaking to me Ruth). There the schedule was work for a month, and off for a while after I got to the home area, but anyway I had more freedom and could do more as I pleased then, and we lived there by the stream (at Stromen) probably for 3-4 years maybe a little bit longer.

I wasn't really working at that time and as it was when we worked in the woods and falling timber we would come home on holidays. During the winters later on, while you kids were small, mamma had to take care of things at home while I left to work in the woods logging.

Tape 5- So than later on I began to think about a place of our own and traded work with Par, mammas brother for the property, these were the days that I was still in the army and I would do smuggling of everything imaginable over the border from Sweden into Norway while I was patrolling the border. Everything from socks to you name it, I smuggled it. Germany was occupying Norway and things were really hard, people went around with mismatched socks and were glad to have them, in Norway they didn't have anything that you would be able to buy there. It was a really a bad time. So I smuggled anything and everything into Norway for about 4 years, skiing over the mountain. After the war was over, there was still a depression for a long time and people had what they called bread cards for food, sugar and shoes everything.

Tobacco too was nonexistence, the old men would sit with empty pipes and sometimes would get just a very, very small amount of tobacco because it was imported, and the Germans controlled everything during this period of time, during the war years.

As I have said before, I lived at home at that time, during 1st World War. The czar (sjeisaren) of Russia and Wilhelm of Germany became angry with each other (osams) and Austria and Germany were partners and relatives also. So during this War, the 1st World War Germany fought with Russia. It seems that Germany has always been a warring nation. The Russians had a czar ruling them at that time. Hitler he too was from Germany so during the 2nd World War he was at war with the whole world it seems, with England and the Russians too. As Hitler fought with the Russians, there were so many troops in this conflict warring with Russia and Finland too that even some in Sweden towards the end of the war was helping with the fighting against Germany. But Hitler did also fight the Russians and everyone else it seemed so at first he occupied all of Norway especially on the south by England. There was a war with England than also, but he occupied all of the Scandinavian countries from the North and of course Finland. But Sweden was kind of friends with Germany so they did not occupy Sweden because they were neutral; the reason was that they had been so for hundreds of years. As you look back through history you will find that the Kings or royalty of Sweden and Germany had intermarried back in history. So even at this time the Swedish king was married to the German princess.

MO & DOMSJÖ A.-B.
HÖRNEFORS SULFITFABRIK.

BETYG FÖR
Karl Göte Norén
(Fullständigt namn)

1114

Född den 19/10 1903
Födelseort St. Luna
Antogs den 4/7 1927
Avflyttar 23/8 1929

Huvudsaklig sysselsättning Skruvläggning

VITSORD:
Uppförande Gott
Arbetskunnighet God

Hörnefors pr. Hörneå den 29/8 1929

Forn. A. Blanketter hos Svenska Teknologföreningen, Stockholm 16.

BETYG FÖR
Carl Göte Norén
(Fullständigt namn)

Född den 19/10 1903
Födelseort Stora Tuna
Antogs den 18/6 1937 o. den 23/5 1938
Avflyttar resp. 20/10 1937 — 1/11 1938

Huvudsaklig sysselsättning Sernverkning vid (lagken 1938)

VITSORD:
Uppförande Gott
Arbetskunnighet God

Gunnilbo den 1/12 1938

Nr 19 L. Hasse W. Tullbergs Blankettförlag, Esselte, Sthlm.

BETYG
för

Namn Norén Karl Göte
Födelsedag 10 okt. 1903
Antagningsdag 2 juni 1954
Avflyttningsdag 30 juli 1954
Orsak till avflyttningen Arbetets fullbordan
Huvudsaklig sysselsättning Grovarbete

VITSORD

Uppförande Gott
Arbetskunnighet God

Stockholm den 11/8

AB SKÅNSKA CEMENTGJUTERIET
BO JONDAL

BETYG
för

Namn Norén Karl Göte
Födelsedag 10 okt. 1903
Antagningsdag 2 juni 1954
Avflyttningsdag 30 juli 1954
Orsak till avflyttningen Arbetets fullbordan
Huvudsaklig sysselsättning Grovarbete. Arbetet omfatta förstärkning och justering av gator och sättning av kantsten och storgatsten.

VITSORD

Uppförande Gott
Arbetskunnighet God

Stockholm den 12/5 1955

The Germans lost the First World War to the Russians and then it became frail again. It was a bad time and there was not much food at that time. We did grow potatoes and carrots so much that we were able to help others too that were without, when I lived with my parents. But at the end of the second world war there wasn't much and we didn't have enough of a growing season up there in the north where we lived (Funasdalen)so we bought most everything there. They did plant some potatoes up there on the mountain side on the Funasdal's Mountain. Mamma did yield some from that.

At this time as I was working on the road crew up there towards Norway, we decided our family was growing, and we should begin to build. We started our small house up there by grandma up in Hållan. I worked there for several years. Ida had some relatives (tremenningar) second cousins in Tännas, that had what they called a (en bondsag) farmers saw, that they used and could cut lumber themselves so than I bought lumber there and I built the house as I could afford by working overtime even on Sundays. There were no get rich skims and no one wanted or could lend money, but I had two persons that I could barrow however much I wanted from. One was a police officer there, I can't remember his name but I remember that I barrowed 100 kr. from him two times and I borrowed also another time from the other man. I needed something special at that time for the building of the house, and did barrow, but I always paid back quickly. During this time I worked for the state, the Swedish government, and for many years thereafter, I worked building roads even until after Sune was born.

I also worked for the state government for one and a half year at a power station that was being built on the river. There were 4 of us on that job there in Kassefosh. I had really good written reports throughout my working career.

(Examples inserted on next page)

In the early fifties there was strange happening, a strong wind probably a typhoon that blew down all the trees on the southeastern part of Sweden there were trees down everywhere for mile after mile after miles, laying (huller combuller) twisted and jumbled everywhere all the way from Gavle, all the way down almost to Stockholm. The woods just blew down; the area was so big that you wouldn't believe, for miles after miles all the trees were blown over!! This is when I traveled down there to Uppland. Einar and AnnaLisa lived there (she was Pappas cousin) they wrote and told me about it, that workers were needed. I had a moped, and I hopped on it with my ax and saw and (damma på) took off to work down there. There were no motor saws in those days but we only had hand saws. There were thousands of men down there sawing wood. I think that the motor saws might have begun to be used and been there, it was probably the beginning of them but I never did see one. I contracted a certain size of an area that I would cut and work in. We were told what size to cut the wood into, so it was just to cut, day in and day out. I remember I got something like 50 öre per length.

*So even when Sune was born 1948, I was still working on the roads, but than in the early 50's I did the work cutting the wood lengths from the trees that had been blown down. I would be gone for 2 or 3 months at the time, and when I came home I always brought fruit and other special items home with me, that you all would like. I came home from down there also the time when I brought you home the accordion, which was around year 1952.

*(Note: We used the paper that the fruit was wrapped in for toilet paper in our outdoor bathroom (pa dass) and that was a good memory, because it was so soft and it smelled so very good. Otherwise we normally had to use hard stiff catalog pages that we would crinkled up to soften for that purpose. To this day I still remember this when I see tissue wrapped around a fruit at the market, as I smell it I am taken back in time. I also loved that blue accordion that Pappa brought home for me and would sit for hours and learned to play some songs by ear.)

THE BEGINNING OF PLANS TO IMMIGRATE TO ALASKA

Karl Tagg (Ida's brother) came from America I think it was in 1952 or 53 I think I was probably working on the road from Sveg and south at that time, but I was home when Karl came to visit. He told us stories of Alaska, and I had another small house there that I had rebuilt from an old poor looking house close to the road, he saw that, everyone called it Göte's playhouse. (pappas name was Karl Göte) Because it looked so nice and it turned out so good, that when Karl saw the house and how nice it turned out he said, "You should come to Alaska; there are many houses there that need fixing up". And when we got to Alaska it was as he said, but there was not so much money in that kind of work, people didn't care or they could not afford to fix them. So anyway that was the first of the talk of immigrating to Alaska. There was much involved with the thinking and the planning, with whether we could make such a move. The money involved, the house had to be sold and much, much more. But I thought if there are old houses to be fixed up and then there was the talk of the fishing also so that was the first of the thoughts.

To get ready for leaving there were many things that had to be accomplished and performed. We had bought the big piece of property at the upper side of our house lot (på myra) in a swampy area next door where we lived. The person that owned it wanted to sell and it was always offered to the closest neighbors first and when the man who owned the property with a companion came up there by our house we invited them in for coffee. I knew the man so I asked how much he wanted for it, he said 500 kr. So I bought it from him. I had just come home from a job and had the cash in my pocket. I had probably another 500 still left to take care of our family needs too. So that was before Karl came home.

But of course than as we started to think about such a move we had to get rid of all we owned. Later as we bought the ticket for our passage to America at a Göteborg travel bureau, I also wrote to a man there and explained that I needed to sell properties in Hallan, Funåsdalen. And then we also had to get rid of everything we owned inside the house besides, so we had to have an auction for that purpose. The cost of land listed in the papers at that time in Funasdalen placed the price of the land at 2 kr. per square foot so the value of the property should have been 20,000.00 kr. So there again it needed to be offered to the closest neighbor, but no one had any money, so I put in an announcement in the Stockholm paper, because tourists came up to our area for many purposes summers and winters, and surly someone wanted to buy land, and I knew that they did. It didn't take long before someone did come up; it was on a snowy morning. One day I came in, I had been out someplace and there they sat by the kitchen table, and they wanted coffee. So Ida put on the coffee pot and they said they wanted to buy the property so we went out to see the lot, there was plenty of snow and it was hard to see it as it went from where we were standing down by Stinas cabin up to the road. So they asked how much I wanted, I told them the price 20,000.00 kr.

SWEDISH AMERICAN LINE   SEE REVERSE SIDE FOR INSTRUCTIONS

Affidavit in Support of Application
FOR
IMMIGRATION VISA, NON-IMMIGRANT VISA FOR TEMPORARY VISITORS AND STUDENTS TO THE UNITED STATES

State of _____
County of _____ } S. S.

I, __Gene E. Snead__
at present residing at __Haines, Alaska__ _____ Street
City of __Haines, Alaska__ County of _____ State of __Alaska__

MAKE THE FOLLOWING STATEMENT UNDER OATH AND SAY:

1. THAT I was born on the __29__ day of __April__ in the year __1923__
   at __Bridges, Missouri__ (City) __Scott__ (County) __U.S.A.__ (Country)

2. THAT I have resided continuously in the United States of America since __April 29, 1923__

3. THAT I was naturalized a Citizen of the United States of America on:
   Date _____
   At _____ (City)
   _____ (County) _____ (State)
   I possess Certificate of Naturalization
   No. _____ issued by
   _____ Court of

   OR:
   THAT I declared my intention to become a Citizen of the United States of America on:
   Date _____
   At _____ (City)
   _____ (County) _____ (State)
   I possess Certificate of Declaration of Intention to become a Citizen of the U.S.A.
   No. _____ issued by the Court of

   OR:
   THAT I am not a Citizen of the United States, but that I was lawfully admitted to the United States for permanent residence on:
   Date _____ (Month) (Day) (Year)
   At _____ (Port)
   on the _____ (Vessel or other means of conveyance)
   and that I have sent Form I-550 for verification of my last entry to the Immigration and Naturalization Service _____ (Date)

4. THAT I am and always have been a law-abiding resident and have not at any time been threatened with arrest or arrested for any crime or misdemeanor. That I do not belong to nor am I in anywise connected with any group or organization whose principles are contrary to organized government, nor do the undermentioned person/s belong to any such organization nor have they ever been convicted of any crime.

5. THAT I am the purchaser of Prepaid Ticket No.: __Immigrant purchased own fare.__
   issued in favor of below named relatives for transportation from __Funäsdalen, Sweden__
   and through to __Haines, Alaska__
   and eastbound Ticket No.: _____ for return from New York to _____

6. THAT it is my intention and desire to have the following person/s at present residing at __Funäsdalen, Sweden__
   _____ come to the United States
   for the purpose here stated: __Permanent residence__
   (State either: Permanent residence, Temporary visit, or Student.)

Name	Sex	Age	Place of Birth	Relationship to Deponent
Göte Norén and family	male	51	Sweden	none

7. THAT my present dependents consist of __Six persons (wife and 5 children)__

8. THAT my regular occupation is __petroleum dispatcher__ with average weekly earnings amounting to $ __150.00__

9. THAT I possess property valued at: Real Estate $ __12,000__, Personal $ __1,000__ and the incumbrance on said property, if any, amounts to $ _____

SWEDISH AMERICAN LINE SEE REVERSE SIDE FOR INSTRUCTIONS

Affidavit in Support of Application
FOR
IMMIGRATION VISA, NON-IMMIGRANT VISA FOR TEMPORARY VISITORS AND STUDENTS TO THE UNITED STATES

State of ...Alaska...
County of .... } S.S.

I, ...Ernest E. Lindquist...
at present residing at ...Corner of Third and View Streets...Street
City of ...Haines... County of .... State of ...Alaska...

MAKE THE FOLLOWING STATEMENT UNDER OATH AND SAY:

1. THAT I was born on the ...2nd... day of ...March... in the year ...1905...
   at ...Snyder... ...Dodge... ...Nebraska, U.S.A....
   (City) (County) (Country)

2. THAT I have resided continuously in the United States of America since ...Continuously...

3. THAT I was naturalized a Citizen of the United States of America on:
   Date ....
   At .... (City)
   .... (County) (State)
   I possess Certificate of Naturalization No. .... issued by .... Court of ....

   OR: THAT I declared my intention to become a Citizen of the United States of America on:
   Date ....
   At .... (City)
   .... (County) (State)
   I possess Certificate of Declaration of Intention to become a Citizen of the U.S.A. No. .... issued by the Court of ....

   OR: THAT I am not a Citizen of the United States, but that I was lawfully admitted to the United States for permanent residence on:
   Date .... (Month) (Day) (Year)
   At .... (Port)
   on the .... (Vessel or other means of conveyance)
   and that I have sent Form I-550 for verification of my last entry to the Immigration and Naturalization Service .... (Date)

4. THAT I am and always have been a law-abiding resident and have not at any time been threatened with arrest or arrested for any crime or misdemeanor. That I do not belong to nor am I in anywise connected with any group or organization whose principles are contrary to organized government, nor do the undermentioned person/s belong to any such organization nor have they ever been convicted of any crime.

5. THAT I am the purchaser of Prepaid Ticket No.: ...Ticket purchased by immigrant...
   issued in favor of below named relatives for transportation from ...Funasdalen, Sweden...
   and through to ...Haines, Alaska...
   and eastbound Ticket No. .... for return from New York to ....

6. THAT it is my intention and desire to have the following person/s at present residing at ...Funasdalen, Sweden... come to the United States
   for the purpose here stated: ...Permanent residence...
   (State either: Permanent residence, Temporary visit, or Student.)

Name	Sex	Age	Place of Birth	Relationship to Deponent
Gote Noren	Male	51	Sweden	None
Wife & Children				

7. THAT my present dependents consist of ...Wife...

8. THAT my regular occupation is ...Mechanic... with average weekly earnings amounting to $ ...100.00...

9. THAT I possess property valued at: Real Estate $ ...5000.00..., Personal $ ...5000.00... and the incumbrance on said property, if any, amounts to $ ...Nil...

We still had everything left to do at this point, we needed to sell the property, the house and hold an auction of all our personal items and things. I needed the money to buy the tickets so we settled for 6000.00 kr. cash money for the property. I told them, you are to send the money to the (handelsbanken) bank in Sveg, I didn't want to have the money in a bag at home and I didn't want to declare it. I got about 1000.00 kr. for hand money that we needed.

Than later I needed also to sell the house and decided to call down to Göteborg instead of writing a letter it was much faster. I had to go down to Funäsdalen to make my calls; there were no telephones in the homes at that time. So they than advertised the house for me by putting it into the newspaper. I did get a letter from someone in Skutkar close to Bollnäs. There were a lot of tourists that came up there to our area trusting all times of the year. They thought it was a bit to small and they thought it was a bit too expensive also. But we did strike a deal; he kept some items in the house but everything else went.

So than as it was we did have the auction just a few days before leaving, and we sold everything that we wanted to, including your accordion. The auctioneer was a good speaker and made it exiting for people to bid on our home items and tools, sleds you name it, it all went! By that time the house was also sold. But there were no airplanes to take us from Sweden so we had to buy a ticket on a boat leaving Oslo Norway on a certain day. I thought of Icelandic Air but decided on the boat the 'Oslo Fjord'.

It was hard for the old one when we left; she didn't like that at all. The cab that we hired had to back all the way down to our door where we had a little balcony to get the box up on the top of the cab and then it was tied down. We drove down by Pär's house (mamma's brother who lived next door to us) and took our goodbyes there from grandma Tagg. There were others there also, you kids were exited and mamma was crying. Grandma was a positive person and accepted our decision to leave, but she gave up her youngest daughter and her family, it was hard for her. There of course was also the chance that we might return too, if things didn't go well, so that helped some. Yes, it was hard for her, but there has always been sacrifice involved in lives in order to move ahead to new opportunities and experiences, and it was so in our lives as well.

(Note: I asked pappa what gave him the courage and the determination and the will and belief in himself that he would be able to survive and be able to support his family in this new world, new language to make this move all the way to Alaska at his age of 53 years old from Hållan, Funäsdalen, Sweden because most people would not make such a move at his age!)

Jo du) Yes, that is true, but I have had such an interesting life with unfamiliar and complicated jobs so I was out from all ordinary idiots, ordinary people. I know that I was different and I knew I would not fail (gå bet), but that I could make it somehow, and some way to be able to take care of the family. There was also (en firma) a Swedish consulate in Los Angeles, and I did send a letter there for information on how to return to Sweden if the need should arise. But we also had 2 names to sign *an affidavit for us to be able to come to America in the first place. (Copy of these *affidavits on the next page) It was Karl Tagg and a man named Smith that lived across from him up there in Haines, they signed that they would help us find the help that we would need if it would come to that. And we did have some dollars that I had exchanged in Östersund. I went to Östersund, Jämptland to exchange the Swedish kr. to dollars before leaving Sweden. Karin and you Ruth came along with me, we also went to the circus and I bought 2 liter of (bränvin) liquor, which was my allotment each month. It was different for each family or individual according to income and lifestyle such a having a business, which could have up to 4 liters. It was decided according to government regulations, and everyone had a book that got stamped. There was no liquor to be bought except in the bigger cities when we lived in Funäsdalen.

I remember some other things about the buying of alcohol. I remember in 1931 there was only one car in Avan Åkers socken and I was the driver of that car ones. It was from France, there were no cars anywhere at that time so this was exiting. This car had big bulky tires, but anyway it was owned by a man named Staka Jonas. There was poker night and it was there by the beach and I had come to go swimming, but he had the car there and I got to drive it. At this time he had the only car in town and it was used for and would be driven around delivering of liquor once a month. People would have their own books that had to be signed and recorded as they bought their allotment of alcohol monthly.

Back to our immigration from Sweden to Alaska, all six of us also took the train down to the big city and went to Stockholm, there to have our physical examination before leaving to America, x-rays, shots and everything possible to secure our health. There was no coming into America without it. All of us also went to (skansen) the zoo and enjoyed that time with the family while we were there. (We have some pictures to insert of this trip) At that point all our papers were in order although it did cost more money for these trips, but we were now done spending money as we bought our tickets for our journey overseas.

Yes, loads of memories! At this time everything was cheaper, money was worth more than now, I think we got 13,000.00 kr. for the little house we sold and property up there in Hållan. That was not much even in that day for that property, but we had to sell, we had tickets for a certain date on the boat from Oslo Norway so we took what was offered, and that was all.

It was just as difficult here or there, for ordinary people that had to work. When we got here and started, it was the same price for all, 21 cents per lb. for the price for sockeye (fish) when I started and now it is 1.75 a lb. So it is ridicules how fast it has gone up so the price we got for the house was probably good for the time we lived in. and we were leaving, we had to sell.

(Note: I asked pappa if he was scared or apprehensive over his decision to go to America, he said with enthusiasm: (Nej, nej, nej, nej)

No, no, no, no, I was excited about this experience, looking forward to this adventure and I knew that if it did not (om det inte passa mig) feel right or go well, I could always go back. I knew about the consulate in Los Angeles. I had it in mind should it happen that I would lose the money and have to go back, so be it. I got the address while still in Sweden to the consulate in California if I should need it. And I didn't worry about the language so much, I just figured that one would just shut up or shut ones mouth (hålla sjeften) and I thought that it will come, it will come when I get far enough, and it did come. At first Ida was out there in Haines helping and working for different women and she was going to learn as much as she could, and my job was to learn how to understand enough to write, because there were loads of letters that had to be signed and returned as we came into the country. So I did have to learn some particular words but I did have a dictionary to help me that I used a lot.

When we started to plan our departure, while we were still in Sweden, which was to leave Hållan and go on a visit to Karl Theodor my brother, while there I saw a nice place down in Uppland close to where Einar and Anna Lisa lived, so I was thinking of buying that piece of property. Einar was going to hold that for me so I had that in the air, but didn't think too much about that. I really didn't want to go there; I wanted to make it on my own. But that is when I came to Karl Theodor (his brother) in Uppsala and stayed there over the night when he offered me the money for the property by the railroad station. It was a nice place and they were building a lot around there at this time.

We also did go to visit with my brother Algot and his family one year; they lived in southern Norway in the city of Sandefjord. We drove into Norway and then took the train down. We had nice weather and there was a beach and warm breezes off the ocean, you kids had fun in the water and visiting with Algot and Nelly and their 3 kids.

Sune was born at our home up in Hållan Funäsdalen. Ebba Lagerborg was the midwife that had come to help mamma with the birth. We (Pappa, Karin and Ruth) went out of the house to paint the (bobbar) bob sleds out in the small storage house at the side of our house. And soon she held a little boy up in the window for us to see, you girls were so excited to have a brother. This was in September 1948.

Gunnar was born in Hede at the hospital I remember, there was not a midwife in Funäsdalen right then, I think Karin went with her. I was in Sveg working at the time. I don't know where you (Ruth) and Sune stayed, probably with (mormor) grandma. That was in September of 1955.

We had loads of excitement and changes in our life over the years. You see when I grew up my sisters and I, we got to learn from our mom (morshan hon var så snäll hon) our mother she was so very kind. But (gubben) the old man was (rättvis) fair of course, but very strict. But we got to learn what needed to be done and to follow through and be responsible. He did teach us hard lessons as he was strict and serious and we learned to complete the jobs given. He taught me to be honest and the way I should live but the lessons were sometimes really hard. He told me that I needed to learn so that I would not have to starve. So I would always have (gröt) mush on the table. He said it was not a time for play and not a time for laziness, but that life was serious. I began to take responsibility with working when I was 10 years old, on small jobs. I knew that work was the only way to make it. In 1916 I was finished with school I was 13 years old in October.

And when we came out to Grångshammar at that time, there was a big (bonds gård) farm with acre after acre, this family owned everything around. There were at least 80 to 100 cows on the farm. I worked there and went home at night. We moved there in the middle of the harvest time when they were falling the hay in the fields, there was (havre, råg, vete) oatmeal, rye, and wheat, all kinds of grain and there was a set time to cut and harvest each kind of grain. And of course it also had to be the right weather for it. But I had been there possibly just a week, when my dad who was a coaler, he took a bid on a certain amount of work to do and he would put the job together, it was a big, big amount about 16 (farmar?) It was 3 meters long and it would be bound together and then it would be put into the slow fire to be coaled down. After that it should be spruce branches on top, and so on. (Pappa explained the process of which I could not completely understand on the tape well enough to translate into English, I listened 10-12 times but his voice was too soft to understand) End of tape# 5.

As we moved out from Borlänge, out to Grängshammar just after midsummer which is about the middle of June in 1916, there were some changes of how grass was cut that year just as we moved out there. Up to this time people had always cut the fields buy hand, with a sicle (lier) and then there were someone else that walked behind and took it up and made (kjärvar) bunches of it. But that summer they had bought something called a (sjelvbindare) self-binding on this big farm. It was as big as a monster, it had 4 horses that pulled it over the field, it would cut than put it together into bunches and something to tie it at the same time and then it would spit it out. So they had 4 horses, two by two, the man that drove it sat high up on the machine and drove and watched the cutting part, it had to be done just so. He went around and around the large field. So than he had to have someone that walked down by the horses and (picka på) peck on the horses to kept the horses moving evenly.

So one day a man came in at home and said he had met the right one, he was speaking of my father, who has a young boy; because he needed someone to keep the horse's moving in the field at harvest time. The horses would pull uneven and someone was needed to keep them pulling even through the field. So he asked if I wanted to earn money, yes, I said. He asked if I had seen the new equipment, I said no, let's go down to look at it he said; I remember it said Canada on it. There were many cars that came at that time from Canada so I recognized the name. It was bran new and it was the first one that had come to Sweden, so I had a whip in my hand and would work by walking all day to keep the horses pulling together and evenly. And it was really needed for there was one horse that was so darn lazy or he was just slower than the rest. You could not hit them but only encourage them to move along.

My mother was so kind and loving to everyone she would give away to everyone in need, times were hard and it was so all over the world in this time period. She baked all the bread that we needed there was long sticks hung in the ceiling; several of them and the bread that was baked were hung up on those sticks in the sealing. It was regular hard rye bread; it was very heavy hard bread. There wasn't any thin bread that was something that came later in time. There was no help at home except the kids, Ester she was good at helping (pappas sister Ester had an illness with a prolonged fever as a small child and never thereafter had her whole intelligence, but her mind was as a young child) she was able to lean the routine and did the same thing every day, every day and at last she was just like a phonograph record, and would know what to do.

My sister Hanna was also there, she was the oldest (the oldest child of their mother Johanna, he also had 6 older ½ siblings from his father's first marriage to Sophia, she died when her youngest child Milda was a baby and Karl Theodor the oldest child was about 16 years old. Later Pappa's father married our mother Johanna and there she took care of and raised all those kids along with raising her own, she had 4 children of which pappa was born 3rd there was Hanna, Ester, Göte 1903 ,and Anna) but Hanna she had to get out and earn money she worked as a maid on a big farm. But all in all we learned to work hard by watching our parents, I was never told that I had to work hard that I remember, but I learned how to stay with the work that I took on and do whatever needed to be done by watching my parents. Mamma (Ida) also learned from her mother, it was even harder for her because she was alone. Everyone on both sides of the family had it hard in those days. And the boys up, Ida's brothers they were as lazy as dung. (dat var bara shit med dom) They were worthless in helping with anything.

So there was not anything left in Sweden that I wanted to be there for or go back to or because of, other than mormor (grandma Tagg). No, no one other than her, I never left anything behind that I felt like I needed to go back because of. *I want to tell you one thing that was important to me, as long as (moshan levde) my mother was alive, I was home as fast as I could each year, I might have been south in Sweden or north up in Lappland but I traveled home at least one time each year just to see her. (Birgitt up in Furudal, daughter to Anna, pappa's sister, told me (Ruth) at the 2008 family reunion what her mother had told her, she said, that their mother was waiting and hoping for Gote to marry so she could move in with him and his family because life at home was super difficult, but Gote never married until he was 37 years old and she died in 1929)

He continued: and I was also home when mother was buried, I was in Woxna at that time. I was in the little store, we lived below the station in the coaling cabin someone yelled at me come up here now for there was a phone call for you from your home with the message that your mother has died, and she is to be buried at this particular time. I had poor clothing when I came up there to fall trees so I went out back to work I didn't have any money but maybe I could borrow a suit when I get close to home. Maybe I could rent a suit in Borlänge. But I had a friend there and I told him about needing a suit and the situation and he said laughing "you can have my wedding suit" he had not used it since the wedding. Yes, I said what does it look like? It had (kransiga rander) fancy lines on it but I tried it on and I remember it so well, he said when you go out you will probably lose your pants. But no, it fit pretty well and so I took it! His wife asked if I had some clean shirts and she said come over here and wash the dirt off of you (tvätta shiten av dig) and take a bath. I had to go to Orsa and to Borlänge on the train.

So than when I went home for mammas funeral I looked like a bridegroom when I got there. Karl Theodor was there in a nice suit and of course Anna was there. My mother died in the hospital in Falun there was something wrong with her stomach. Anna went with her to the hospital; they had to take the train to Borlänge and then to Falun. So she said that the doctors (skar ijär na) cut her to death, yes, a woman said that there was a helper, a nurse that said they cut a (en tarm) cord or vessel and she died.

She never had any problem on the inside that I ever remember. But she had a problem on her leg it was called a (roseben) problem, a sore that was deep and red looking, it came from or started thought the neighbor who was helping from a time when she went wading in the water in the Dala river (Dala älven). I saw what it looked like, every morning when she would take off the cover over it to redress it. It looked almost round deep, deep, and red just as if an iron had been placed on her skin. And it turned completely black after a while. There was that neighbor who was a helper to mamma and she tried everything possible and laid on the soar, it was all homemade doctoring, trying everything she could think of to lay on it. But it didn't get better it just got worse over time, it went through (it sounded like it traveled through her leg to the other side?) and when it came out here (don't know exactly where?) she started to have pain and stomach problems. So this is when they traveled to the hospital and they said that she did not die from the stomach problems. There was never a doctor involved; she never did go to a doctor, until she went to the hospital. (Note: She died in the year 1929. She must have had the problem for a long time, as pappa saw it at first and then was home for the funeral?) But the neighbor was sure it came from the wading in the river. Anyway I did make it home for the funeral on the last day before it took place.

Life continued:

I was home ones after that time when he (his father) had the housekeeper who was Karl-Ivar's mom, he was just a little guy, he was just beginning to walk a bit stable and this was the first day that he had raised up by himself, he saw me too sitting there on a chair visiting and talking. I was going to sleep there over night; I just came from working on the roads in Jokkama.

I got a free ticket from the state all the way from the North Sweden where I was working on the power plant down to South Sweden, it was as far north as you could go up to where there were people still living. (Jacopokonu?) I was working up there on a power plant (kraft station) that the state was putting in, but after a job was finished or if it closed for the winter you would get a free ticket to wherever you wanted to go, here or there from the state of Sweden. And I heard talking going on from a bunch of guys about a job here and there. It was very popular there by the coast that sounded good. This was a winter job up there because in the winter the river that ran by there was frozen so the water didn't run fast and they worked fast and furious (som tusan) to get as much work done before the river started to run fast again, so I went there and they said I could have a job. I took the train down and I came there to Borlänge, and drove home and stayed there over night and that was when I saw Karl Ivar just that one time when he was very small, until he got older of course, I did see him then. They (the parents) were not married but did have this one son together.

Life was hard work at this time, but it was not hard for me for many went without work. I began with the state because they were building loads of things about this time, so I always had work.

There were roads being built all over the country. When I was born there was not any help for families like it was later, with money for families and children (socialistic government). No there was only to work yourself for what you had, no help for anyone. There were no doctors not even midwives, but maybe a lady in each town that would help with things like that. And that was all there was to it, these were hard times for families.

The reason for our move when you (Ruth) were small was that we were going to move from Hållan anyway, because there was trouble with (kåringa) (Brita our aunt) with the lady next door she was so foul to Ida and Karin, I don't know how it was with you and Sune (I responded, I did not have any problem with her) But to Ida they were terribly ugly, mamma had a moped and the boys would close the fence gate right in front of her and then they would run and yell and she would stand on the steps and hollered really negative foul things loudly at mamma, so we were leaving and moving from there, there was no question about that. The question was where?

I don't know how Grandma Tagg felt about our moving, but she lived with us that last winter, she would sit there and say Alaska, Alaska, and shake her head. We, mamma and I couldn't even speak of it with her or even ourselves at first for we didn't know what was going too happened or what lay ahead. If we went to Alaska, I only knew that I needed enough money so as to get back again to Sweden if I should need to, if things didn't work out.

Funäsdalen in the
distance -
Mormor's house 1930-40

From left to right:
Göte
Ida
Inger
Jenny
Åsenwald
Grandma Tagg
Stina
Kristian
Johan
Axel

In front:
Solvig, Ingeborg
Fredrick,
Mola, Axel Jr.
(1939-41) Dog

- Fredrick and Ingeborg, mamma Ida's sister.

- Our little home that pappa Göte built - the wood shed - bathroom behind the house -
- Small house for visits and building in below.
- In Hållan, Funäsdalen

- Our little house from the front. Basement enterence below.
- Uncle Pär's house in the distance.

- Visit at Midsummer Celebration, Sala, Sweden. 1949 - Sune in Ida's arms. Karin and Ruth in matching dresses. — cousin Solvig in the middle.

- Visit to Trondheim, Norway (1947)
- Friend and two boys
- Ida and her two girls Karin in the Middle Ruth on the end.

The Norén Family Passport Picture

Ida Sune Karin
Göte Gunnar Ruth
(1956)

Our house our dad built for us.
Karin ↑   Ruth ↑ (me)

Karin   Ruth ↑ me

me → Ruth
Grandma Tagg
Karin →

← the spot is where I lived. We

Our My Church ←

Our My school house the kids went to ↙

↓ Tea party

Per-Bertil
Ruth
Karin
Lucia

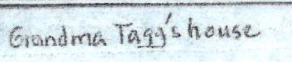

Grandma Tagg's house 1951-52

↑ Our house

Cousins house ↙

Friends Ida, Sune, Kristian, Karin, Mormor, Ruth, more friends

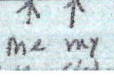

friend
Cousin Per-Bertil   Me my

Per Kristian Johan (Mormor) Ida
Brita   Fredrick Ingeborg (Grandma)
              Solweig

Well, when we decided to move or started the plans, Ida and I at that time began to talk very, very much about it together. It was so difficult to sell properties, the banks had at that time put a stop on all the loans, the banks had absolutely stopped all loans. It didn't matter how much property you might own, no one was able to get loans at that time. So I advertised outside of Funasdalen in a couple of newspapers, Ljusnan and (Dagens nyheter) in two Daily News. I paid taxes on our property and house for 30,000.00 kronor, but there was no one that had that much money, at least anyone private that was for sure, because we wanted and needed cash money. We got several letters. But there was one that could pay 10,000.00 on credit, but we needed cash because we were not returning to Sweden anymore and he didn't have cash.

At this same time there was Karl Theodor my oldest brother, as I went down to visit him in Uppsala, he said to me, you are an idiot to go to America. He had talked to someone that knew about people that had starved to death over there and other problems and having to return. So he said to me, here I have 3000.00 kronor in the dresser drawer in bills, so he said, you can have this so you can buy a lot down here in Mehede, there is a nice lot down by the train station. I know the man, and he will sell it to you. I will help you with the foundation and to build and help you with everything, if you just move down here. For to go to Alaska, America I've only heard terrible things about it over there.

Then I went home and Ida and I talked and worked our plan and exactly what we needed, we needed a particular amount. We knew how much the tickets would be, I had contacted the travel agency down in Stockholm, so we knew that and we needed that two times, so that we could get back to Sweden if we needed to, and we needed enough to make it a couple of months in case I couldn't find work and we had to turn around quickly, but we had a little extra, there was enough to make it a couple of months.

Leaving our home in Hållan:

So we did leave Sweden on June 17th 1956 and took a taxi from Hallan, Funasdalen to Roros Norway where we met Johan, mammas brother from Trondheim Norway for lunch and then continued the travel on to Oslo. We stayed there overnight in a hotel, than we boarded the steam liner the next day and from there we took the steam liner the 'Oslo Fjord' as it took 5 days and 5 nights onboard to reach New York City. I heard it said that this was the fastest and nicest trip they had had to date. The weather was nice almost all the way, as we came close to the harbor and as we entered into Pier 42 there was a bad storm.

There was very much thunder and lightning and it rained really hard, it was totally black when we came into the harbor, wind and lightening were going on to the point that we could not go out to see the 'Statue of Liberty' as the ship passed by it! There was myself, Mamma, Karin, Ruth, Sune and Gunnar he was 9 months old; I remember it cost 10 kr. for his ticket. (pappa he laughed as he told me the price of his ticket) We slept onboard through the night and in the morning prepared to get off the ship in our new land.

The next morning there were 4 officers that came in, everyone had to have a passport, and no one could come into the country without one. So when we came and it was our turn to get off, I had all my papers ready, I knew they would all need to be shown. All the ones with American passports got to go off first. So we began with me and worked down to the kids, so that was while we were still on the boat, for there sat 2 men checking all our papers as we got off. There were other men standing guard and had to see that all the papers were in order.

After we got off we were led into the place where we had to go through all our stuff (our luggage) as we walked into what looked like a big warehouse we were led to our big box which had to be opened along with our two suitcases and mammas hat box, than the custom agent went through checking all our belongings. There was a black man that after I unlocked the big box began to go through our stuff, he just looked through a bit and he said, naaa, and I think he swore in English and closed the lid, than I had the papers ready for the box to be sent on by railroad and boat to Haines, Alaska. It took a long time for the box to get there, more than a month as I remember.

After we were done there, there was a lady that met us with a taxi; she was able to speak Norwegian. It must have been pre-planned; she helped us and took us to the airport there in New York. We flew down the streets and passed the tall skyscraper buildings. She was a big help, she told us where to go and what to do. Well, I had everything ready and mamma too. And after that we were to pay her, I think it was three and a half dollars, something like that, well it was under five dollars anyway for all of us.

On the plane trip from New York it was interesting, it was a long trip. We flew on a Pan American a propeller plane in those days (no jets yet) to Chicago, where we had to change planes and they said they were full booked. There were long flat benches to wait on and there were people everywhere, but just inside the door was the stand with a person by it. It was a long wait, so I went around in with all those people trying to see if anyone spoke Swedish. And one man said "Jeg snakker Norsk" I speak Norwegian, I said yes, I understand that language. So I asked if he could help with this and that, but he just kept saying "Jeg snakker Norsk" over and over, he did not speak Norwegian. So I went back and sat down, and after a while there came a man and led us outside into the dark, and there was another man that took us up into the plane and gave us some very nice seats in the front of the plane. It was completely full booked with people. We had one stop along the way. I got off the plane to walk around a bit and I took Sune with me, and he said pappa, pappa see over there, look over there, there is a real cowboy and his horse is over there too, he was so excited. There were also 10 or 12 soldier there; they were sitting on the floor. I think it could have been in Denver that we stopped for some to get off and others to get on, than we continued the flight on to Seattle. There we got to sit and wait and wait for a long time, and after a while everyone left, no one was left in the area. A man came over and motioned with his arms, telling us to come with him. Just as we walked out into a hall there was a little door and he led us out through it and there were all the people waiting to get on. So anyway the plane was just outside there and we got to get on first after all, there too.

In all the plane travel from New York to Haines, I think took us 2-3 days, and we did get special help and treatment and got to go onboard the planes first before others boarded. We had many small children along with our language problem. So in Seattle I do remember there were so many people on that flight and everyone went out and we were there alone. I showed my ticket the lady smiled so nicely. So she took us out a small door on the side into a long corridor and we were the first to go aboard and we got to sit in the front of the plane again. Across from us there sat a man

Haines

1956-57

our uncle Karl Tygg who was the reason for our immigration

- Pappa Karl Göte writes this post card to Mormor in Sweden. It is well with us, we fish for salmon bought food and a motor. I fish by the cross. Gunnar is walking now. Hallo and a hug Göte

- Ida writes Göte was always good to Mamma she loved Him, He fishes by Pyramid Harbor.

Haines + Port Chilkoot from the air.

A walk on the beach — an end to a perfect day.

Craftsmen of Alaska Indian Arts at work on a 30 ft. "Friendship" totem.

Hotel Halsingland

Gateway to the Interior

Port Chilkoot

Haines Alaska

E-4527

KARL TAGG FAMILY — HAINES ALASKA

Merry Christmas and a Happy New Year from The Tagg family in Alaska 1947

Alice, Karl, Karl Jr., Jenny, Louice, Donna and Gale Tagg

Haines, Alaska 1956-57

1956- Alice, Ida, Gunnar 1 years old in Haines

1957- Inger, Ida and Göte at coffe at Lindquist (sunny day in June)

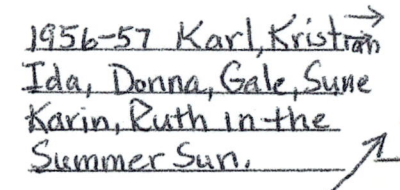

1956-57 Karl, Kristian Ida, Donna, Gale, Sune Karin, Ruth in the Summer Sun.

Pappa Göte was going to build a house for us out this old shack but it was to damaged and rotten.

STATE OF ALASKA
COMMERCIAL FISHERIES ENTRY COMMISSION

1974 INTERIM-USE PERMIT NO. A2-03 1494

THIS CERTIFIES THAT: IN ACCORDANCE WITH THE REGULATION OF ENTRY INTO ALASKA COMMERCIAL FISHERIES

KARL G. NOREEN
217 5th Street
Douglas, Alaska 99824

SOCIAL SECURITY NO. 574-12-8759   DATE OF BIRTH 10/10/1903

HAS BEEN ISSUED AN INTERIM-USE PERMIT TO OPERATE

UNIT OF Drift Gill Net GEAR IN ADMINISTRATI[VE]

AREA "A"-Southeastern

BY: _Clement Compton_   DATE 01/08/74

COMMERCIAL FISHERIES ENTRY COMMISSION

SIGNATURE OF PERMIT HOLDER _Karl G. Noreen_

THIS PERMIT IS VALID THROUGH DECEMBER 31, 1974. APPLICATI[ON] FOR 1975 RENEWAL OF INTERIM-USE PERMIT OR FOR A PERMANE[NT] [W]HICHEVER IS APPLICABLE, MUST BE MADE PRIOR [TO ...] 1, 1975.

T[HE] HOLDER MUST HAVE THE PERMIT IN HIS POSSESSI[ON] [TI]MES WHEN ENGAGED IN THE OPERATION OF THE GE[AR] [FOR WHICH] IT WAS ISSUED.

STATE OF ALASKA
VESSEL LICENSE
EXPIRES DECEMBER 31, 1971

No. 38783

RESIDENT	NONRESIDENT
$10.00	$30.00

AREA SALMON NET FISHING: 1
ADF&G NO. 13009 AREA KING CRAB FISHING

VESSEL NAME: Ida Marie
OFFICIAL NO. 508 732   KEEL LENGTH 33'
COAST GUARD NO. _____   NET TONS 10
TYPE OF VESSEL: Gillnetter
TYPE OF GEAR: Drift Gillnet

X OPERATOR: Karl Noreen
  ADDRESS: Box 367 Douglas, AK 99824
X OPERATOR
  ADDRESS
X OPERATOR
  ADDRESS

ISSUED AT Juneau, ALASKA 3/18, 1971
BY: _Kathleen G. Gillrich_ (ISSUING OFFICER)

IS LICENSED AS A FISHING VESSEL IN CONFORMITY WITH APPLICABLE LAWS DURING THE CALENDAR YEAR ENDING DECEMBER 31, 1971.

X _Karl Noreen_

(INVALID WITHOUT SIGNATURE OF LICENSEE) LICENSE MUST BE KEPT ABOARD VESSEL AT ALL TIMES

DEPARTMENT OF REVENUE
DR-FG-234

COMMERCIAL FISHERMAN'S LICENSE
EXPIRES DECEMBER 31, 1971

No. 25145

NAME: Karl Noreen
ADDRESS: Box 367 Douglas, AK 99824
SOCIAL SECURITY NO. 574-12-8759

RESIDENT	NONRESIDENT
$10.00	$30.00

AREA SALMON NET FISHING: 1
AREA KING CRAB FISHING

TYPE OF VESSEL: Gillnetter
TYPE OF GEAR: Drift Gillnet

ISSUED AT Juneau, ALASKA 3/18, 1971
BY: _Kathleen G. Gillrich_ (ISSUING OFFICER)

PHYSICAL DESCRIPTION

SEX	AGE	HEIGHT	WEIGHT	COLOR EYES	COLOR HAIR
M	67	5'2"	155	Blue	Gray

X _Karl Noreen_

IS LICENSED AS A COMMERCIAL FISHERMAN IN CONFORMITY WITH APPLICABLE LAWS DURING THE CALENDAR YEAR ENDING DECEMBER 31, 1971.

(INVALID WITHOUT SIGNATURE OF LICENSEE) LICENSE MUST BE CARRIED ON THE INDIVIDUAL WHEN COMMERCIAL FISHING in front of me spitting his snuff, I didn't have any snuff but I did buy some on the dock in Juneau, the Norwegian man (Jorgensen) got some for me, but it tasted terrible and I threw it away. I did have a pipe though at that time.

It went as nice and smooth as it could, all along the way, so we made it to Seattle and then Northern Airline to Juneau and Costal Air to Haines; we had to go into town from the airport for a pontoon plane with 6 seats to Haines. But the plane that we were to leave on was really full too. But then mamma had to take Gunnar (for han hadde skitit I byxan han) he had messed his pants and she needed some warm water for changing him and cleaning him up. Anyway I went out and someone, I understood that they said there was a man who spoke Norwegian down the street, downtown Juneau (Jorgansen) and he had warm water there. So I got out and went to find this place. He was very helpful he came along and mamma was able to clean Gunnar up and he also gave me a pack of cigarettes. Then he and another man named Rude spoke for us and were able to get a smaller plane and then of course we left Juneau and flew to and landed on that dirt runway at the airport there, and all of us were in Haines. This was June 27th 1956.

HAINES ALASKA June 27th 1956

When we first got to Haines we stayed with Karl and Alice Tagg, with Ida's brother and their 5 kids. We stayed in an old shack in their back yard for a few months, through October anyway.

This shack had terribly thin walls, with no insulation and it was an early winter that year, I had to buy a stove so we would not freeze, it was the most expensive stove anyone could get a hold of, I paid 350 dollars for it. But we had to have a stove and at that time I did have money, I had 200 to put down. After fishing I ordered some food for the winter for that is what Karl did each year. Than I was working out at the tank farm so I did have some money coming in right then. At that time it was starting to look up and it was getting a bit better for us as far as work was concerned. (In the picture of Haines, Karl's house is the big looking white house almost middle on road next to the beach on the lower part of the picture, later we moved to Port Chilcoot the 2nd white house up from the dock next to the woods. The x is where Pappa built his fishing cabin and where he had 2 set nets off the beach for several years.)

We had planned out our finances, so when we arrived in Haines we did have a little extra money left over after the trip, I think that we had 80 dollars or was it 180 dollar, that was what we had to keep us until I found work, but I had to find work. I did find some small jobs, the first job was at a small sports store down the hill there in Haines, I think his name was Kiggs, he had some small carpenter job so it was there that I bought that radio that we had and then I was also paid for the work of course, so it looked pretty good and so it didn't begin to badly anyway. But it was so cold out there, it had no insulation in the walls it was just a cabin there was just 2x4 and plywood, it was not a place for people to live and we had to have a stove to keep warm, the first thing I had to do was to fix a toilet room, we had a drawer there and the smell was in the whole place so I had to make a hole in the wall for the smell to escape. I saw a chainsaw sitting there I asked Karl how to use it, he wanted to know want I was going to do with it? I told him there had to be an opening for the smell to escape to; he could see that that was important so he told me how to use the saw. I understood how to use it without his help but thought it would be good to ask. But it soon got too cold to stay in there our mattresses froze to the walls and would be soaking wet in the mornings we had to set the mattresses out in front of the stove during the day to dry to sleep on again that night. We had to find another place to live for it was so cold that we would all get sick if we stayed there so we had to move.

We took the stove with us too, and we moved over to Port Chilcoot into one of the old army houses. We got to live there free except for electricity; he needed a carpenter who could help fix up old rotten buildings and problem areas for Mr. Hainmiller who was the custodian of the old fort. There was so much work there; someone could keep busy for a long time. I did get paid for working though along with the free rent. At that time there was no money put aside for maintenance of the buildings, so I got a dollar here and there. After we moved to Juneau, I got a check in the mail for 375 dollars back pay from Heinmiller. The first year that I did set net fishing off the beach on the other side of the bay past Pyramid Island it was just the last 3 weeks of the season. And after that I fished there set nets for 5 years I think. I also after that leased a fishing boat from the cannery for a few years before buying my own boat that I named the "Ida Maria" I did fish for 25 years (1956- 1981) until Gunnar took it over, I still have the first fishing license I got I think.

But it was <u>as very close</u> as it could be that <u>we did return</u> and go back to Sweden. Things were tough, I couldn't do anything myself because I didn't know the language so I had to go through Karl, mammas brother on everything because I didn't understand, speak or write English, I had to get his help with everything to do with communications. I started to worry a bit and wanted to be ahead of the problem should it arise. So I wanted to get a hold of a Swedish counselee, but in those early days it was through a layer (a Swedish vise counsel) there was one in Anchorage and one in California so he was going to get the address for them so I could write to them there in California, there was a layer here in Juneau that Karl contacted, there were no real layers here than and there were only two doctors in town, but there was man who did work as a layer, for he helped us later when we had been here long enough to need new passports, I think it was 3 years when we needed new ones. But anyway he contacted the consulate in California and I thought I would get a letter back. The reason I needed to contact the counselee was in case we didn't have enough money to return, I had to go through the Swedish counselee to get help, and the only help we could get through them would be money for tickets back to Sweden. We could not get any other help from them, only emergency money for returning.

But there was so much to do with that too, that it was almost hopeless, you must be totally on your own with no one to help you, you must be totally (sopren) destitute to get any help from anyone there. I was thinking that we might have to return; I at least had to know how to get the help in case it turned out so I couldn't find work, so we could make it back. Anyway it took weeks and weeks and more weeks so I kept working a little here and there. I didn't know if we would make it, that's was why I wrote to the Swedish counselee. But I never did get any real

YEARS OF FISHING

1956 cirka.   aprox. 1978

Sue

AT THE CABIN

SEP · 59

SEP · 58

SEP · 59

Mamma Sure Ceuauar   pappa   IN HAINES

information back about it; I got something in the mail that they were going to take care and look into it. It was difficult and frustrating. I didn't know anything because I didn't understand enough; everything had to go through Karl Tagg, for he was the one who spoke for me. Well there was Kristian too but he didn't know much more than me, he had come over just the year before us.

Than after that our outlook was that we were not in control of that situation, we could not decide, say or make decisions over anything, when you come like we did and don't know anything. We had to take it just the way it was and the way life came to us each day. And believe and have faith in the future, but there were times we lost all hope of making it here. But how it was, Ida she also hacked along and found some work here and there. We had a feeling if it had only been Ida and I and no children it would have been different, but I was thinking of the children.

Ida (tappa humöret ibland) lost hope and was sad once in a while and that was no wonder about that. I also (tappa humöret) felt overwhelmed and was sad and didn't know what would happen and how it would go, and then with Ida down and pale looking, that also took strength and courage away from me too, for I of course had the first and the biggest responsibility to provide for and be dependable for the family needs. But we couldn't blame anyone; we had to take things just the way that it came each day. We realized that we had also come into a situation with the family there in Haines, where their lifestyle was different, there was only party time and drunkenness all the time, and this was also very difficult for us. It was lucky that mamma had that Lindquist lady there; mamma was with her a lot. So anyway you know we fought our way forward, (krångla oss fram) and so it was that we moved forward just a little bit at the time.

So however it was I went looking at the (skiffs) boats that were there for sale. And I thought if I only could build something like that myself, so I must have mentioned it to Karl for he was the only person I could talk to. So I said if I just had lumber I could build a better skiff than any of those, Karl said well if you can do that, you can get lumber through the canary and then you can get a fishing license for only 5 dollars, but it was 15 for a non-residence. So we went out there and talked to Jack, the canary had regular shipments come up on a freight boat monthly and it was just the right time to talk to him, for it was the time of the month that they were putting in their order for food and fishing supplies and so on for their store. So I told Karl what I would need, how many and what kind of boards of this and that and so and so long, and how many ribs for the sides and so on. I listed everything that I should need, I had it written out. And my golly it soon came, I got it on credit from the canary.

(Så jag sat igång) So I got going and started building myself a fishing skiff. When I had almost gotten it finished there came to me an acquaintance of Karl, a fisherman he was some sort of relation to Alice, thinking about it he was actually Karl's wife's brother, Mets was his last name, she had two brothers. He asked "do you want to sell it?" I of course said "maybe so" he offered me 650 dollars. He was serious so I had to really think about, I had planned to use the boat for fall fishing. So I decided I didn't have time to build another boat before fall, so I didn't sell it.

I also needed one fishing net, Karl had an old one he sold to me and I also needed a motor for the boat, I got one for 200 dollars from one of Karl acquaintances. I was able to pay later so in that way I got started. But it was poor fishing that fall. After fall fishing they began building the oil tank farm and I got a job out there than, so it kept sliding along and so we kept making it.

But we saw that there was really nothing to depend on up there in Haines. So we decided to start to make planes to a move to Juneau for more work opportunities for mamma and me. I continued to fish up there in Haines with the set nets for at least two more seasons there along the beach on the other side of pyramid harbor next to Katzik family. Then I leased a gillnet boat from the Haines cannery and after about 4-5 years of doing that, I was able to put a down payment and buy my own gillnet boat which I named the 'Ida Maria' (this was Mamma's name) in which I fished with until I retired from fishing when I was in my 70's. (He loved life here in Alaska and could wish for nothing more. He worked hard but according to him his life was perfect!)

This is the **end** of Pappa Karl Gothe's recorded memories. ---
----

*Mamma Ida Maria Tagg now adds her thoughts about leaving Sweden, preparation and immigration too far away Haines, Alaska, afterwards seeking of Citizen Status as she continues her recorded memories after coming to America in the next volume.

She begins: When I think of leaving our homeland Sweden, this was the biggest step that we had ever taken and that has happened to us in our lives. We spoke often of Alaska because of my brother Karl, who had himself immigrated to Alaska. He visited us in Sweden after having been gone and lived in America for about 31 years. (This was the year of 1952-3 or 4) He found his wife in Hoonah, Alaska. She was a full-blooded Thlinket Indian woman, Alice Mets by name. They raised their family here in Alaska and resided first (bosatt) in Hoonah, Alaska. After some time there they moved to Haines, and there he started fishing salmon (lax) for a living. When he at last decided that he would fly the long way home (to Sweden) to see his little mother and siblings, this is when our own life's plans also became completely altered. This is a true story right out of our own life. It's hard to believe it happened but we, the 6 of us came here to Haines, Alaska with everything that we now owned in the world, everything was contained within two suitcases, one hat box and one big wooden packing crate that pappa built. (approximately 4x4x3) We could not speak or understand the English language. There were many things Göte had to organize and figure out while we lived in the small tourist community in Hållan 5 km north of Funäsdalen Sweden before we were able to be ready to leave our home there.

We had to sell our wonderful little home that Göte had worked so dilligently to build and move us into. It was not difficult at all to sell; the area where we lived was a beautiful place, ski slopes on every mountain peak. Pappa put an advertisement into the Stockholm paper that our house was for sale. A tourist company from Stockholm (Mackmyro) bought our home very cheaply. We sold it much too cheap back then and this grieved us at that time very much. But we had everything ready; we had passage already booked on the steamship Oslofjord, out of Oslo Norway on a set date. And we didn't want to miss the departure date. If we had missed it, we would have to wait a long time until the next available date and cabin room.

Everything was so hectic; everything had to be sold, all my small cute knick knacks that I had collected in our home there. Everything had to go. Mr. (Herr) Busk was the auctioneer, yes, we had a **big auction**. The people in our town of Funäsdalen were all exited to call in their bids for

Passasjer Liste

TURIST KLASSE

Nielsen, Nils H., herr	Oslo
Nilsen, Alf, herr	Staten Island, N.Y.
Nilsen, Erling, herr	Oslo
Nilsen, Berit A., fru	—»—
Norén, Göre, herr	Funäsdalen, Sverige
Norén, Ida, fru	—»—
Norén, Karin, frk.	—»—
Norén, Ruth, frk.	—»—
Norén, Sune, herr	—»—
Norén, Karl, herr	—»—
Olsoy, Einar, herr	Rissa
Omland, Solveig, fru	Lyngdal
Ommundsen, Warren, herr	Brooklyn, N.Y.
Ommundsen, Marion, fru	—»—

14

- We left Grandma Tagg sad standing on the Poarch

PAN AMERICAN WORLD AIRWAYS SYSTEM
Issued By PAN AMERICAN WORLD AIRWAYS, INC.

PASSENGER TICKET AND BAGGAGE CHECK — PASSENGER COUPON

FORM 0263-21 NUMBER 076148

CONJUNCTION TICKET(S) Form NAL Serial 14912

FARE US $ 85.
EQUIVALENT AM'T PAID VK. 440.
TAX US TAX EXEMPT
TOTAL SKR 440

FORM OF PAYMENT: CASH

DATE AND PLACE OF ISSUE: AB NORDISK RESEBYRÅ OVERSEAS DEPARTMENT STOCKHOLM

ROUTING:
- NYC — NWA $41.50
- SEA — PAA $27.50
- JNU — ACA $8.00
- HNS

VALID UNTIL: 7/0 JUN 12 1957

FROM: NEW YORK / SEATTLE / JUNEAU / HAINES

NAME OF PASSENGER: NORÉN, SUNE G. MASTER

FARE US $ 85-

Ticket 1

PAN AMERICAN WORLD AIRWAYS SYSTEM
Issued By PAN AMERICAN WORLD AIRWAYS, INC.
PASSENGER TICKET AND BAGGAGE CHECK — PASSENGER COUPON
FORM 0263-21 NUMBER 076144

- Conjunction Ticket(s): Form NHL Serial 19711
- Fare: $170.00
- Equivalent Am't Paid: VK 881.-
- Tax: US TAX EXEMPT
- Total: SKR 881
- Form of Payment: CASH
- Free Baggage Allowance: 20/30

Routing:
From	Via Carrier	Fare Construction
NYC	NWA	$99.-
SEA	PAA	$55.-
JNU	ACA	$16.-
HNS		

Valid Until: T/0 JUN, T/0 12, T/0 1957

From NEW YORK → SEATTLE → JUNEAU → HAINES — OP

Date and Place of Issue: AB NORDISK RESEBUREAU, OVERSEAS DEPARTMENT, 12 JUN 1957, STOCKHOLM

FARE US $170.-

NAME OF PASSENGER: NORÉN, K. GÖTE MR

Ticket 2

PAN AMERICAN WORLD AIRWAYS SYSTEM
FORM 0263-21 NUMBER 076147

- Conjunction Ticket(s): Form NHL Serial 19712
- Fare: $170.-
- Equivalent Am't Paid: VK. 881.-
- Tax: US TAX EXEMPT
- Total: SKR 881.
- Form of Payment: CASH
- Free Baggage Allowance: 20/30

Routing:
From	Via Carrier	Fare Construction
NYC	NWA	$99.-
SEA	PAA	$55.-
JNU	ACA	$16.-
HNS		

Valid Until: T/0 JUN, T/0 12, T/0 1957

From NEW YORK → SEATTLE → JUNEAU → HAINES — OP

Date and Place of Issue: AB NORDISK RESEBUREAU, OVERSEAS DEPARTMENT, STOCKHOLM

FARE US $170.-

NAME OF PASSENGER: NORÉN, IDA MRS.

Ticket 3

PAN AMERICAN WORLD AIRWAYS SYSTEM
FORM 0263-21 NUMBER 076149

- Fare: US $17
- Equivalent Am't Paid: VK. 85.-
- Tax: US TAX EXEMPT
- Total: SKR 881.
- Form of Payment: CASH
- Free Baggage Allowance: 20/30

Routing:
From	Via Carrier	Fare Construction
NYC	NWA	9.90
SEA	PAA	5.50
HNS	ACA	1.10

Valid Until: T/0 JUN, T/0 12, T/0 1957 — INFANT

From NEW YORK → SEATTLE → JUNEAU → HAINES — OP

Date and Place of Issue: AB NORDISK RESEBUREAU, OVERSEAS DEPARTMENT, STOCKHOLM

FARE US $17.-

NAME OF PASSENGER: NORÉN, KARL R. G. INFANT

M/S "OSLOFJORD", Norwegian America Line

Voyage No. 64 West, 1956.

Tonnage Gross 16844, Length 577 feet - 176 metres, Beam 72 feet - 22 metres.

Captain LEIF HANSEN

Oslo—New York via Kristiansand, Stavanger og Bergen.

Date	Lat. N.	Long.	Miles		Weather etc.
June 21.	59° 45	W. 2° 10	217	N.W, fresh br.	Slight. Overcast, p. cloudy.
" 22.	58° 16	" 17° 23	479	W.SW, strong br.	Rough. Overcast, fog.
" 23.	55° 02	" 31° 08	493	Var, "	Overcast, light cloudy.
" 24.	50° 36	" 42° 35	494	S.E, fresh br.	Slight. Overcast, fog.
" 25.	45° 59	" 52° 44	493	Var, "	Overcast, light cloudy.
" 26.	42° 25	" 63° 18	502	" mod. breeze.	Overcast, fog.
" 27.	40° 28	" 73° 35	486	" "	" "
" 27.			10		

Left Oslo June 19th at 0:06 p.m.   Left Bergen June 20th at 11:11 p.m.

Sea voyage: Marstein Lth. — Ambrose L/v.

Pass. Marstein Lth. June 21st at 0:53 a.m. Pass. Ambrose l/v June 27th at 0:45 p.m.

Dist. 3174 n. miles.   Time 6 d. 16 h. 52 m.   Av. speed 19,7 knots.

Arrived New York June 27th at 3:00 p.m.   Total dist. 3622 n. miles.

Total time 8 d. 7 h. 54 m.   Clock set back 5 hours.   AU REVOIR.

How To Reach...
PIER 42 NORTH RIVER
FOOT OF MORTON ST.
NEW YORK, N.Y.

NORWAY N·A·L DENMARK

Norwegian America Line
AGENCY, INC.

M/S. OSLOFJORD

OSEAN-BILLETT Nr V 19712

Passasjerens kopi

Den norske Amerikalinje / Norwegian America Line

Skip: "OSLO-FJORD" Seilingsdato: 19 Juni 1956 Klasse: TURIST
Fra: OSLO (Ombordstigning) Til: NEW YORK (Landstigning) Lugar: B 69 Køye: A11

EFTERNAVN	FORNAVN	Alder	Gift/Ugift	OSEANPRIS Dollar	Kroner
NORÉN	Ida Maria	38	G	200,-	1.036:-
"	Sune Göte	7	Ug	100,-	518:-
"	Karl R.G.	9 mån	"	10,-	52:-

Hva slags visum: Q.
Total: 310,- / 1.606:-
PREPAID nr.:
Forskudd:
Verdi $:
Restbeløp betalt: 1.606:-
Omregningskurs: 5.18

OSEAN-BILLETT Nr V 19711

Amerikalinje / Norwegian America Line

Skip: "OSLO-FJORD" Seilingsdato: 19 Juni 1956 Klasse: TURIST
Fra: OSLO (Ombordstigning) Til: NEW YORK (Landstigning) Lugar: B 65 Køye: A11

EFTERNAVN	FORNAVN	Alder	Gift/Ugift	OSEANPRIS Dollar	Kroner
NORÉN	Karl Göte	52	G	200,-	1.036:-
"	Karin	13	Ug	200,-	1.036:-
"	Ruth	12	Ug	200,-	1.036:-

Hva slags visum: Q.
Total: 600,- / 3.108:-
PREPAID nr.:
Forskudd:
Verdi $:
Restbeløp betalt: 3.108:-
Omregningskurs: 5.18
Agentur: NRB, Stockholm

Adresse:
Hjemsted: FUNÄSDALEN, Sverige

Dato: 11 Juni 1956
for Den norske Amerikalinje A/s

'Oslofjord' 1956 voyage

• Outside of the Hotel in Oslo

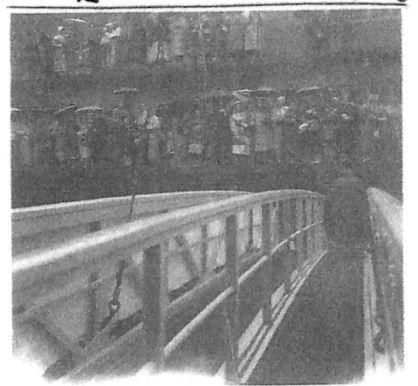

• We are here in New York

• pappa Göte

• Ruth

pappa Göte - Sune

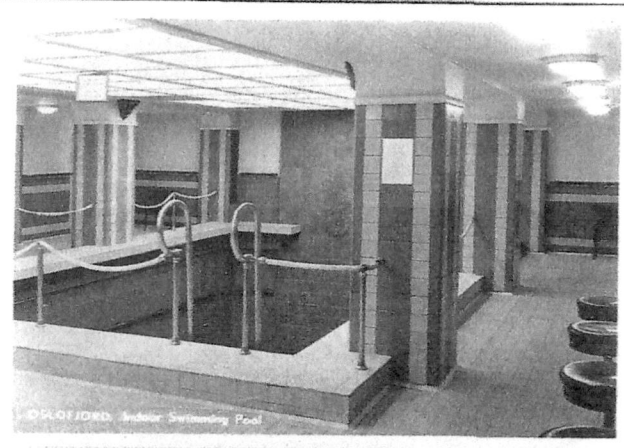

• Swimming fun

OSLOFJORD

June 19 through 27

OSLO, NORWAY to NEW YORK, USA

- OSLOFJORD, Norse Dining Room
- OSLOFJORD, Star Dining Room
- OSLOFJORD, Library
- OSLOFJORD, Garden Lounge
- OSLOFJORD, Ball Room
- OSLOFJORD, Ball Room
- OSLOFJORD, Salon
- OSLOFJORD, Smoking Room

Northwest Orient Airlines Stratocruisers — Finest... Fastest

Karl Göte Norén (June 27)
Ida Maria — " —
Karin S.M. — " —
Ruth I.J. — " —
Sune Göte — " —
Gunnar Karl Ritz — " —

info.
← found on the back

We flew on this plane to Alaska 1956   Ida

PAN AMERICAN WORLD AIRWAYS SYSTEM
Issued by PAN AMERICAN WORLD AIRWAYS, INC.

PASSENGER TICKET AND BAGGAGE CHECK PASSENGER COUPON

FORM 0263-21   NUMBER 076147

FARE $170.
EQUIVALENT AM'T PAID VK. 881.-
TAX US TAX EXEMPT
TOTAL SKR. 881.
FREE BAGGAGE ALLOWANCE 20/30
FORM OF PAYMENT CASH

ROUTING:
NYC — NWA — $99.
SEA — PAA — $55.
JNU — ACA — $16.

FROM NEW YORK
TO SEATTLE
TO JUNEAU
TO HAINES

VALID UNTIL: JUN 12 1957

DATE AND PLACE OF ISSUE: STOCKHOLM

FARE US $170.-

NAME OF PASSENGER → NORÉN, KARIN MISS

FORM 0263-21 | NUMBER 076148

PAA

PAN AMERICAN WORLD AIRWAYS SYSTEM

ISSUED BY
PAN AMERICAN WORLD AIRWAYS, INC.
MEMBER OF INTERNATIONAL AIR TRANSPORT ASSOCIATION

PASSENGER CONTRACT TICKET
AND
BAGGAGE CHECK

The System of the Flying Clippers

Each passenger should carefully examine this ticket, particularly the Conditions on the next page.

PAGE (1)

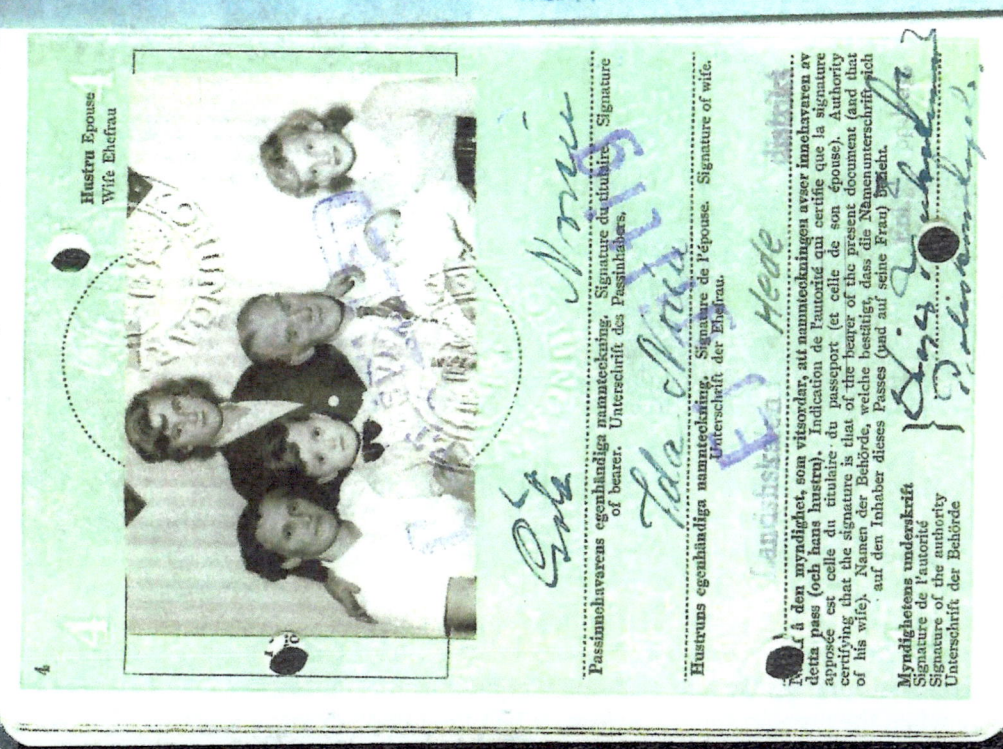

ISSUED BY
NORDISK RESEBUREAU
Stockholm, Göteborg, Malmö, Örebro
Member of the Swedish Travel Bureau Association

PAN AMERICAN WORLD AIRWAYS SYSTEM — PASSENGER TICKET AND BAGGAGE CHECK — PASSENGER COUPON — FORM 0263-21 | NUMBER 076146

Issued by PAN AMERICAN WORLD AIRWAYS, INC.
SUBJECT TO CONDITIONS OF CONTRACT ON PAGE 2

COMPLETE ROUTING THIS TICKET AND CONJUNCTION TICKET(S)	Form NHL Serial 19171	FARE $170.00	DATE AND PLACE OF ISSUE
ORIGIN		EQUIVALENT AMT PAID VK 881	AB NORDISK RESEBUREAU OVERSEAS DEPARTMENT
DESTINATION	ISSUED IN EXCHANGE FOR	TAX US TAX EXEMPT	STOCKHOLM
ROUTING FROM / USA Carrier / FARE Construction	Form Serial	TOTAL SKR 881	
NYC / NWA / 99	DATE AND PLACE OF ORIGINAL ISSUE	FREE BAGGAGE ALLOWANCE 20/30	AGENT:
SEA / PAA / 55	FORM OF PAYMENT CASH		
JNU / ACA / 16			
HNS			

FROM NEW YORK TO SEATTLE — JUN 12 1957
TO JUNEAU
TO HAINES

FARE US $170-
NAME OF PASSENGER: NORÉN RUTH MISS

NOT TRANSFERABLE

CARRIAGE/TRANSPORTATION hereunder is subject to the rules related to liability established by the Convention for the Unification of Certain Rules relating to International Carriage by Air signed at Warsaw, October 12, 1929, unless such carriage is not "International carriage" as defined by said Convention.

all our small cute things that we had, such as furniture, radio, skis, clothes, sleds (bobbar), moped, and a whole bunch of homemade jam that I could have used here in Alaska, especially the lingon berries. The kitchen stuff, bedding, rugs, lamps, axes and saws, everything we owned, everything had to go. (Ruth's accordion was also sold.)

But the absolute worst thing of all was that I had to leave my sweet, loving little mamma, she who had sacrificed everything for us all her whole life through, she looked so alone, standing on my brother's porch. IT WAS SO VERY HARD. (We all cried rivers). We had always lived so close to one another. Life tears bits and it tears pieces from us, especially when we become separated from our loved ones. This was the hardest thing I have ever done, to say farewell to my sweet mom. My dear mamma said to me. "The path that God has set before us, that is the one we must travel, and may God bless all of you." These were my mom's last words to me, as I left with all of my family to travel on my new path, a new direction, to a new life that God had given me. This was on 16 June 1956 that we took our farewells from Hållan, when we the six of us climbed into the taxi for Oslo, Norway!

There was a great loneliness and sadness that entered into my mamma when we all left Hållan. I remember when she was living with us in our little cottage there that last winter before we left, she would sit and be deep in thought and then she would shake her shoulders like she was shivering! And I can hear her saying so often, oh, so often "Alaska, Alaska" Mamma had already lost two of us to Alaska at this time. My brother Karl who left Sweden around 1930 and came home to visit in 1952 and my other brother Kristian, who had immigrated in 1955 about one year before we did. That was the reason the word Alaska was ringing in her ears, as a constant reminder.

And because of that she would be lost in her thoughts shaking her head with concern and shivering at even the thought. When mother would just sit and stare we knew her thoughts were on how unbelievable far away her sons were, and waiting for letters that so seldom came and wondering. It was hard for my little mamma to write letters now. And now of course in 1956 it was I, her baby (youngest of 10 children) that had gotten the same idea into her mind to also move from Hållan to Alaska. I know mother had a secure and safe feeling with us being so close by, her whole life circled around us. Göte was so godly good to (mor) mother. And Göte would make her so happy when they would sit and talk and when they would reason together, than there would be a happy feeling. And she so loved the children, it would be so lonely for her.

IT WAS SO HARD WHEN WE LEFT. I NEVER SAW HER AGAIN!!! (She capitalized these words, as if crying out inside!) Even today many years later, it is the hardest thing I have ever done. And still today I ask for forgiveness. She took it so very hard when we separated from one another for that became the last time we saw one another. It is still to this day, a pain in my heart!!! My heart breaks as I think of leaving my mom; I never did see my little mother again! She struggled with her livelihood, living alone in her little house in Hallan for a time (she was 83 years old in 1956 when we left). But however she struggled against leaving her home, after a time she was not able to make it there by herself. She lived with us the winter before we left, it was hard for her to make it on her own, to bring wood and water and all else. God, please forgive me for leaving! Did I do the right thing?

So than my siblings that were left there took care of mother here and there as they could for several months, (it was only Per and his wife Brita were there in Hållan) but poor mamma struggled, and wherever she was living after that, she wasn't ever happy again. So then by winter she was moved to an old folk's home in Vemdalen. She was a total stranger there and was never satisfied or happy there, everything was unknown and strange, my poor mamma! I feel in my heart how hurtful this was for her. I plead 'God forgive me for making her so sad'. It was very hard for all of us to leave her and everything we had known. I pray God will forgive me, because I left mother when she needed my help and company the most. I took everything away from her!

But I had to go where my family was led and where we were driven and I remembered her statement to me, which gives me strength. Mammas words were: ("Jaa du Ida, det är hårt att bära for mig") "yes, dear Ida this is difficult for me to bear, when you travel so far from me and I will never see you again! But, the road that God has marked out for you, that is the road you must follow". (Underlined by mother Ida) And that is the thought and feeling I still carry with me, it gave me the strength I needed, even today as I sit here and write my memories about days long passed away, I am grateful for her wisdom and love. But as we left Mamma she was now in need of others around her to help and give her attention sometimes and she was longing for us after we left, and longed for all her other children's attention too, for she was in need of help, even though she wanted to do things for herself. But I thank God for the blessed years that I have been given with mamma, for all unthinkable difficult years mamma strived to bring us up and teach all ten (10) of us respect. It is with great gratitude, love and happiness I have to mention about all the good qualities that she taught each one of us, to meet lives problems and to find solutions, along with always having respect for one another. This keeps me very strong and grateful for all the happiness we have had together.

**This knowledge is like gaining the richest of kingdoms in our lives, the greatest of those that we can possibly have, for with *this attitude* we can meet all kinds of different difficult situations. Even though we sometimes must live through a variety of situations, challenges and difficulties and over the years I must say that we certainly have done that, in the past 28 years in our new homeland of Alaska. I can certainly say we have had to use all the senses that we have received and learned and gained throughout these years, keeping our minds clear and never ever give up. And the years only move forward with us. So I must say like mamma "No one has been given more than what they need in understanding, and we do need and should use all of what we received." That is so very true!   (Mothers underlined these words)

Now here we begin what happened as we were leaving Sweden and our travels began to Alaska.

16 June 1956 Hållan, Funäsdalen. Life gives us hard choices; we had everything packed and ready to go. We had ordered a taxi which took us from Hållan, Funäsdalen to Oslo, Norway and the children were so happy and so excited for all new things that they would meet. I shall never forget how empty my heart felt when I took a hair from mamma's 1/2 meter long hair. I took one long strand of hair and rolled it around one of my buttons on my leather jacket. This became a reminder of our departure. Oh, oh, can you believe how difficult this was for me to leave my sweet mamma. On the way we stopped in Röros Norway where my brother Johan came from Trondheim to meets us and to see us off, we had lunch together and he wishes us well on our journey, and we all wept. Then the taxi continued with all of us and took us further and further away from Funäsdalen, we drove mile after mile, all the way until we arrived at the big harbor city of Oslo, Norway with all of us the 6 Noren's where the boat was waiting our departure.

We spent one night in a hotel with all our baggage, mainly a big wooden trunk aprox. 3x3,1\2x 4,1\2 tied to the top of the taxi. We all were a bit nervous that night that someone might get into our stuff. After all it contained what were our most important possessions in the world; it was all we owned after the auction at this time and as we left our little home in Hållan. The next day we were to board the Oslofjord to cross the ocean, one step closer toward Haines, Alaska. So thereby we took our farewell from the Scandinavian countries. (On the dock there was a band playing and we all threw streamers off the deck as the ship moved away.) It was a wonderful trip over the Atlantic Ocean, wide and deep going to our new promised land. We took God as our helper and went out onto the ocean for one week's sailing, this was on June16 we left Hållan, June 17 1956 we left Oslo, Norway. This was a trip that made all of us in the end, citizens of the United States of America. Pappa, Mamma, Sune and Gunnar became citizens in 1964 in Juneau, Alaska. Karin and Ruth were over 16 years old and had to seek their own citizenship. We have important photos of this happening to look at and remind ourselves.

Everything was new and difficult until we learned the language and the value of the dollar. We found a tolerable back yard shack for all of us to live in through that first fall into winter in Haines. The memory of that first winter cannot be described; when I think of pappa, myself and four kids in that shack, it was really tuff! It was quite a bold and daring existence and it is amazing how we were to live through that first winter with all six of us in one small room.

1956-57- This first winter was a cold one with loads of snow, there were drifts covering the roads in October and the wind blew so cold. I had a habit of standing by the 1 small window in the shack we lived, that was frozen over and I would blow on the glass window until I had a clear hole so I could look out. The thing that saved our health that winter was that we decided that we would buy a wood burning stove and pappa he installed the stove into this outhouse where we all were placed into, this was in the backyard at my Brother Karl's house. I think it was an old woodshed. Pappa nailed some beds together, and we decorated the walls. I bought some sturdy wool military blankets from Dock Allen (at the cannery) that I covered the children with. We had the stove on around the clock for heat. We were so very poor, but we were strong and able to work. The walls in our shed were very thin, they were made out of cardboard so with that it was to wake up and find the walls all wet and frosty every morning. (I remembers the blankets frozen to the wall, as you read on you will see, mom and dad through it all, were so positive and courageous.) But a new day came and it was good to hope for a better life. Our health and strength was good, (mamma Ida capitalized and underlined where so done) BEING TUFF, THAT WAS THE WORD. We made the best of every situation. Karin, Ruth and Sune started school there in Haines Alaska that first year, and it went o.k. They learned English faster than their father and mother of course. Gunnar had now begun to speak and run around with anyone who was kind and gave of their time. The little man grew quickly; Gunnar was nine months old when we came from Sweden. So in 1956 in Haines we had the worry to find work so we could live, send the kids to school, care for our little man (gubben Budi) (an endearing name mamma Ida gave to Gunnar) he was helpful in being with us in all the new things we met. We learned something new every day. I have wonder and thought often about our leaving Sweden and our immigration to America, and how we had to truly believe in a new luck in an unknown land, and looking back how we have had to have strong nerves. God really was with us and He has continued to bless us very much.

We move to Port Chilkoot later that winter, one mile from Haines, there we rented a giant of a house from the company of Karl Heinmiller who was the boss there at that time. We knew it needed fixing up for they were old army barracks. The roofs inside were high, 10 foot tall, big rooms, but we had a roof over our heads. So we fixed up, put up wallpaper so we could live there at Port Chilkoot in these old army barracks. There was also a great thing about Haines, we found some wonderful Swedish friends. They owned a hotel named 'The Hälsingland Hotel' they gave us a lot of help, some old tourist beds with mattresses, sheets and pillowcases for the whole Noren family, all 6 of us. And new days continued to come and we had to go forward with the days also. We had to find work, and earn money, and begin to learn. We could not sit still, for than there would be nothing to fill the hungry mouths that were around pappa and me. Here we were in a foreign land, but we said 'we'll make it, all of us'!!! Pappa took a job, he could not speak English but an old Indian man named Paddock had some carpenter work to be done, and pappa knew how to work. (Note: Uncle Karl helped translate what the employer wanted done)

Yes, I guess as we were learning the new language there came, maybe a couple of new words into our mind each day. But it was really hard for us to learn and to speak English, so we spoke mostly Swedish until we learned a whole sentence or a whole meaning. But I thought everything was very interesting. And the desire to learn became stronger and through God's help and His peace we succeeded. After a while I started working as a janitor, cleaning at the Pioneer Bar. And then I became overloaded with people that wanted help when they heard that I wanted to work. So here and there in this little place we landed, we got work, so the program went full speed, for all of us every new morning. Soon we had all the work we had time for and needed.

The children grew and soon no one thought much of our homeland. There were new excitements for them to do and become used to as they grew. Everything was new, in this new land for all of us the six Noren's from Sweden. Sune started the 2nd grade in Haines. He has also kept in remembrance to write the Swedish language, and your Mother thinks that this is super wonderful. Gunnar learned English and understood and spoke it, because of his growing up here in America.

Göte and myself and with our 4 trolls, left Sweden towards our new adventures, with desire and looking forward to our new experience in an unknown land. As we left we couldn't even count to 10 in English, the first black person we ever saw was in Chicago, she was a taxi driver, she was able to say "I can speak Norwegian" (jeg kan snakke norsk) but that was all she could say. We took God with us in the boat, and went out on the Atlantic Ocean. It took seven days and seven nights to get to New York from Oslo and Gunnar was just nine months old when we left Hållan. But we were firm that we would make a change in our lives style. And we made it to Alaska, and we became stuck here in our new life, but we have found health, happiness, and we learned to like it here in time, for we received a new exciting life here, for all of us both large and small, we began, you might say, our new school of life here.

As we left the old country, we sailed with the steamship 'Oslofjord' from Norway to New York. In today's society we fly wherever we go, so we can get there faster. Göte and I we have worked together these many years. He upon the water by the silent ocean coast, he has been fishing for 25 years, every summer for 4 months of hard days, in the mostly stormy waters, waves so very large and as high as a house has cut in around the boat, the Ida Maria. The skipper Göte, can bear witness that there were many hard, dark, cold miles to hold the wheel and the boat on the right course night after night, hoping that the nets would be full of fish, which would mean $$$$$.

The nets that we used for Salmon fishing were 200 ft. long. Every stitch on the net is 6 and ½ inches long with 60 stitches deep. On the top of the net there were corks tied to hold the net up from sinking. When the corks would go up and down pappa would know there were fish in there. Father (far) he was a tuff man and so willing! When the 4-5 day opening for the fishing week was over either in Haines or Juneau it would vary, the Ida Maria would be parked at the Juneau harbor till the new week would begin. Father (far) wanted very much to come home for the 2-3 days between openings, there would be much to do to fix the holes in the nets. No time to rest. All the fishermen are tuff, happy and hope the next week will be better than the first, and so on it goes. And we hoped before the fall that between everything that had to be paid out, more has been brought in.

I am so very thankful and want to share this happiness with all of you; we have been fortunate and so lucky, that we have had health like steel. FATHER GÖTE GAVE EVERYTHING HE HAD AND MOTHER IDA TOO AND WE THE TWO OF US WERE ALWAYS UNITED and that was needed if we were to begin a new life in a new land together. Father is a good example for all of the Noren's, and for all the extended family. Thank you pappa!! I chose to stay on land and build our future. I packed fish in the Haines Packing co. I have been a cleaning helper in Haines and Juneau homes as well as a (custodian) in the two schools (Juneau Douglas High School) for 15 years. From that I can now take it easy and receive my pension, social security checks each and every month since 1979. So now my back has been able to be still, relax and have had time to rest. And since that time I have had my 65th birthday, I receive 250 dollars every month as long as we live in Alaska and about 1000 dollars in oil present yearly. This is a new law and it visits every one and is welcomed by all. But who knows maybe a new law will take this help away again, we will see?

Mamma's memories continue about our arrival in Haines 28 June 1956: When we were dumped at the Haines airport full of glass beer bottles and garbage blowing hard around us everywhere, my 2 brothers Karl and Kristian met us to welcome us. From there we were taken 4 miles into Haines and there we met Karl's family for the first time. For about one week we slept in the big bedroom at the top of the stairs and then after that we were dropped off and moved into an old fallen, little back yard shack, called a house, this was in my Brother Karl's backyard. Father (far) had the biggest responsibility. But I had to be home and take care of that rough and awful place we were to live in that first winter. It was an old dirty full of spiders and old garbage storage shed. On the walls there was dampness from just breathing and body heat and cooking, oh, and so cold at night. For the kids it was the worst, what if they should get sick?? No, we had to do something right now. Yes, we were in a simple word, in **despair**, not knowing what to do? Both father and I agreed. It can't be helped; it can cost whatever it will! We have to fix this somehow! So after some searching, we were able to find and bought a big stove that could use oil, wood and electricity and this helped us live through that first hard winter and kept us alive. The stove cost 250 dollars.

Father (far) he organized and kept the stove going and there was warmth all through the day and night, we kept burning wood to keep us dry and warm. We took turns checking around the room, looking to see if and making sure the children had their bed covering over them through the night. Yes, bed covering on them, let me tell you this was not the luxury hotel! We had brought two wool blankets with us from Sweden and then we had some we barrowed. We heard someone say that at the place where we had bought the stove (the cannery) they also had military wool blankets for sale. So we went directly out and bought 6 wool blankets (from Doc Allen). Pappa also bought an old red International pickup truck (see picture) from him the next fall 1967. Father took a carpenter job for an Indian man; we could not speak English yet, but knew how to do the job and could work, than we didn't have to say much. Soon things became a little easier to understand and so life became easier with time. (In Haines Mamma Ida holding some salmon in the boat papa built, probably Sune in the foreground.)

Pappa he had his own interest: soon he began building his own 21 ft. wood skiff that later he would pull salmon up into. This skiff or boat was the help we needed for our new start in this salmon land (lax landet) Alaska. THE DREAM IS TRUE, so we will take and do everything that we can, WE WILL MAKE IT. Göte was 52 years old. I know that it was an adventure for Göte and a very exiting one to start fishing. We bought an old net from my brother. It was old and rotten, but we paid 80 dollars for it, it was not even worth half of that.
So than he went out the first time in his boat with nets, motor, and slid out on the calm seas with clucking waves beneath to try his luck.

At that point he knew that fishing would not be a hobby any more. But now it became the way we made our living for us in Alaska. I will add here that Göte never did enjoy sport fishing when we lived in Sweden. It certainly is interesting how times changes in our lives. I don't really know how we made ends meet, but we were never without strength, we had the gift of health and the will and the drive to strive forward. There was no chance to give up and so we had of course to learn the way that people lived and did things here. There was too much partying going on though, I think. I had decided that my lives program from the very start would not include that, that it does not work to party and roll on however one wants. If a person has a family that one wants the best for, than one must think and give respect and thought about their growing up, and hope that this will give them a life that they can learn to believe in themselves from, and by that they will become honorable and will be able to make and live their lives in this difficult demanding world that we must live in.

But we had to have something to begin with. We learned quickly that everyone wanted to have theirs in America, yes, we learned that from the very beginning, and we learned it even from our own, it wasn't that we wanted to have anything free. But it was not easy as we began our life here.

Göte started in with his work at fishing that first September, in his new boat he himself had built in July and August 1956. What a new adventure for all of us!!! Göte was 52, I was 38, Karin was 13, Ruth was 12, Sune was 7 and Gunnar was 9 months when we came on June 27th from Sweden.

So Göte he took off for the first time in his boat, with motor and net, out on the ocean blue with the clucking of the waves against the boat, there to try his luck! We knew from that time on that fishing would never be a hobby ever again. Now it would become our livelihood here in Alaska. I have to add here, that Göte never had desire to go out sport fishing even when we lived in Sweden. It's strange how time can change things.

I really <u>don't</u> know how we made ends meet that first fall and winter, but we were not afraid to get out there and try. I can't tell you even half of how we felt, our hard work, our prayers and trust in God and our belief in our own abilities too, we just knew that things would work out, and we were not without courage, we also had the gift of health and the will to slave and fight forward. There was no chance that we would or even could, give up hope.

We made it on two weeks fishing in **September 1956**, he made 300 dollars and the season closed. But it was wonderful fishing, father (far) was strong and willing but he had a fishing net and other equipment that was poor,(spent countless hours fixing the net) and the wind in the fall was hard on the equipment too. That fall and winter pappa took some small jobs here and there. Working for Karl Heinmiller for example at Port Chilkoot (fixing ups, doing carpentry on old army housing) and for Paddock and Kings Store. $$ has to be made, we had a large family, and had many responsibilities.

But through all this we still could not understand or speak English, but we knew how to work, so everything moved forward, but at the time we thought it seemingly went terribly slow. We brought food for the winter, approximately 300 dollars' worth and we struggled through. But by Christmas we were without money and the Lindquist's offered us that we could borrow. They came specifically with this intent and through two men's hands, spoke and Göte barrowed 2000 dollars from them, there was no choice. That was paid back in full the next fall. Note: this was a lot of money at that time in life for us to barrow and pay back.

Gunnar was just a little tyke, and I was fully busy taking care of that horrible place (elandiga kåken) we had to live in, the space was so small and tight for all of us for that fall and winter. (Ruth's memories: This first winter it was a very cold early, several feet of snow by Halloween, and oh, so windy, the inside walls had frost on them, everything froze, even the toilet water, I remembers that our blanket even froze to the wall while we slept.) Back to mothers writing: During the day we had to pick up the mattresses and place them in front of the wood stove, so that they could dry out and so that they would be dry when it was time to lie down on them again. It was horrible, horrible. (huva, huva). It is strange now to think about how <u>we strove in our poverty and filth (dynga), till we were able to get on our feet.</u> I had to have my children and my home clean, so we all could stay healthy. Göte and I have divided our work and picked out all the thorns in our life that we could through the years, and continue working with our children, and for them we hoped for all that is good.

There was no choice in giving up hope, we had to go on! We have all been able to learn the way and how people live here. I think they party way too much here. I decided on my life's program from the very beginning, that it will not go well if one parties and carry on however one wants. If we have a family we must give the best that we can for them, than one must work and think about them and with respect for their upbringing, and hope that it will give them a life that they can learn to think for themselves. And by doing so they will grow up with respect and will make it in this demanding world we must live in. God has been so good to all of us. And I am glad that I have been able to write up a little of what has happened to us.

There were plenty of invites to parties and favors, for they call this "the free land". But from the first moment **27 June 1956** when we landed in Haines all six of us in that plane, it became our family that we must have the extra plans and strength for, Göte Noren, Ida Noren, Karin, Ruth, Sune, Gunnar, and the extra time and place for in Haines. No time to party.

My first thought at the airport, there we stood with four small children was, "well now, now, we have ended up in the wrong place". It looked anything but (inbjudande) inviting; there was nothing to give me a peaceful or happy feeling as we arrived. On this particular day the wind was blowing very hard and my two brothers Karl and Kristian met us to welcome us. At that point the wind blew their hats off, and we saw those hats for the last time. But now we were here, we had reached our destination with our bags and with tired kids at a small dirt runway airport and it looked very lonely. All around us we were enclosed by sky, high mountains and water, (huva) I had a dreadful feeling, there are tightly grown spruce trees, deadwood and bushes, (urskog) total wilderness, a very rugged terrain and the ground was decorated with empty beer bottles everywhere. TO LATE TO TURN AROUND NOW, but we had all at least arrived safely from the long trip we had undertaken, but I felt locked in in a no man's land (inmurade i en ingen man's land). And then to begin to learn everything from the beginning, this really would indeed be an enormous challenge. It was hardest to talk to my brothers because those who did not understand Swedish when we spoke to one another were not happy, they were suspicious and thought that we were talking about them, and at times they were right.

**(Ja, herre min hatt) Yes, my goodness gracious, there were episodes, but when I don't make notations some of the most important things that have happened to us and have passed by, than there is much that goes on also and is not said or noted, but is than forgotten. But for my own deal, I wish to write down as much of my memories, from the many memories as I can of our family's life, in our new land.

So, that first winter we lived in a very poor shack like dwelling, it was only one little room and a toilette that did not help a family our size very much. Thin walls, damp and cold, small window holes that had thick ice on them so one never saw out of them. We bought up the most important thing for us; some food stuffs that we ordered and came by boat one time a month, the whole town bought their food in this way. This was new for me that came from little Hållan, Funäsdalen. So I thought that it was kind of fun to learn what we needed, which type of groceries would last till the next boat came. But then I was never used to wasting anything so it went very well for us, and we had good food even though it was different from what we were used to eat, but very interesting.

*In another memory about our arrival in the U.S. she wrote:

When we were dumped off down at the airport in Haines, it was full of glass beer bottles and garbage blowing hard and wildly around us. Karl and Kristian my brothers met us and welcomed us. Then when we finally stopped, we were to stay in a badly fallen shack; this was where we were to live. In the fall it was very cold and the walls were very damp, we had to buy a stove for 250 dollars. This kept us alive through the first winter. Before Christmas we had no more dollars and then the Lindquist's offered and told us we could borrow some money.

Karl Tagg my brother got sick and died at the hospital in Juneau, Alaska around Christmas 1957.

Our life in Haines ends here. January of 1958 we boarded the ferry 'Chilkoot' in Haines for Juneau Alaska where we would make our new home for the next 50+ years.

------

*So here begins the memories of our mother Ida Maria Jonasson Tagg in her early years, living with her mother Karin Ingeborg Backman Tagg in Hållan Funäsdalen.

Ida Maria Jonasson Tagg Noreen 1918- 2010!

This is mother's life story as she wrote it and as it was told by her, starting the year of 1977 through the year 2000 approximately when she made her last main dated entry at 83 years of age. However some notes and inserts of writings are of a later date and can be found here and there in her handwritten notes.

Mamma spoke and wrote in Swedish, she was a Swedish girl through and through, so I am translating her words as written and spoken to me in her native language, into English for the benefit of her children and grandchildren to come. In this way they might get to know her and learn from her personality and strengths and how she dealt with her life experiences, and perhaps learn and know where some of your own characteristics and strengths come from, and through this learn the skill of patience, that each one of us too might learn to endure our individual challenges and trials as mamma Ida did. I regret that I cannot translate into English with her same wit, style and flair, as mamma's communications were written or spoken in the Swedish language. But as I have the privilege to translate her words from Swedish to English, my hope is that you also can feel her spirit of communication, for she truly had a great talent in the way she used unique words and expressions in her native language at times. This has been assembled, recorded, translated and written by her daughter Ruth.

She writes on the inside cover of the journal I gave her in hopes to learn more about her life:

Today is Sunday the 23 September 1979 Ruth, Dennis, Kristina, Travis and little Trent Dennis, 6 months old came to visit, they gave us Far and Mor each a book that we should fill in and write all our memories back as far as we could remember. This will certainly be a big assignment, but fun to try to make the wishes of Ruth our research specialist who we have in our family come true. I hope that it will bring old forgotten and newer ideas to memory and be worthwhile to all when it will be read. There was then and is now such a big difference from my time, when I was a child and as I grew up compared to today's life, the differences are like night to day. But I am sure I will remember and write many a memories. So now, I will begin the first chapter, thank you Ruth for the idea.

I was born the March 3rd 1918 in our home in Hallan, Funasdalen, Harjedalen, Jamptlands lan, Sweden.

I am number10 in a long line of children of our mother. Over the long time period that I've been alive, there always was something exiting going on. I've written a little bit now and then so this will be kind of fun as I think and try to remember back through the years, this is the first time I have ever been asked to recall my memories

(Note: Mother did keep a record of sorts, they are found on some regular large written pages, sometimes several pages of writings together, but also on small scraps of paper, these have been put into (mamma's binder) if you should ever want to see the notes she has written. She also wrote unrelated notes in her recipe books, on calendars and on any other small scraps of paper, even a tissue rolls or any item she could find to write on at the moment. She even wrote on a piece of fire wood, on her baking board and inside a large turtle shell, I have found some of mammas writings in many strange places. She was indeed unique and frugal in every way!!!)

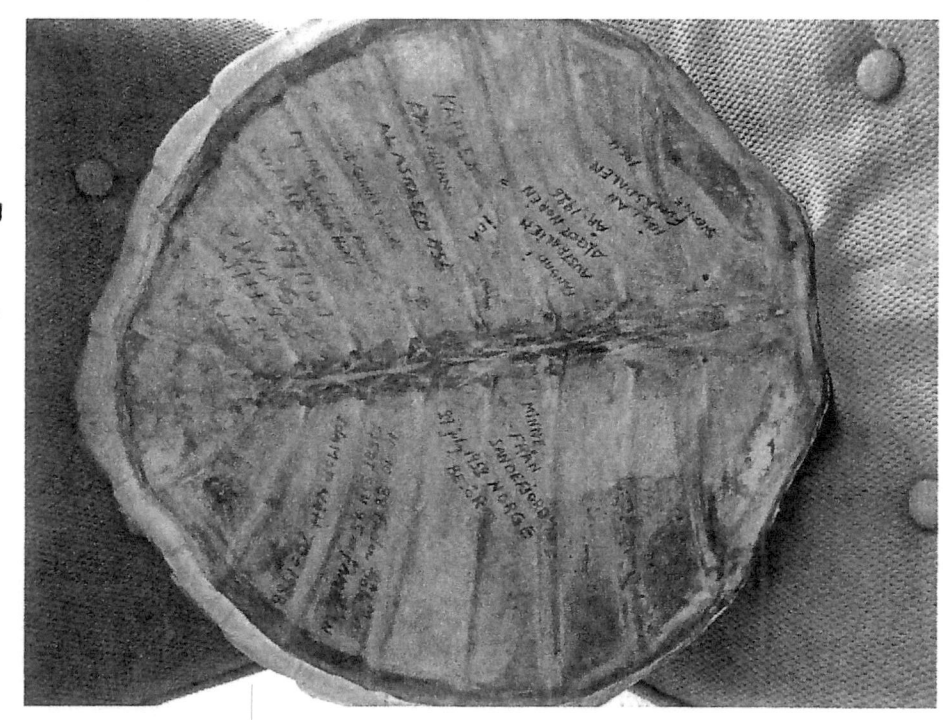

Our mamma (Ida) also used to make multiple entrees many years apart on the same page, even the same piece of paper, sometimes commenting on how things were now and again at a later date. And again, she even made notes relating to totally different things on places such as I said on her recipe pages, on wood blocks, inside a turtle shell, on toilet paper rolls, on a piece of wood, on padding, on her baking board that pappa made for her, even on a piece of fire wood was found writing, you name it, as said, there you could find a note from mother, her experiences, thoughts and concerns. It seems she used writing as a confidant, dear friend, someone she could share thoughts with and trust that somehow they would be remembered as she shared her inner thoughts and feelings. It seems that this was her way of gaining relived from her challenging life, hard work and sometimes loneliness from her mother and sisters in Sweden and Norway as she missed her association with them, or just everyday stress, but also happiness and days of satisfaction in her day to day life experiences. I am so glad she did, as we that knew her, certainly miss her very much! ☺)

Look ↙

This next quote was written at a much later date on the same page with her usual wit and style, she writes: "And If I become famous from my writings after my days are done, I hope that you Ruth will make more copies so that everyone will have the tale of the immigrants Noreen, as they left Hållan Funäsdalen to go to big adventurous, much talked about Alaska. Where we became pioneers, 30 years here in Alaska on June 27 1989, not to bad! (I am now complying with her request) We have had and tried many different days together and we have been successful, and all in all, we have really done quite well. There have been many years that I have not made any record of or writings about our family's life, which I regret, for there have been many things of great worth that we have experienced and lived through. So I am now thinking, trying to remember as I begin, and it is hard to relive this time that has now passed away from us. (A still later entry) Now on march 3/3/1999 Ida has reached all the way to 81 years.

These are her words: recorded, translated and typed by me Ruth, as written down in notes or spoken onto cassette tape recordings by mamma "Ida Maria Jonasson Tagg", this is how she begins her life story that she was asked to think about, try to remember and write down.

So here we go as she begins her remembrances:

Memories from my early days of my life in (Sweden, and Norway)
(Her mother's picture: Karin Ingeborg Backman Tagg)

As I think back, first of all I remember my mamma wanted me to know and taught me that there was a God; she really wanted me to know that fact and this was a very important thing for her, and for me too that I needed to hear and learn from her. Everything that I believe in, I have as a gift from my mamma. She truly said that we must pray and trust in God, she was a great example to me.

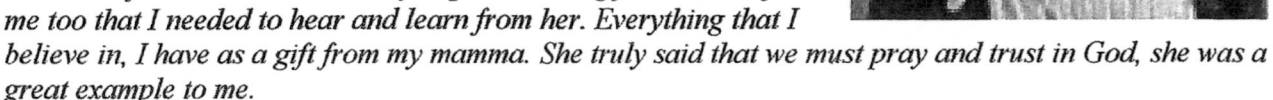

About our food that we had, it was very plain, we had a lot of salted (sill) herring, we didn't have much of bacon or meatballs and such food, foods like that, those kinds of foods were very seldom had, it wasn't anything like we have it now. We did go to Norway as often as someone was going, but we could buy Norwegian salt herring in Sweden too, so we always had that, and it kept a long time. Mamma was really good at cooking soups, fruit soup (from dried fruit) and meat soups and it was easy to make and then there was food when they the boys (Pär and Kristian) would come in. For breakfast we had pancakes, waffles, hot cereal, thick and milky (grot och valling) we had mush at night a lot of time. It was very plain foods (ingen krusifix) not fancy stuff like now, no, no!!

Our home was not fancy but our furniture was nice enough, old beds of course, nicely made, my mamma would weave her sheets herself from old cut up (white) shirts and I still have one here which I gave to Ruth, if anyone is interested in seeing it she has it now. These rugs were used for our sheets and we slept on them. The mattresses were made of old rags but the cut up clothes had to be totally worn out before mamma would use it for making rugs or stuffing mattresses. There was something really good in the woods to use, but we used the first and best that we found or had. In those days they also used stuff like hay, for fill into making the mattresses. There was no choices if we had something we used that or we could lay on it hard too. But Mamma also wove her own sheets (rugs) they were usually white she also wowed colorful rugs for the house. She was really skilled.

She had a spinning wheel and also spun her own yarn for knitting socks. *We had a wood burning stove and had to have wood of course to feed the stove, it was loads of hard work getting prepared, for the winters were very long. I remember mamma was usually mad at the boys* (brothers Pär and Kristian) *for not helping more and she would say "its best that I go out there myself" and she went out and began chopping or carrying in the wood herself. She was left to do nearly everything herself.*

I was probably 7 years old when my father died; (picture of Jonas Jonasson Tagg) (he died 25 May 1925) *I remember how I cried when they took him out and laid him in (bua) an old outside shack we used for storage and such, so anyway I remember when I thought about, that there is father out there, and I remember how I screamed and cried really loud☹! We decorated around him where he laid with (tallbar) spruce branches and then of course he was put into his casket out there, and was buried down the hill at the graveyard in Funasdalen. It was a really sad time; my father's name was Jonas Jonasson Tagg.* **I remember how I loved to sit on his lap; he was so very kind to me.**

Mamma lived a really simple life, she didn't have much to choose from, she took that which came to her, and it took everything of what she had to fix food for us each day. We never went without food though, we never starved, and she was always baking, so I learned to do that from her. We didn't have waffles with whip cream on it kind of food, only plain and simple food. But we did have goodies, in the summer we would pick (hjortron also called smultron) cloud berries and that is what we lived on all winter.

*We did **not** buy apples, oranges or bananas at this period of time. They were too expensive so we couldn't, we didn't have a job, but we never starved. But the berries were important to us and raisins and (stor fika) dried prunes in bags, that could be laid in water and soaked and we could make fruit soup from that. There were a couple of small stores in town to buy some supplies from. We bought eggs and milk from the small farms our neighbors had; they also had a few chickens and cows. It was a long way to go, and heavy to carry, we usually got 4 liters of milk and that was my job to go and get that. We never had chickens ourselves, but we had some goats for a while and at one time some cows.*

We lived a bit far from town so we could only buy a little at the time because we had to carry the food all the way home and it would be very heavy, so we had to go many times and take a bit each time. Every time anyone went to town we always brought something from the store. I couldn't say no to mamma when she wanted something, she was always so kind in every way. It seemed like she always had some money, I don't know where she got it. (Gamelmor) Old Mother as she was called (this was grandma Tagg's stepmother who raised her, as her mother had died in childbirth with her) *she got 25kr. pension each month and I think we lived off of that. I can't understand how we made it, but we did. Old Mother was known also as Jo Gulliks Christina.*

(Christina Olofsdotter 1850-1933) She went to live with some other relative for a while, but she didn't like it there so mamma went and got her, so she came home and lived with us from then on. She was really good to us she would give us candy and stuff and I liked her very much. She died when I was around 10 years old I think. (Note: looking up her death date, she really died when mamma was 15 years old.)

I remember as a child I was deadly afraid of the dark, someone must have scared me or something and I would not dare go out after dark for anything. But on this particular night it could not have been any worse, the night (gammel mor) old mother died, mamma said I had to (knalla ivag) get going, out to get some help, out into the dark, tall trees all around on my skis, it was the night of February 23. I remember it was such a super dark night. My job was to get help to carry 'old mother' out of the house. I went down to Erick Dalsten first and he wasn't home, so I had to try some other place but I couldn't find any help and the houses were quite far apart from each other, so I went back to Erick Dalsten's house and he was finally home. He came along home with me and helped mamma carry 'old mother' out of the house. They took her down to an old enclosed shed that was kept really cold, further down on the property down by the hay shack. Oh, my God in Heaven how difficult this was, it is hard to remember all that happened, but this was an experience that I do remember and it was very hard! The weather was starting to get a bit better at this time, so this must have been in the spring that old mother died. Life was terribly hard for us at times.

We did have some pets as I grew up, we had a dog, I remember and we had a cat too, I also had a goat named Quilka, it was a black in color, it was such a sweet goat and I loved it. But it seemed that we didn't have the pets to long, they just disappeared from time to time. I think someone just took care of them??(Mamma Ida was laughing real hard when she remembered this) She continued; mamma she couldn't stand the cat so maybe she took care of it? Anyway we were so poor we had to be so careful about food for the family and the milk too, there just wasn't any extra. I can't remember just how expensive the milk was but it was probably really expensive and it was such a long way to carry that 4 liter bucket. We bought the milk from Kristian Dalsten and Hendrika his wife; she was from Norway. It was quite a distance to go up to their house. This much probably lasted us a week, we kept the milk in the creek in the cold water, but it was always cold there anyway, so that was not a problem.

In the summer I had a special place I went to play, this was mostly before I started school but probably for a while after that too, it

was a little ways away from out house in the woods nearby, there was a dip or an indentation hole in the ground there, and I found a good-sized rock that became my baby and this was my house, I played there by myself and talked to that baby and dressed and drug things out to play with in my play house. I made a shelf in there for the bed, I remember it fondly, and it was a fun place to play.

My father and mother they were all over trying to make ends meet, as I just think how they worked and strived for everything and trying to find the best way, they were poor as could be their entire life, but never, never did they complain, no, never did they complain. And now, in today's world it has to be everything and still it doesn't seem to be good enough. People are in general (forstord) destroyed and really messed up now. ***I think there will come a different time, that they (the people)will have to wait a bit, a time without everything so easy, yes that I am sure of, if I live so long I think I will get to know such a time again even in my day. (She died 12 March 2010) There will be trials ahead; I don't believe it can continue like it is now, a time of such plenty. No I am sure it cannot continue with expectations so high!

Our winters were long and hard in Hållan Funäsdalen where we were born and where we lived and we had as much as 3 meters of snow some winters, but it went just fine. There were horses that pulled old wagons along the streets to plow the snow off the roads so we could get through. I am telling you, that was the life than, and no one seemed too complained. And oh my goodness, how we kept chopping wood to keep the wood stove going. It was a big job to stay warm in the house during the long, long winters. Mamma kept after us to bring wood in all the time, but the boys didn't do much.

I started to go to school when I was probably 7-8 years old in first grade. I had to go about 5-6 km. from home to school; we walked or in the winter went on skis. We lived up in Hållan and our school was down in Funäsdalen, our school was in a very old building, torn down long long ago now. You Ruth and Karin and even Sune went to school in the new school that was built later. We sure had fun in my day though on the way to and from school, my friends would wait for me, hiding and scaring or surprising me playing along the way, we had a lot of fun in our poor circumstances. It is interesting how it is when one is small and poor, I still have such wonderful memories from my childhood, and these were days that never ever can come back again. I don't remember a lot about school other than that I didn't like to read, but I could sing, I had a really good voice for singing and if they were not nice to me, I wouldn't sing, and I had to give them the tone where the song should begin, and that was one thing that I could do. And then I knew how to be mischievous too and I was, and the kids would laugh at me (she laughed really hard at herself as she was remembering and sharing her childhood with me.)

I was probably a little imp and a troublemaker. (jag var nog en satunge.) There was a room in the school where the woodstove was kept, that the whole school was warmed by and I would sneak off and stand behind it, making faces at the kids when they were doing their lessons, I didn't care about the lesson (jag struntade I lektion, sa jag fick sitta kvar pa kvallarna) I didn't give a hut or care about the lessons, so I had to be kept after school in the evenings to do my work that I missed when I was misbehaving, and then

- Ida Maria Tagg - and her pet goat "Twilka"
- Grandma Tagg's House and property in Hållan.
- mamma Ida was born here -
Funäsdalen in the background.

- young Ida Maria -

Mamma Ida 20 years old

I had to walk home by myself,(5km) but I didn't care. Yes, I just had to walk home all the way up to Hållan by myself, when my time was up. On my way home I had to walk past the graveyard and I didn't like that, but that time passed too. But I remember that I did sing well, and that is what saved me. Of course I did learn to read and to do my lessons but it was so that sometimes I had to stay after school; it was probably when I had to stay behind to finish my work that I learned the most. But it was such a long way home, to walk by myself, but I did it a few times.

I remember also that I did have a lot of friends, that was for sure, everyone wanted me as a friend and to be around me, we played loads of games too, we threw ball, up on the wall, around our back, under our legs, and all kinds of modes, and played a game called sink, it was a eight sided piece made out of wood that one would throw and find and put it on again and do it again? It was really fun; we should try to find that game, I think the kids would like it too. We also jumped rope. We had a lot of fun playing many games with friends. In the winters when it was snowy we would ski. When I was small the first skis I had were homemade from a plank or board with some rubber glued to the top to put my feet through. And of course than we put something on the bottom that would make it slippery and so it was how we started. It was some man nearby that made them, but we couldn't buy everything that we wanted to have.

And I had to ski to school and home again. Later I think I got some skis from my sister Stina and her husband, some good ones, they were so good to me!

Any time when someone died I had to go to the funerals, to the graveyard to see what it was like, I was just a little scared about going but I was (sa nyfiken) so curious that I had to go there to see what was going on, but I remember that I left really fast in a hurry after, and I didn't really like it at all, but I had to see what it was like anyway. I was always very curious. I cannot remember ever really being sick when I was at home, I think there were fewer illnesses back then, than there are now. I guess we had colds and such, I really can't remember any bad sicknesses though. I guess we had measles and the childhood stuff. But I do remember that I stole something one time, I can't even remember what it was now, but I remember that I had to go back with it because I was feeling so sick about taking it. ☺ (She laughed at the memory, and continued) We are always learning!

My mamma was very kind and very well-liked by everyone, she had a very outgoing way about her, but she also had the other side, she could tell them what she thought, and if it was so, they just didn't have to come back again if they misbehaved. Mamma always read the bible every night, there was not an evening that she did not read in her bible. She had other books too that she read and of course it was by the light from a lantern. It was a yellow one, that was the only one we had and if we were really lucky and we could afford to buy candles to light, that was especially nice, but that was very seldom that we had that. I remember how we sometimes opened the wood stoves door and saw from that light to read the letters of the paper or something like that when we didn't have light. So we were not spoiled at all, but I think that is how we turn out real people, these become the strongest individuals, those who don't get everything all

the time. I do remember being cold, we all slept in the same room with the stove. There were no electric things to warm us up in those days. I was taught this prayer by mamma and said it every night before bed.

"Gud som haver barnen kär, se till mig som liten är, vart jag mig I världen vänder, står min lycka I Guds händer, lyckan kommer, lyckan går, den Gud älskar lyckan får" Amen.

God who has all the children dear, look after me because I am small, wherever in the world I wander, my blessings are always in God's hands, happiness comes and happiness go, but the one who God loves, receive happiness ever more. Amen.

She went on: If I think about who I am mostly like, I think I take after both my mamma and pappa because they were both very practical and they had a great understanding about everything and they didn't want to make anyone sad, and I too am like that and try to make it the best way possible, yes; I believe that I am much like both of them. But mamma was also very firm, she would give us a spank if we misbehaved, even I who was her baby, the last love, as I was the youngest. She wanted us to grow up well behaved.

We had many relatives, many cousins in Funäsdalen and around neighboring communities. Ljusnedal, Hede, Tännäs, Sveg. We also had a lot of family in and around Trondheim, Norway. I remember Ingeborg and Fredrik Fast would come to visit every year, they were from Sveg, he was a salesman, and he sold machinery. He had a car that he used for work and I am sure I got to ride in the car, Per he had a car too and Stina and Aksel also came every year to visit and they also had a car. They moved the storage building (bua) from way down on mammas lot to further up and they stayed there when they came. I don't know how long that lasted; they finally moved it to (Vemdalen) Norway.

My first job could have been babysitting, but probably I worked at (fornminnes) the former days memories park in the buildings, these were old buildings moved there or perhaps a recreation of old buildings from the 1700-1800 where we made waffles and sold refreshments to the guests that would come there to hear the history of Funäsdalen. We would dress up in the old style clothing in the Swedish traditional dress. But the thing I really loved was to pick cloudberries (hjortron). We used to pick the cloudberries up in the mountain bogs, I remember I almost lifted and carried myself to death, that is part of the reason why I have such backaches now and my problems now comes from that beginning. I would pick the berries and then sell them. But I really enjoyed doing that; it was really a fun thing to do. We picked lingon berries in the fall but I didn't sell them, it was just for home. The types of food we mostly ate were oatmeal mush, and sometimes rice mush, but that was very seldom because rice was very expensive. But we boiled potatoes, made meatballs and gravy and mixed and ate it all stirred together (pytt I pannan). We had the same kind of food most of the time, also carrots and cabbage things that was grown there at home. We didn't have at that time and use as much vegetables as we do now. Maybe that is why I am so healthy and strong☺ (she laughs).

We also did at times go to a show of some kind, or maybe a gathering of people putting on some kind of show but that was really seldom, there were no movies when I was small in Funäsdalen. And we had to walk wherever we went so if we went out, we first had to walk the approximately 5 km to get there, and then after the show was over to return home by walking 5 km again in the dark, we just didn't have the strength for those kind of outings very often. We didn't go to church very often for the same reason, but we read the bible and learned to pray from the very beginning, mamma she was so kind. When we went to church everyone sat together on benches in a big church building and there was a warm feeling there. At that time there were loads of different preachers that came preaching and mamma liked to go when they came. I too thought it was fun to go and so I was especially good the whole day so I would be able to go with her and so I did go with mamma on those occasions. There would usually be some nice music and preaching.

Christmas was as festive, yet as solemn as it could be. We dressed a tree, sang songs, and had some extra special foods. Everyone got together and I of course always received gifts from my sister in Trondheim, she has always taken care of me, what a special person she was. She was wonderful! Someone always dressed up as Santa Clause (Jultompten) and they would say "you better be good now because he might live here or there?" As it was always someone that lived close by and we knew that. "Then he will see you and then you won't get any gift!" We had Lute fish and potatoes and good gravy; we had hot rice pudding or mush with a cinnamon stick in it. And all the good berries we picked during the summer we could use on our hot mush. Easter, we ate eggs and sometimes went to church but there again it was so far to walk to and from.

(Note: I asked mother if she remembered her first boyfriend. She started laughing and saying that she would never reveal that information. Oh, his name was, must I tell you his name? I said no, of course not, and she blurted out "His name was Olle Eriksson, I met him when I was a maid (piga) in Sveg. In a little community called Eggin outside of town. She said I thought it was so silly to remember that☺ (I asked her, what else do you remember doing as a youth?) Oh, I was a troublemaker; no not really we did everything other kids did. I was a happy person I loved to dance, so as soon as I knew that I could dance I had a lot of fun. I danced the vals, the hambo, and the scottish; the dances were fast and exiting. There is nothing so exiting in the music now as it was back then. I guess each generation feels like that about our own music. We were usually in a dance hall location; there would be accordion and guitar and other instruments too. But sometimes we also had music from record players too, but usually at the dances it was live music.

I had the very best of clothing when I went and of course, my sister had sowed the dresses for me. I also cruelled my hair, by warming an iron of sorts on the wood stove and it would sometimes get to hot and I

65

burned up an awful lot of hair that way (she laughed as she reminisced) ☺ but of course we had to curl our hair. But mamma was very angry about that, she screamed at me when I was working with my hair, especially when she smelled burned hair, I would hurry to comb away the burned hair and I would say, oh, I'm done now! No, she didn't like that! But I did burn my hair many times and it did smell. I warmed the iron on the top of our ordinary wood stove or put it into the stove and held onto it with something so I would not burn my hand.(I commented, oh that would be bad.) She said, no, it went really well. We did have an iron too for ironing our clothes which we did all the time. We put the cast iron on top of the wood stove too and it got hot, and the ironing went just fine.

I never got in real trouble with mamma where I had to be restricted or anything, but did get a good spanking a time or two when I was small. She didn't say very much or very often, but when she did she really meant it! We had music and it was mostly guitar, violin, accordion and (citra?) and the record player of course, just like now. I can't ever remember movies in my youth; I don't think that had been invented yet. We would go skiing though, up onto the mountain, just once in a while, but not too often. In the fall there were those times that we had to cut the grass and hang it on wooden racks to dry making (hashor). We were busy doing the work that needed to be done in the fall after the hay was completely dry, than it had to be taken down and put into the shelter (lada) for winter use to feed the goats. Sometimes we had to buy some hay too.

I never really went on a formal vacation, but I did go home with my sister who lived in Norway. I was quite young the first time I went along. I had a lot of friends there too, we played and had fun. I would stay for a month or more until they again went to visit mamma and of course they then took me home. When I got a bit older I did go and visit and stay with my other sister Ingeborg in Sveg, Sweden. The only hard times I can really remember was when someone died. Such as when my sister Karolina (Lala was what I called her) she died (in 1924) and was buried in Trondheim, Norway. I remember mamma got a message, a letter I guess and she left right away and went there to the funeral. Than I was home alone and my sister Ingeborg came up and stayed with me. It was an especially difficult experience for there were no cars for transportation at that time between where we lived Funasdalen and Roros Norway. (We lived approx. 18 of our American miles from the Norwegian border, and from our home to Roros (another 35-40 miles)? mamma had to go by horse and from there, there was some sort of train the rest of the way to Trondheim. But at least 40-50 miles by horse, so she had someone take her there. These were difficult times for us especially for mamma; she wanted to go of course to see her daughter one last time. But maybe that was why we were so tuff.

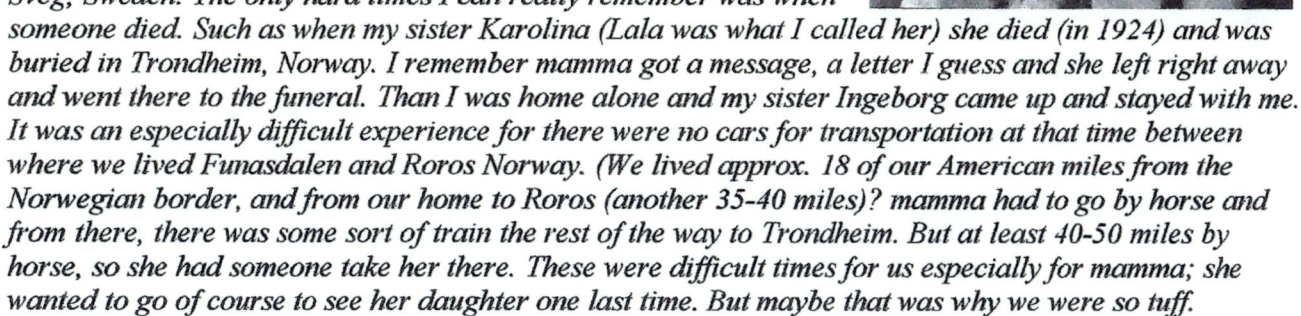

Hallan was just a small housing area 5-6 km from Funäsdalen up in the mountain toward the border with Norway. There were probably 20 families spread out up there within a couple of kilometers and maybe a 1000 people in Funäsdalen. This was a big ski area for tourists and of course there were hotels and restaurants to help service the people. Inger Lysholm my brother Johan's daughter would come and visit her grandma, my mom, and of course me also as we were the same age and that was every summer and we would have fun together, go dancing and have a good time running around. We had loads of fun times

during those many visits from Norway or on my visits to Norway. Mamma taught me to trust in God and that prayer should be an important part of our life during those early years of my life.

(In the picture: Ida middle and Inger below also 3 boy who were friends, view is from behind Ida's house in Hållan-, Funåsdalen is in the distance)

Tape #2 (This interview is dated January 23, 1999 in Douglas, Alaska at mammas house, on a snowy day Mothers comment to me was, " I forget and don't know what to say" but I said, I will ask you good questions to help you remember.

That was our conversation, as we began again!) (I suggested, we will start with remembrances of the older brothers and sisters. But then she began and we went another direction as her mind was indeed working at remembering, as she must have been thinking about her Mamma.)

So she began: But I do remember going to church at times, but it was such a long way to town from where we lived to go to church. So it was quite seldom that we walked the 5 km to town and 5 km home again, but there were prayer meetings and discussion groups in the individual homes close to us, I would go with my grandma Jo Gulliks Kristina, She was like a mother to my mom (she was the stepmother who raised her) she used to love to go to these meetings and I liked it too, and it was fun to go with her, so I did go with her many times. She was really nice, but she used to go away and visit a lot as I remember, but I too liked to go, because I was just little and I wanted to listen to what they had to say. They would talk and discuss, and sing beautiful songs, songs that I still remember even today when I am 80 years old, yes I still remember many of the songs and all of the different houses we went to and the preaching (pingst vanner) that was going on by the women. And of course I learned much from that too.

Mamma did a lot of reading of the bible too as I said, so I was taught mostly by my mom, I think my pappa also believed, but he was more easy going, but he taught me many other things like to save and such things. People that lived in our community seemed to have jobs and money only enough to make ends meet and they probably had a small pension, there were small farms and such. But I really don't know how my mamma made it from day to day; she never had more than 20 kr. in her purse maybe 25 at the very most. There was no child support money in mammas day, like it was later in time when you were small, (talking to me Ruth) No, I don't know how she made it! And we had to walk wherever we went of course, but there were bikes too and sleds and skiing during the winter.

There were those who came visiting the ski areas and stayed in hotels around there, but not as much as in later years. But we, No, we just lived our lives up there in Hållan, went to school, were confirmed and grew up. I did have acquaintances and friends but no dates or steadies, we did have fun but I was guarded *pretty close by my mom. I had to adhere to being home by 8 or 9 each evening or (morshan) my mother would come after me and find me, she was strict. I did have a few dates but we mostly had fun at dances with everyone. There was not anything steadier until I met pappa. Life just continued day after day!*

Around 1937- 1939 *-He (pappa Göte)would visit at our home, mamma liked him really well and he liked her too, but he didn't get to stay there, it was not so at that time period that we would sleep together before marriage, but we would sneak away at times though, walk around and have a good time. I could never bring a man home to stay, not ever. It is different now in some households. But we were out having a good time together, Göte Norén was a really good dancer and that was something I really liked to do too. So we had a lot of fun visiting together, we listened to the radio, and did a lot of walking together; we just enjoyed spending time together.*

He left for a while with some other road work and we kept writing to each other during that time and did what we could to keep in contact, and believed things would turn out right. He did come back up and that is all it took. So we had a wonderful wedding in the Funasdalen Church, it was new only a few years old at that time. So we got married there then, on 31 August 1941. The picture that was taken of our wedding is just awful I think, but it is a picture.

There was no contact with his side of the family, no one came to the wedding either. It was too bad, but we had more contact later as time continues forward. I learned that he was kind anyway and that we would make it together (vi skulle klara oss) and build up our ideas and home, that is about all we thought of. We lived at home with mother for a while, we didn't have anything, if we had had anything it would have been nice but we didn't have anything, it took us a while before we had our own place. Göte he worked and we got a few kr. as time moved forward.My goodness, how we had it back then, now we have it so good that it is shameful to even complain at all. Therefore I cannot understand how anyone could wish for more, we didn't have anything and we were still always satisfied. We had clothes and we didn't have anything that we were sad about, we were always satisfied, wasn't that a gift from God?

My clothes were all made by my sister Stina, I was the most elegant person around. Our underclothes were clumpy though, they were thick and were homemade with (womuls) wool and they rubbed in on my (lära) inner leg until I was beside myself. But we could make pants of material that didn't hurt by the time you were small (Karin and Ruth) you guys were lucky. I couldn't sew really well, but we sewed underpants anyway, but when Stina would come home from Norway where she lived, every time she came, she would have made nice clothes for my kids. (The Coats in this picture for Karin and Ruth).

We didn't have it very big and it was not super comfortable but it was a really lovely home, I really loved it and fixed it up of course. We had beds that were built into the walls, a set of bunk beds and one that pappa and I slept on.

(Note: In the picture above the whole house was probably only about 24x35? we just had only 3 rooms, kitchen, living room and bedroom, with a very small pantry) (Above is our house in a picture in Hallan with Karin and Ruth in our beautiful coats sewn by our aunt Stina, mamma's sister, she had just come from Trondhaim Norway to visit. Below is shown matching outfits for Karin and Ruth also made by her. We were lucky girls!!

We had some small gardens too over the years with potatoes, turnips. We continued to plant and work up on Funasdals Mountain they always planted potatoes up there and we continued over the years to work for winter potatoes up there. We had fruit very seldom. In our home there in Hallan we did have electricity but no running water. So we had to go over to the little stream that also ran past mormor's house and we got our water from there for the first few years. We had to carry it in buckets quite a distance, for drinking and washing. This was hard work. We also had a wood stove that we cooked on and that kept our house warm that we had to have wood for. We got the wood from the woods around there. If a tree fell down or sometimes pappa would buy a load of wood. But we had to cut and saw lengths to fit into the wood stove and then chop the rounds to fit, yes it was really hard work, it is no wonder that our backs are now broken and gone. Ohj joj joj, (expression, like oh, my, my, my or oh, my gosh) but no one complained. We didn't know anything else and so there was never a complaint uttered about any of our conditions. Pappa would keep sawing and cutting and our home was always warm and nice. It's hard now to understand how we did it, but wood and water was carried in continually. Isn't that wonderful? Isn't that a wonderful memory to have? (I agreed, yes, it is a wonderful memory to have, as we their kids also experienced some of that.)

(She went on :) and we made it just fine and we even were able to come to America and we got better and better homes, lived in and built and sold! Life has been great!

Göte worked away from home for weeks at the time and then would come home to see us for a little while. I had to take care of everything at home of course while he was out working. (I asked her if that had any effect on any of us). *She said jokingly: I could get away with spanking you more while he was gone☺ No I think you all had everything you needed, and you also had friends around you so everything went well. I baked at times and we also had a party and you children were satisfied, and you never went to bed saying that you were hungry and that is really nice. You children were not ever cranky or sad. We didn't have any of that in our home. Our life was good there.*

After starting the wood stove in the morning, I used to warm up your clothes, I would put your clothes into the oven to get warm and then I would bring them to you and Karin and you had to get them on in a hurry while they were warm. We also listened to the radio that we had in the morning, (We woke up to the song that started (god morron, god moron, tral lal a lal a and so on, wishing us a good morning.) We also had our bathroom outside across the yard from our house or we sat on the (påttan) potty on the porch and I, mother would carried it out, especially in the winter. We had very much snow in the winters, it was extreme snowfall, and I remember you kids had a lot of fun; you made snow caves outside of the kitchen window with candles inside. And you children would take out the washbasin to slide down the snowdrift in it; you did have a fun time. We had no electrical heaters that would have been too expensive. No, my goodness no, we always had to heat with wood. We were not involved in any outside things, because we had a full job just keeping up with the bringing in the wood and the water in the middle of the snowstorms, and then to go out with the waste. Our life was not one of real comfort, but we had nothing to complain about either, we really didn't know anything different.

You kids were all very good; I never had any problems with any of you. Karin played the violin in the school orchestra and you Ruth sang in church on an occasion when Karin's violin orchestra played the Lucia song and you also sang for the Härjedalen promotional film just before we left Sweden. Sune was out there riding the sled and having fun, he was too small to be involved with other things. Good memories!! We went to church sometimes and we sang and listened to the windup record player at home and of course the radio.

To all those of my family line who I will never probably meet or be able to visit with, I say you must find out for yourself, and to learn as each of us before you have done. We were born on this wise, that we had so little that we never expected any more than what we had, we didn't ask for something that (far eller mor) father and mother didn't have and could not give us and so then, we were happy with what we had. We had to be! We were satisfied, we were never unhappy because we didn't get what others might have had. So be happy with what you have, and be grateful for what you do have, and don't wish for what you can't have. It has got to be so when you don't have it, everyone wants more and more it seems, like there in never enough now, but always want more but I hope you will be happy with what you have. And work diligently, and keep working even if it is hard, take a break if you are sick but be sure to do the job you said you would, be true, and hardworking, and take life the way that it comes to you and be satisfied with what you have, that is what happened when we came to America.

There was a few sayings that I remember, that the four leaf clover was really good luck, we always looked for those when it began to grow. If someone got sick there was not much that we could do other than to lay down and drink something until you got better, we didn't run to the doctor to spend all our money. If there was an earache we put some (bomull) cotton into the ear, mormor (grandma Tagg) used to put a little bit of oil on the piece of cloth and then into the ear and wrap the ears with a scarf, and then it would warm it up and be soothing. There were home remedies that we used. We took care of the colds and problems at home and were lucky that we were healthy.

① mamma and Gunnar in Haines ② Stina, Axel, Ida, Göte and Sune ③ mamma Ida and Sune.
④ Mamma Ida at the bus stop in Hållan with Gunnar in a baby basket. ⑤ Ruth and Karin on a bench outside in Trondheim Norway

Feb 1956

GUNNAR I VÄSKAN
5 månader
VAccinerings dag
VÄNTAR på Bussen
i Hållan

- 1954 Funäsdalen, Sw. Karl Tagg came home from Alaska to visit his Mother and siblings —
- Family Photo (from left to right)
  Ingeborg Fasth, Karl Tagg, Kristian Tagg, Stina Garmo, Pär Tagg, Ida Norén, Johan Tagg
- in front: grandma Karin Tagg (Happy times)

Ida's Parents
Johan Jonasson
Karin Ingeborg
Tagg
Johan + Stina
Children (Karin) →

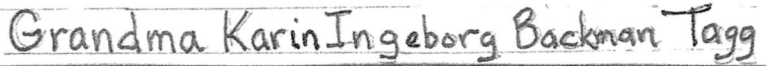

Grandma Karin Ingeborg Backman Tagg

1943-44 Ida - Göte
expecting Ruth

Ida and her mom aprox. 1940

1956 Our Family with Grandma Tagg

Karin
Sune
Ida
(mamma)

Ruth
Göte
(pappa)

(Mormor) Grandma Tagg, Gunnar 9 months

We were happy that we had the four kids that we had, yes we were lucky daddy and I. ☺ For birthdays pappa would usually buy something and of course we baked a cake and sang, 'yes we hope you will live for a hundred years'(ja må du leva uti hundrade år) was our Swedish birthday song.

We really liked Christmas; we went all out and put everything we had into it. Everyone got something, usually something that was needed, and there was a special something for everyone, but not so much that they didn't even know what they have gotten and from whom. Today there is much too much of everything, absolutely, ush, so we don't value things like we did back then, we were so satisfied with what we had. We decorated for Christmas about 3 days before Christmas and live candles, mother didn't like that. We had a (jultompten) Santa clause that came with a bag of goodies☺ it was a fun time of the year!

We took some trips too, to Trondheim when you Ruth and Karin were really small, in 1947-48 my sister Stina and her family and my brother Johann and his family lived there. And then our family went to Sandefjord, where pappas brother Algot and family lived in the year 1952, both of these places are in Norway.

Look at Pictures of both visits in Trondheim and Sandefjord.

At that particular time while we were gone there was a young man Rune Ahlgren and his friend that came on motorbikes to see pappa from down south in Sweden, we understood him to be about 17 years old and that he was pappas biological son from a previous relationship. I feel so bad that we missed him, I am sure he would have liked me and I would have liked him, I feel so bad we didn't get to see him. Maybe we could find him?

(My Note: Karin wrote letters for pappa to try to find him and I also did send out letters to seven Rune Algren's listed in the Swedish phonebook, but no one replied. It was our aunt Anna, pappa's sister who told us about this event, that he (Göte) her brother, our father, was father to a son and the mother's name was Alma Ahlgren. (She was a cook on a road crew) Anna's daughter Birgitt also remembered what her mother Anna had said, that an uncle of Birgitt, another man had also fathered another child by the same woman. I Ruth also heard our aunt Anna relate this to me when I was home to Sweden in 1978.

Pappa told me at another time that he had a son named Rune when I was ready to name Sune after his birth, and therefore could not name him that name.

We also went to Sveg where my sister Ingeborg lived to visit, I really don't know how we made ends meet and still go on vacations being as poor as we were, I really don't understand how we made it. It is fun to remember though. Ruth you got to go to Göteborg to a camp when you were probably about 8-9 years old, It was a program and camp for children that needed more sun, you were so pale and skinny, ☺ you poor thing, you have had it bad. The state sent you to the beach and sun for 2 weeks, we didn't have any money.

In our home in Hallan we had a small pantry just off the kitchen and we had some food stuff always on hand but it was simple food in a simple lifestyle.

EMIGRANTS FROM HÅLLAN, FUNÄSDALEN TO ALASKA 17-27 June 1956

God has been so good to all of us and I am glad that I have been able to write down a small fraction of that which has happened. I have not even written down though but a small part of what we have experienced, but we have done the best we could each day to give our children a strong understanding about that they must choose their own course. Nothing is simple. The years go past and we all more and more are called to respect life and to answer for ourselves.

But with God's help we will with love be completely triumphant and victorious. But I thank no one personally except God, and my Mor and Far for the valuable feelings of learning given me, to be able to deal with life for and through myself, and all mine, whom I love the most of anything in life, Göte and all my children, whom I am so thankful for. This became a wonderful memory and notation, and it is also true.

I found a note I had written to mor (my mother) in Sweden, that came back to me from her, that states: In the greenest part of my youth, when life with my beloved Göte was blooming and our interests were in common. When life was at its best, our responsibilities were and seemed so easy. We didn't find any objection to each other's ideas, and we felt that we had plenty of what was really important. We left for Alaska in 1956. When my brother Karl came home after 30 years **(in 1952)** we became captivated by his encouragement to try our luck in Alaska. The year we immigrated Karin had just received her confirmation. Ruth finished the 5th grade. Sune had finished the 1st grade in the school in Funäsdalen and Gunnar was 9 months old when we took all of our 6 healthy bodies, into a taxi to drive to Oslo Norway and then sail via boat across the Atlantic Ocean to an unknown land and destination.

She continues: The first time I saw pappa, he lived close by in a neighbor's house up there in Hållan, they were building the road, our road up through there was a very poor before that time period, so than Göte and his crew lived there, in several (kåkar) homes and houses renting monthly. Göte was the boss. That was the first time I met Göte. Inger was of course with me, she had just come from Trondheim and I said to her there is a cute boy here, so let's go out for a walk. So we did and he got to see us and I have to tell you he came out in a hurry. They didn't know there were girls there because we had both just come home from Norway. So that is how I got my little Göte, we dated for probably two years, there was loads of road improvement work all around there, so he had work there for a long time.

Tape #1 **that which is written in Italics** *is inserted remembrances from a recording on cassette tape interviews spoken in Swedish by mother Ida, this was started on December 30, 1998 when she was 80 years old.)*

That which is written in (**Book Antiqua type)** indicates writings found on individual little notes, found on scraps of paper and also on individual sheets, with add on notes from many different years on the same sheet or piece of paper, found here and there throughout her home, written over many years, these journal entries were made by our sweet mamma Ida mostly in the years beginning in 1970 and forward.

This is where mother Ida's writing in the Journal that Ruth gave to her begins (in this type).

1918-1925: I was born in Hållan, Funäsdalen 3/3/1918. As I begin to write it is my first year in school, I was a happy lively little being as I went to school that first year, we lived up in Hållan 5 km from the town of Funäsdalen. It was necessary for me to go on skis with a backpack on my back, when going to school and I remember it was a long way to school for a little girl.

But we had a very healthy life and lifestyle, my mamma would make me a lunch the best she could each day, but I remember there wasn't much to it.

My Mamma's name was Karin Backman Tagg, my father died when I was 6-7 years old his name was Jonas Jonsson Tagg. *I think I was born at home in the old red house, not the one we had later. I think it was (gammel mor) 'old mother's house where mamma probably grew up too (grandma Tagg's stepmother). We always lived there in Funäsdalen when I was small, I haven't asked my mother enough about her past life to know much about her life, but we had our home up there in Hållan. We had our house and a small barn with 4 or 5 goats, a male goat and some cows at one time. I gave you (Ruth) the bell that the cow wore. My memories of my pappa are that he was always so good and loving and kind. He was old but he took good care of me. I was always up in his lap. I was his little girl. He worked down town at the hotel landscaping and on farms in the community and other work and had to go there every morning. He died from a hart attach I think, he died while he was at work. They found him sitting there (1858-1925) he was a really hard worker. In his years that he worked in the woods, he was known as (Skogskungen) " The forest King" because of his strength and ability to work hard and accomplish much, Yes, he was a hard worker, people would say "here comes Tagg, the king of the forest".*

After he died and because he was not there anymore that meant that mother was alone and bore the burden of providing for us and raising us. *My mamma, she just was my mamma and always, always kind and loving, but firm. She was always a very hard worker, she had the animals to care for and she would milk in the evening and the morning too, mostly in the morning. She also had a potatoes and rutabagas garden. The farmers from around there they had big potato fields up on the Funäsdal's mountain. They had the very best yields up there on the mountain. They were so very good, we all worked up there during the summer and at harvest time putting the potatoes into bags, it was really hard work but it was fun anyway, we got to share good food and stuff that the farmer had brought.*

Mamma had 10 children in all, I am the youngest. There were 3 of us children left at home at this time when mamma was fully responsible for us, my brothers Per, Kristian and little me, Ida. It was not easy to have enough food for us we were like hungry wolves. That we were poor like Lazarus is true, these were my whole childhood memories, but we were brought up to eat whatever we had in the cupboard, and that was all there was to it. If it didn't taste right, it was only to wait long enough until we were hungry enough to eat it, then it had to be good enough, for there was nothing else. We never had good butter or fruit or anything that cost a lot, we could not throw away money on such things of luxury. But there was nothing wrong with our appetites. But even though our life was like that, I felt my childhood was good anyway. There was no way for mamma to earn money; she had a small pension and that was where everything came from. Mamma had it very difficult, as she tried to support us three that lived at home. I always looked to mamma to provide and take care of everything I needed throughout my childhood and the many years thereafter.

I learned how to play the guitar when I was just a little girl, my brother Per had a guitar he played it really good. I remember mamma also did like to sing but she sang really off key (mamma laughed) oh yes she sang out loudly sometimes ☺ It was really funny! I was the youngest of all the children (of 10) and I nursed from mamma till I was 3 or 4 years old. If I got really cranky at times than she knew what I wanted and I would pull her behind the door and if I got a little nursing than I was good again. I was a really cranky little girl till I got my way. (She laughed) Gosh, I don't think I am telling and doing this right! (I assured her there is no wrong way; we are trying to preserve her memories, and she was doing a great job remembering!)

We were not in terrible need as I got older, mamma had a pension and my older sisters helped sometimes. Pär and Kristian were 5 and 7 years older than me. As I remember they were not at all willing to help with the work, they were lazy and spoiled, and they always would have an excuse when mamma would ask them to chop wood or carry wood or water in, they snuck away the fastest they could, and they seldom did anything worthwhile. But when they became hungry, then they found their way home and emptied everything of the little that mamma did had. I remember it so well! Mamma was usually tired of all argument that went on with us kids. But it went one day after the other anyway, mom being worn out and seemingly never done with her work.

I have to mention here that we of course had the wood burning stove to heat our little house and to cook on all the years as I grew up. All my years of growing up we also got all our water for cooking, drinking or washing from a little mountain stream that had the most wonderful fresh tasting water, it ran right next to our house. We didn't have any spring water all of my growing up years. We had to exert ourselves and carry it in every day from the creek that ran past our house. *When wash day arrived we had to carry the water into the house in big buckets from the creek and warm it on the wood stove. And we would cook our clothes, can you think of it? But we had clean clothes, that I can tell you, there was no dirt there. We had green soap for all washing (lye soap) we made it at home we used it for washing ourselves too. No it was not very fancy but we had that which we needed. We never bought soap; we would whip it up ourselves at home.* In the winter when it was frozen or if the drifts of snow were much too high, we had to melt snow for water.

When I compare my teenage years then and how it is now, there sure is a big difference from that time and how we live now. But it was a wonderful time when I stop and think back, how little we needed to make us happy and very thankful for everything back then. I got a backpack for Christmas with two new dresses one year from my older sister Stina, blue overtop with dark blue bell skirt decorated with a checkered band on the bottom. I remember I snuck in and took a peek in the mirror, it hung to high on the bedroom wall and I thought that I was the most beautiful of all. Mamma didn't say anything just then, but other times she warned me when I stood in front of the mirror to long that "pride is the worst thing of all, and that God is not patient with those who possess it". I feel like I can hear her say it now and how serious she sounded. She continued "God has suffered for all except for the sin of pride". I knew anyway that I was pretty and I was very happy; I snuck in and took another look in the mirror, and thought everything in my life was so perfect!

I was a mamma girl, I held on to mammas skirt until I was 15-16 years old; we were very close to each other she and I. No, we didn't have much but we had that which we needed and always seemed to make it. Because she was alone raising us, my older sisters Stina and Ingeborg helped us out mostly especially during the summers. *This was the way it was with us until the time that Stina started to come home each summer, and Ingeborg also came home and helped us, so things were better than. I too was supposed to help at home of course when I was little and of course I did learn how to do most everything, but I think I got away without doing too much, I remember my sisters said to me, you get away without doing anything, you don't have to do anything. So I snuck away after hugging mamma and got away without doing much. I was naughty and mischievous at times. But of course I did learn to help.*

I have mentioned before that nothing was ever thrown away, we were always grateful that there was at least one meal for each day. I remember through the years from a small schoolgirl on until married and grown up that my dear sister Stina and family would come from Trondheim, Norway in their car and it was always filled with food. Than throughout the summer months as they would visit mother and us that there was delicious food for all of us hungry wolves for our meals. Every day it seemed we would fix the very best meal yet. There was nothing wrong with our appetites as I remember; everything went down into our stomach just fine.

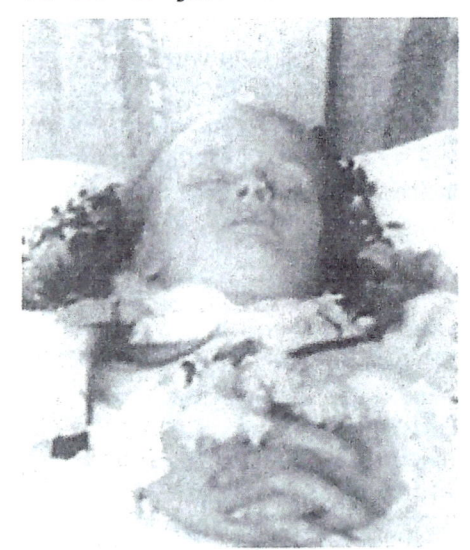

My sister Karolina she died in Trondheim, Norway (1909-1924) she was 17 when she died, I was maybe 4-5 years old then. She was so beautiful, yes, her life ended early, I think her death had something to do with her heart. She lived there in Trondheim with Stina and Aksel, she was working and earning a bit of money. But she went away early, I can't even remember the last time I saw her. But as it was I grew up and started my own life. All of my brothers and sisters were older than me of course. They were here and there out on jobs. Johann he was married in Norway too but he had a daughter Inger with another woman, but they were not married. But her mom died early when Inger was about 8 years old and Inger at that point moved in with Johann and his wife. But she said that they were kind to her. (Mamma Ida and Inger were the same age and they were like sisters all their lives.)

Then there was Karl who went out traveling and came over to America, but that was later, I was probably about 14-15 years old at that time. I remember how sad mamma was, she said "this is the last time we will ever see one another" and it almost was that, but he did come home about 30 years later (1952) to see his mamma. There was also Jon Backman he is my half-brother, he was the first born but he has died. (1891-1941) There was another Karl that died as a baby (1898-1900) that was in Folldalen, Norway, they lived in Norway at that time. And of course Pär and Kristian that was just a little older than me.

1926-1930: My dear sister Stina (Karin Kristina) that lived in Norway she also sowed all of my clothes for school; I was the fanciest and best dressed person in my class during this time period. There were not any styles to choose from but I felt very beautiful, each year she would have sown some new clothes for me. When it was stormy and very cold I had thick wool pants with a matching vest, the pants it had two buttons on each side that I fastened my homemade knitted wool socks to. This was very warm, but as I grew older I really thought that they were baggy and uncomely. But we still had to wear them because that is what we had. *Our pants always were under a skirt, girls didn't wear just pants in those days, but we wore thick pants under. I had a cute skirt that I liked to wear. And every pair of socks (they were long ones) that I had as a child were home spun and knitted by mamma. We had an outhouse where we went to the bathroom, and when it got to full in there, the outhouse was built so we could go behind and shovel it down ☺ and so than there would be room again. In the winter we still had to go out to go to*

the bathroom of course, but during bad storms we used to go out on the porch and sit there on a bucket. What a life!

Stina she also made me a backpack and I will never forget it, I was probably in the 5th grade, it was made out of (Norwegian) sealskin and my homework was never wet. I remember that I used to sow and hand stitch on my linen things but it was far from fancy, and then when I clumped on all the outside clothes over that, those things mamma told me to, the fanciness didn't matter anyway.

She would always say to dress warm when it was so very cold and snowy. Also because of the long way to and from school, if I did as she told me, I was not frozen even though my short eyelashes became thick with ice and my long braided hair had ice clumps in it. As I said most all the time in the winter we had to strap on and use our skis which had old fashioned leather binders on them, I would stick my feet into them and fasten them extra tight with rope, so that they would not come off till I got to school. If I was forced to take my gloves off to fix them than my fingers froze, so it was only to ski forward quickly so I would not be late for my class that started at nine o'clock.

In the winter there was so much snow that the beautiful mountain stream that flowed past our house disappeared under the high mountains of snow, after a snowstorm we had many hard of hours of digging to find our little water house that we built over the creek, it had a little door on it and then, there was the wonderful sight of the blessed water hole. Than I was happy to fill as many bucket as I could find to fill for drinking, washing and cooking. When the snow storms came we would wait a whole week sometimes for a calm in the storm to shovel the snow to get to the water, because it was so hard and exhausting to shovel all the snow away and it (the snow) would just bury the wonderful water hole we had made just while I would have time to fill and carry in two buckets and I didn't want to risk that. Than after we got the water, then there was the wood that needed to be brought in and put by the side of the wood stove so it would dry, thereby it would be easy to get the fire started. Sometime it took long to get the fire going but after a while we could feel the stove becoming warm and that was wonderful. Mamma and I usually had to put extra clothing on before it got warm in the house.

I lay in mammas good bed with her, there I kept myself warm. We had sheepskins with mountain long hair, in our bed layered with home woven white rug for under support and they served as sheets. It was warm and wonderful; we had it as clean and hygienic as it was possible for our poor circumstances. But I do recall that mamma wanted order and cleanliness. But once we had a big problem, there were black bedbugs that hopped around in our bed but we got rid of them somehow. Anyway Saturday was bath day; we carried water in from the creek or melted snow. We always had to warm the water on the wood stove and then splashed around in the tub and got clean in it the best we could. We had homemade lye soap. We certainly did get clean, my hair would be combed and braided, and after that we put all our dirty clothes in the tub in the same water to soak overnight. The next day was washday and mamma had made for her a wooden stick to stir the wash, from a birch tree. It was squeezed dry and hung out to dry.

I was very shy and backward when it came to boys and dancing but I still enjoyed going out. Mamma was very strict in her way, she could not stand to look at me when I was going out with my friends, because than I would want to cruel my hair and make myself fancy looking. I had a big nail that I would put into the coals in the wood stove. When I stood in front of the mirror and curl my hair, she saw that my hair got curly she shook her head and said" Pride is the worst thing, and God will not stand it or put up with it". My mamma was a very good God-fearing person and because I was the youngest of 10 children, she was careful and concerned about me and held me close, she loved me very much, that I know. She never would say much but I felt it, whether she approved or not. Mamma taught me to pray.

It was the same prayer every night; it went like this in Swedish: Gud som haver barnen kar, se till mig som liten ar, vart jag mig I värded vänder, står min lycka I Guds händer, lyckan kåmmer lyckan går, den Gud älskar lyckan får.

Translated into English: God who has all the children dear, watch over me who so little am, wherever in the world I turn, my happiness will be in your hands, happiness comes and happiness departs but those who God loves will peace and luck receive.

Mamma she was a very strong woman, she had it difficult and there were many challenges in her lifetime, from birth until the particular time of her death. (Note: grandma Tagg's mother died from complications when giving birth to her, she was just 21 days old at the time of her mother's death). Mamma she was also so very poor, but oh, so very thankful for every new day that she met, yes, she was strong and seemingly not afraid of anyone or anything even though she was alone with us. What a great example she was!

Most of the time for transportation we kids would use skis to go everywhere if the snow was deep, otherwise I was really happy to take the (spark stötting) that mom had, when I was allowed to take it I was really happy. (a standup sled with handles, one pushing and one riding down the hills, walking and pushing uphill, with a seat on the front for one person to sit on and ride another standing on the back) Mamma had paid a good sum of money for it, so she warned me not to put it on the side of the road so someone would barrow it. Had I lost it and not brought it home with me after school, I wouldn't have gone home, because than I would have heard it, loud and clear!!!

I learned to embroidery we did that a lot, on tablecloths, pillowcases. I learned how to crocheted and knit. My mamma taught me everything. I learned how to sew too, mamma had a sewing machine that you would turn the wheel with your hand and later on there was a peddle machine too. Oh, I had to be so careful and I could not break the needle because there was no money to replace it with. We had a radio to listen to and a harmonica too. There were record players at this time too but we didn't have that until much later in our lives.

We had a loom for weaving rugs and a spinning wheel for making yarn for knitting that stood there in the room. Everything was homemade including homemade socks. Mamma was a remarkable person. I remember learning all homemaking skills, everything including learning to fix food from very small recourses. We took and used what we had and everything taster wonderful. There was always homemade bread in mammas tins in her cupboard. When I grew and got older I knew that it was not an easy thing for mamma to bake from a sparse supply that she had. Sometimes foodstuff such as bacon bits, a margarine package would be forgotten until it would have a rancid taste. But mom could do no wrong, I love her heart. She always had some kind of food. Sometimes I got newly baked half thick bread (lefsa) with syrup on it; oh I thought that was sooo ☺very good! I used to have to go shopping at Konsum's, one of two stores in our little town and pack one half kg margarine, yeast for 5 ore, only that which was mostly needed. Karin my older sister did most of the shopping. We lived far enough from the store that mamma had to take a full day to buy bigger and heavier things. *In the winter we kept the frozen foods outside or in the porch, when we didn't want it to be to frozen.*

No, there were not very many sweet bread days in my early life at home, only on special occasions and holidays, it was just mostly from hand to mouth, but it is with gratitude that I sit here and recall and share my memories of how we really had it, I have only good memories. But we had to be so very economical, limiting and not using all our recourses as they were so limited, so that everything would come together for each day. We never felt a real lack or need in our lives, because we didn't know any different, but now in these new times when there is too much of everything and it seems very luxurious and everyone and things are wasted and squandered and people are taking everything for granted. I sometimes will be found sitting and thinking with most wholehearted respect of how mamma was able to hold her family together. I have on many occasions thanked God for the things I learned from my home during my growing up years. Maybe that is the reason I have been lucky to make it thereafter in the years after and way that I have had.

"Health is a precious gift" is what my mamma used to say, which I believe I have inherited as I am now 60 years old as I write this, sitting here dreaming myself back in time (Note: Mother Ida just turned 89 and I Ruth am 63 tomorrow as I translate this pages and must also have gratefully inherited that good health. New entry 2014: today as I am close to finishing this portion of our parents' lives and find myself at 70, time really flies.) Now back to mom's writing: To remember everything that has happened to me and my family up till now this will be impossible to write, but it will certainly be quite a bit to read, and maybe even worthwhile to my posterity. One thing is sure; it is the beginning of a lively life and my story and its related accounts. The words and memories are a little hard to bring out, but a little bit at the time and soon it will come and soon the continuation will follow.

I admit and remember that I was also like by all other children. I wanted to go to my friends and play most of the time. Kristina Norberg was probably my best friend through the school years, and after that it was all the other kids in the school play yard after I got to school.

Yes, my childhood and my growing up days were not at all hard for me. I really think that I was probably a spoiled child, because of my siblings. *I still slept with mom till I was 15 years old.* (Note: I remember grandma's house and only one room was heated by the wood stove and there was only one built I bed in the heated room, therefore she slept with her mom in those early years.)

At home we had the bible that we read but we also had the books from school that I had to read and of course my writings lessons too, because we had to do our homework every day. My teacher was a woman teacher the first several years, and then a man the last two years, his name was Herr Bergquist. I began school in first grade when I was 8 years old. I can't remember anything special about any of my teachers except that they were very strict, we had to be obedient or we had to stay afterschool and that we learned we didn't want to do when we lived up in Hallan which was 5 km away. I did have to stay after a few times but I learned to listen and do what I was told. I had many friends and I remember I was well liked by everyone. My very best friend though was Stina Norberg and Elsa Sandvoll, Lina Roos I had many friends. I had lessons in school in music and dance and singing and that is how I learned everything I knew in those areas or I wouldn't have known anything.

*Now that I have receiver this request of my dotter Ruth Cunningham to write all my memories from my childhood to this day, as I sit here in my home in Douglas, Alaska in 1979, it probably won't get written in the exact order of what I remember from my childhood but those who will get enjoyment in reading this will at least know that I have at least started to write a true record of my life and as I record my time, I'm sure it will be enjoyable reading. Stormy and difficult years, only gives more lessons in life to learn from.

There was no modern machinery in those early days, which we could use while we grew up. But we lived a wholesome, healthy lifestyle and it seemed good even then. There were no comfortable switches to press on for lights and heat and so on when I was in primary school. But soon the men in our town and community began to think more and more that close to us there were strong water power, so many years later (aprox. 1930) they installed an electric lamp in mamma's sealing and also in others houses up in Hallan. We thought it looked magnificent; there was almost no money for anything else but the basic needs, we were living under the poorest of circumstances, we lived from day to day, but mamma wanted to pay for the lights. Whatever our circumstances were, mamma was very skillful and thoughtful, and she handled and managed to get along with and in every situation somehow. She would sneak away a little; and this is what she did her whole life through. But heath and the desire to succeed and to go forward, that she certainly had and she thanked God for everything continually!

We her kids knew where mamma kept her pocketbook!!! There was no money lying around in those days that is for sure, like in our day now. Yes, mamma had a woolen vest with a big pocket on the inside that buttoned. She went into the back room by herself when she took out some money. We really wanted to know how much she had in there, but when we asked her she laughed away our question and forgot or went on the something else. So that was a question that we never got answered in our lifetime, but she always had what we needed as far as food was concerned, and after that there was no more even to ask for, and we knew it. We always had the benefit and the advantage of a deep love from her, that has stood as a strength my whole life through, (Tack älskade mor) Thank you my wonderful loving mother.

1932: This particular year when the school years over, it is spring time and it was time for my confirmation at the Lutheran Church. I was 14-15 years old; everyone of course had to be as beautiful as could be for this special occasion. I knew that my sister's Stina, who was 17 years older than myself and lived in Trondhaim, Norway would help me out again as she always did, she would sow me a new confirmation dress, I knew that. The time was almost here. I waited and waited for the package to arrive, my mamma always trusted completely in my sister's help.

It was only one week left and no package had arrived yet. Mamma she was calm, well there was nothing else that we could really do. I thought well, I guess I can wear the dress that I already have, because there was no airline transportation at this time, and as I grew up and mother didn't have a savings account to go out and buy me beautiful clothes, that just wasn't done before in time, we didn't even think about that, there was no such a thing. So I guess I would have been confirmation in the dress that I had and it would have gone just fine, but I waited and wished that it would come. It was a long ways for it to come from Norway to our little town, and then we had to pick up our mail and packages downtown in Funäsdalen.

I waived through the snow, sometimes unplowed roads with a backpack and of course on skis, 5-6 km to get to the post office which was in the store where we bought everything, this was also right by the big beautiful white church in Funäsdalen. At times like this we always had strength and the day came that the package did come to our address, with my name on it, just a couple of days before the big date of my confirmation in the church, this was the biggest day in my life as yet. I remember like it was a dream when I opened the package from my kind sister. Within the package there was always something extra, as it was this time also, other than the black confirmation dress, I found therein a blue dress length coat that fit me absolutely perfectly. My joy was great! When I think about it now, I think that I might have been happier and felt better about a lighter, maybe a white dress but I thought that there was not found anyone that had such a nice outfit as little Ida had just then, and at this time it was a black dress. I didn't have any jewelry, not even a little flower so it was simple and beautiful and I was happy. To get to the alter for confirmation it took 4 weeks studying with the priest, we had to learn the contents of what the bible had in it. To memorize the Ten Commandments and to learn about forgiveness of sins (repentance) and there were some Psalm verses that had to be memorized. This was a wonderful time to gain a good background and respect for God and a foundation for the whole life ahead wherever I have gone.

This was a special time to become confirmed in the church. This meant that a person would get to learn about and study the bible and what was in it. It took a whole four week of classes and then be asked questions after to see what we have learned. We had to read almost the whole book. At the end there is a get together and we received a certificate. And I did become confirmed this year.

I really liked to go to people's homes and visit, it was the most fun I could think of and there were always goodies to taste. Mamma liked it too, to have coffee and bread and other goodies ☺ Fun! In my teen years we still lived about 5 km from town where the church was and all the activities that were held, were held in town, this was when life was like a game, the road wasn't any further than we would walk, and we did it sometimes two times in a day. Especially if I had an existing meeting, yes, and especially to get together with my friend Kristina Norberg, at that time and through the years she was my most steady and sure friend in every way. She even helped me with homework sometimes. She always knew the answers and sometimes she would whisper the answers to me, otherwise I seldom would rise up my hand. But we grew up and away from school and of course chose our personal life and times and that meant we chose our own and different companions and other friends. We began to go to dances and we were very wholesome and shy. Our life was at that time very fun. We would laugh with and tease the boys and sneak away. Life was fun and free. I had lots of friends in both Sweden and Norway.

I took a trip to Trondheim, Norway every summer. I was like a daughter to my sister Stina, and I really liked the big town too after growing up in the small community like Hallan. Wow, this time of my life was a wonderful adventure, to be able to be part of. I became a little maid for my sister during the summer. There I learned cleanliness and order. She fixed me up with new clothes and shoes so I looked just as great as the city youth. Friends and fun and more excitement for every day it seemed, but I had to be in by ten o'clock every evening. It was difficult at times to hold to the time expected, but I have heard in later years that I listened and followed the rules and with that which was decided pretty well. So I was an obedient girl. Oh, I had it super fun and I love to think back in time to my childhood and youth, a wonderful lucky and fun time of life.

From my sister I learned so much and had new experiences and wonderful happiness then and throughout my life thereafter. She was remarkably particular but so happy and kind. In the fall I would return home from Trondheim, the big city just in time for school to begin. Than I would be dressed up in new beautiful clothes, shoes and backpack for my books and material and a messmor sandwich to eat. (like a peanut butter, but made out of cream) Stina would come home to Hållan every summer I remember, than we always had good food to eat. She stood in the kitchen and cooked faithfully every day. Then my mamma had a good summer, ate, enjoyed life, took it a bit easier and was at peace. We could count on her (my sister Stina) sewing new clothes for us, mamma liked to look nice too. With my sisters and I there has always been a strong bond between us, we have always held together.

1937- 1939 Youth is a fun time; I was in my teenage years very excited to go to dances. We, Inger and I and sometimes other friends we would sometimes barrow old bike cycles. It was especially fun to ride to the neighboring towns. And we looked at the boys and enjoyed our youth, looked for a good-looking companion, this was a special exiting time just like it should be. We would ride our bikes on summer evenings up to Tånndalen 4-5 km further up into the mountain towards the border. Inger Tagg as I said was my older brother Johann's daughter; we had some wonderful years growing up together, she lived in Norway and came to our house during the summers to visit. There was dance on the weekend so Saturday was the day we longed for all week. **Tånndalen was the place where I met my life's friend, as he swung me around the floor in a stirring Tango.**

My brothers and sisters were by name and years:

Jon Backman (1891-1941) he was first born to grandma in Norway before she was married, I don't remember my older half-brother at all, he lived in Norway. He was married and he had two good looking boys, Einar and ? I can't remember his name, they lived in Lokan, Norway and the boys were also born there in Lokan.

Johann Tagg (1896-1956) he was always very nice and came and gave me hugs, he came home to see mother as often as he could, he drove a car, he was a car salesman I believe, he was really a handy person, he was married too and had a daughter Inger, and she was the same age as me.

Little Karl Emmanuel (1898-1900) was born and died shortly thereafter, I never knew him.

Karin Kristina (1901-1988) She took care of me just as if I had been her child, she came home bringing food and everything we needed to mother and me, everything we needed for the rest of the summer. She was so kind words are not enough. Think what memories! Her husband always drove her to our home it was 24 Swedish-Norwegian miles. It is not so far, a day drive each way. Stina was home several times each summer. She also made all my clothes all my life until I left for Alaska.

Karl Emmanuel (1904-1957) He was the brother that came to America in the 1930's. I don't remember him so much at home he must have been gone working a lot. He was here many years before we had a thought of coming here.

Ingeborg (1906-1993) she helped mamma when she traveled to Norway to visit Karolina and everyone that took care of her, then Ingeborg came and she took care of me who was little. And we had a small barnyard only 35-40 steps or maybe more and we of course had to take care of them, we had cows, goats and some sheep so we had a little bit of milk from them back then, but in the winter we still had to buy some of our milk because we did not always milk them.

Karolina Johanna (1909- 1924) she lived in Trondheim mostly after she finished school (7th grade) she was 8 years older than me. She must have gone to Norway before the time I started School at 8 years old. So I don't remember her other than she was really beautiful. She died there when she was about 16 years old (maybe it was from the Spanish flue).

Per Gustav (1911-1995) Per and Kristian lived there all my life while there in Sweden. They were like twins and got in trouble together all the time (var odygdig tilsamans) they were always together. But they were nice to me but I don't think they helped mom too much. It was we the girls that did that, Ingeborg,

Stina and I did the most to helping. But they always came home when they got hungry and knew food had been made. That is typical of course.

Kristian Ingemar (1913-1968) Kristian was a good jultompte (Santa) at Christmas time for our family later when you kids were small. And then after Karl had been home from Alaska he decided to immigrate to America also, he left in 1955. He died in a boating accident up in Haines.

Ida Maria (1918-2010) I immigrated in 1956 and all this talking is all about me and my memories!

Then came the time when the construction of a new road through our mountain area began. There came a whole bunch of road construction workers to our little town. I did some cooking for the road crew home at mor's house and earned some extra money, but it wasn't very much money.

Mamma liked Göte really well, she was always happy when he would come to visit her and I am proud to tell that she was always very comfortable with Göte when he visited us. Göte he was working on the road crew, so after we started seeing one another it was he that started to paid for all our fun times together.

The first radio that we ever listened to at home at mor's house, it was Göte that bought it for us. It was a battery radio so once a month it had to be sent by bus to Ljusnedal and Lars Helgesson would charge them up for us. Then we were able to turn it on and listen to the Swedish good music programs again. Mor thought it was such a big thing to have the radio. There were not many that had that luxury yet. It was only us up where we lived. Soon it seemed that Göte was very comfortable and close, and in my presence and I in his and we both had the same feelings. So after some time, both Inger and I began to be kidnapped by the men that we would finally marry and make our life with and we have been married to now for many years. Both of us also in later years happened to end up in Alaska. (I must count how many years it has been) yes, Karl Göte Noren and Ida Maria Tagg met in 1937; we liked each other and always stayed close together thereafter.

Then came the time when the construction of a new road through our mountain area began. There came a whole bunch of road construction workers to our little town. I did some cooking for the road crew home at mor's house and earned some extra money, but it wasn't very much money. (Göte was föreman on the road crew).

Mamma liked Göte really well, she was always happy when he would come to visit her and I am proud to tell that she was always very comfortable with Göte when he visited us. Göte he was working, so after we started seeing one another it was he that started to paid for all our fun times together. The first radio that we ever listened to at home at mor's house, it was Göte that bought it for us. It was a battery radio so once a month it had to be sent by bus to Ljusnedal and Lars Helgesson would charge them up for us. Then we were able to turn it on and listen to Sweden's good music programs again. Mor thought it was such a big thing to have the radio. There were not many that had that luxury yet. It was only us, up where we lived.

1939- We decided to become engaged in 1939, so we told mamma that we had decided to become serious and to share engagement rings. On a cold winter day we took a trip on S.J. Bus line 15 miles (abt. 70 American miles) from Hållan, Funäsdalen to the town of Sveg. We were not rich but had a strong belief that we could make it, so there we took our entire savings that consisted of (42 silver two kronor) we walked a bit embarrassed but proudly and happily into the first and best gold smith in Sveg, the name was Eriksson's and picked out our 18 karat gold rings. It was a cold windy night we stepped out into the street

Karl Göte Norén
and
Ida Maria Tagg
Married in
'Funäsdalens Kyrka'
30 August 1941

attendents: Axel Garmo,
Solvig Fasth, Mola Garmo

WEDDING

ENGAGEMENT PICTURES

Vigselbevis

Karl Göte Norén

och

Ida Maria Tagg

för vilka lysning till äktenskap avkunnats i Tännäs församling i Jämtlands län under n:r 11 år 1941 hava härstädes denna dag blivit av undertecknad enligt svenska kyrkans ordning i äktenskap sammanvigda.

Funäsdalens kyrka

den 30. aug. år 1941

Georg Granberg
v. d. m.
Kyrkoherde

and put the rings on each other and had a heartfelt good laugh, because we had become serious and had defiantly decided on one another!

Back to our engagement, after we put the rings on each other's hands we went together up to my sister Ingeborg and brother-in-law Fredrick Fast who lived there in Sveg, we stayed with them a couple of days. As we walked out of the store, we felt that the rings shone really brightly from our fingers, so that I personally thought that everyone noticed that we were newly engaged.

We felt lucky and in love even though we were without those silver kronors now, however we did have our return ticket, so we got back on the bus for Hållan, Funäsdalen. We really had everything we could wish for, but we couldn't afford to throw away the silver kronors that we had left.

We lived with mamma during this time; I was actually in (fortsattning) homemaking continuation school, so my (min älskade) loved one would meet me every day after school and we would wander long distances together and talked. Oh my, how interesting our conversations were I those early days as we walked and spent time together.

Göte worked as a road construction worker on a crew when I met him that first summer, Mor really liked him too. After some time we decided we wanted to be together so later when Göte had to move down to Lossen to work on the road down there, and I wanted to go too. So we built a roomy barrack, it had four isolated walls that were screwed together, the floor and the roof was also screwed together, it was only one room, there was a big window, a wood cooking stove, table and a bed. It was finished really quickly.

We lived there together for what seemed like a long time. It was very choosy in there; it was everything we could have hoped for. It was a really sweet home. I should mention that Göte was (ingensor) the foreman from his job, came and sat on a stump outside of our little house, we had no furniture then, but there I offered coffee and rolls served in four different sizes of bowels that what we had. It went just fine, and the men said it tasted good, and I smiled happily. There were many that lived in larger barracks that could house 8, 10, or 12 men and they had cooks. Lossen was a lake down south from Tannes and there was a road being built there. It was a warm and loads of hard-work that summer, but a wonderful life and such good memories; we were young and full of energy. Pappa was from Dalarna and I was from Harjedalen and we felt we could concur anything together.

It was a truly wonderful little one room house and we moved it home to Hållan, down onto mammas property and we lived there for a time. Then when the fall and winter was on its way, is the time when we decided that there should be a wedding. When we got married and had the wedding reseption home at mamma's place, so in the (i ladan) storage barn we built a plank floor and fixed it up and invited the whole community and all the road crew and Göthe's friends too.

In those early days at home, we did not have any luxuries not inside or outside, but mamma was a very strong and resourceful woman in soul and body, she was very strong in every way. And we were satisfied with what we had. I learned so many good things from her that later I have used with my own family, and have always appreciated and I have had much benefit from her teaching through the years. Mor (mamma) gave me love, faith and strength. We have made sure that all of our children have also been given the same work ethics, desires and skills, so that they can go forward to become strong and skilled and able peoples also, so they can make it without problems or at least overcome in the years ahead just as well as we have, even though there have been enormous changes since these early days. (The most important thing is our health, which is the richest gift of all and that will aide us as we need it! Then it becomes possible to make it through whatever comes our ways.) Mor's sayings came often (Health is the richest gift of all.)

1941- So now we had actually tied the marriage knot, so our lives together had begun. We were poor but strong and proud. Our hope was that we would have the best of health through the time ahead that we would now begin to share. The Lutheran minister Georg Granberg preformed our wedding ceremony in the beautiful church in Funasdalen on August 31st. There were many guests and gifts. When we were finished at the church we all gathered in our home up at mamma in Hållan (this is aprox. 5 km north of Funasdalen) we had cabbage soup and sandwiches, frickadeller, and cookies and coffee. There were also stronger drinks, and soon everyone began to dance and move around and the happy party lasted for two whole days. Wonderful lively accordion music and everyone that could still stand on their legs danced, the tempo was as high as the ceiling. We received extra benefits (ranson) for the wedding, and everything was used up. What a party, the next day the old men were out hunting for their false teeth☺. That was our wedding, and I know that everyone that came to our party had good memories and spoke with laughter of the fun time they had for a long, long time thereafter. I must say I chose a wonderful companion, for us in our lives the clouds has never covered up the sun!

So in **1941** was the year we Gote and Ida rented an old summer cottage from Mattias and Elisabeth Persson up in Hållan for a while, they had bought new furniture and fixed it up so homey for the two of us. It was close to mamma (Karin Tagg) we could actually see the smoke from the chimney of her little home when we looked out from where we lived; it was only a five minutes' walk away. We rented as close to mamma as we could, and she was glad that we were close. We often had wonderful heartfelt visits from one another, and mom liked my cooking and then she ate a little extra god when she came to see us. Everything in our home was orderly and in its place; I had small newly woven rugs on a white scoured wooden floor. It was so intensely homey and good when it was newly cleaned and fixed up and when homemade bread had been made made, it smelled so inviting and tasted so good! There was always someone of our favorite old folks who came to visit and began a conversation and they always got something good and maybe a spirited drink (sup) from far (pappa). Solid, respectful, beautiful people to remember! It seemed as though everyone took it more slowly and peacefully in those days, even though it was so much harder work back then, then now.

__1942-__ But time went and soon we were expecting our first baby and at that time we started to rent an apartment further down towards town by the stream, (strömmen) and then as I was close to delivering her (Karin) I had to go to Sveg, that was the only place to have the baby back then. Pappa was working in the woods right then, but he came as fast as he could to see her. I can see him now in my mind as he came, walking with it and holding on to the bike.

After Karin was born we of course went back up to Funäsdalen, and we continued to live down by the Stream. We had a nice home there; pappa came home from his work to see you guys there. Pappa was home from the Army when Ruth was born. __(1944)__ He had to go on the (sparkstotting) stand up sled, all the way up town to pick up Ebba Lagerborg she was the midwife. But he got her there in time for your delivery. Karin was such a mamma to you, you couldn't tell her anything of how she was to take care of you☺She was so cute! Ruth, you fell down the stairs there and twisted your ankle you had to have a half cast on for a while, Karin was a big helper to you then too. We were satisfied with everything, but we did decide that we needed a bit more room and began plans to build a house. We bought a lot from Per, my

Åldersbetyg
(för äkta makar)

Uppslag i förs.-boken __11__

1. Att _svenske medb, anläggsarb. Karl Göte Norén, Funäsdalen 2:14_
2. är född den __10. 10.__ år __1903__ (_noll tre_)
3. i __Stora Tuna__ församling i __Kopparbergs__ län,
   att hans hustru __Ida Maria Norén, f. Jagg__
   är född den __3. 3.__ år __1918__ (_aderton_)
   i __Tännäs__ församling i __Jämtlands__ län,
   att makarna blevo kyrkligt—borgerligt—vigda den __30. 8.__ år __1941__
   och hava följande barn: d. _Karin Sylvia Maria, f. 23/12 1942,_
   d. _Ruth Inger Johanna, f. 11/3 1944, s. Silve Göte,_
   f. _12/9 1948, s. Karl Ritz Gunnar, f. 24/4 1955_
4. betygar __Tännäs__ församling i __Jämtlands__ län
5. den __27. 1.__ år __1956__.

Kyrkoherde — v. Pastor — Komminister — Kyrkoadjunkt — Pastoratsadjunkt

Nr 171 A Svenska Kyrkans Diakonistyrelses Bokförlag. 4-51

ens namn med mera:	Födelsetid och -nummer:				Födelsehemort:	Dopt:
	år	månad	dag	nummer		
...in Sylvia Maria	1942	12	23	824	Sveg	ja
...Jager Johanna	1944	3	11	822	Tännäs	ja
...e Göte	1948	9	12	825	Tännäs	ja
...Ritz Simon	1955	9	21	823	Tännäs	ja

...e uppgifter överensstämma med kyrkoböckerna, betygar

(namn)

(ämbets- eller tjänstetitel)

Tännäsdalen
Myndighetens postadress

Utfl.-nr: **10**
Uppsl. i förs.-b.: **11**

Infl.-nr:
Uppsl. i förs.-b.:

Observera!
Har den, som uttagit utvandringscertifikat, icke inom tre må... lämnat riket åligger det honom att ofördröjligen och senast in... efter denna tids utgång återställa utvandringscertifikatet och betyget till den myndighet, som utfärdat detsamma. (Folkbo... ningen 23 och 24 §§).

Utvandringsbetyg

utfärdat den **31.4** 1956

1. Karl Göte Norén
2. och hans hustru Ida Maria Norén, f. Jager
3. från Tännäs församling i Jämtlands
4. blevo med varandra i äktenskap förenade genom kyrklig vigsel den 30.8.

	Mannen			Hustrun	
	år:	månad:	dag:		år:
5. född:	1903 (mollöre)	10	10	född:	1918 (aderton)
6. födelsenummer:	847			födelsenummer:	824
7. födelse(hem)ort:	Stora Tuna			födelse(hem)ort:	Tännäs
8. i	Kopparbergs	län		i	Jämtlands

9. är — döpt och / är — döpt och
10. inom svenska kyrkan konfirmerad / inom svenska kyrkan konfirmerad
11. har inom svenska kyrkan begått H. nattvard / har inom svenska kyrkan begått H. nattva...
12. ___
13. åtföljas av å omstående sida förtecknade barn under 15 år:

29 aug 55 — Nu är hela sommarlovet förbi. Sune pojken min, Karin o Ruth knogar iväg till skolan. Tycker jag känner mig så ensam när jag har hela huset ja mig själv. Tänk Sune börjat skolan, stor spänning för oss båda men önskar det bästa för oss alla i hemmet. HÄLLAN

PS. HÄR ÄR JAG, FET, HAVANDE
Vi har just kommit hem från Solveigs bröllop 27-8-55 Trevligt minne.

Sune o Eva Brudnäbbar.

Programmet gäller i år stora familj — men jag är så glad i alla mina. Tack Gud och FAR FANS. När jag började denna bok o antecknade om Karin får ½ år nu trodde jag det skulle räcka med henne. Nu är jag lycklig o sitter o väntar på min 4:de i ordningen o barnen mina stora glädje, arbete ansvar är det. Farmor Ida under väntan, o Fet Rund.

29 aug 1955
Här kom vi hem från bröllopet Bernt Solveig. Några härliga dagar i bröllopen och mycket mera tack för gången. 29-8-55 Måhänning Johan Gretha

SKRIVIT AV Broder min

1 sept 1955. N:o 4 i Norens barnskara
Ja nu har det stora hänt igen. Karl Ritz Gunnar har kommit. Den 29 sept. kl 20 min. i fyra 1955 fick jag honom i Hede. Det var en hård biltur men desto gladare är jag när allt är väl över. Vi reser o kunde tillsammans. Gunnar är 6 veckor nu o matfrisk o skriker det är programmet för dagen, men jag är lycklig i mina fyra barn, min rikedom OCH FARS VÄRDE ÄLSKAS AV ALLA

nov. Karin skall konfirmeras till våren 13 år.

Ruth går i femte klassen 11 år

7 år Sune har börjat skolan i år 1955. o det går fint han stavar o ritar bilar så han klarar nog sig gott.

Ritz Gunnar bara ligger i korgen än o stirrar på mor men tiden går så fort så han blir snart stor också han är ung på 6 veckor när detta skrives.
FAR VAR stolt av sina härliga barn. SKREV
Sune har fått en bror nu klämmig kille Karl Ritz Gunnar som är BRÖDER
FAR BEVITTNA NÄR DET SKER

Gunnhild agare av DARIS NILLS TILL 1949
313 Douglas ALASKA
är 1955-56
1955

NOREN KAN DET — språket fri gamla "

Ms. Ida M. Noreen
PO Box 632
Douglas, AK 99824

MIN FJÄRDE HAR JAG FÅTT NU Karl Ritz Gunnar Ousslag barnet 21 sept 195
MIN LEVDE PÅ DEN TIDEN I HÄLLAN, I EN RÖD LITEN STUGA VID FJÄLLETS

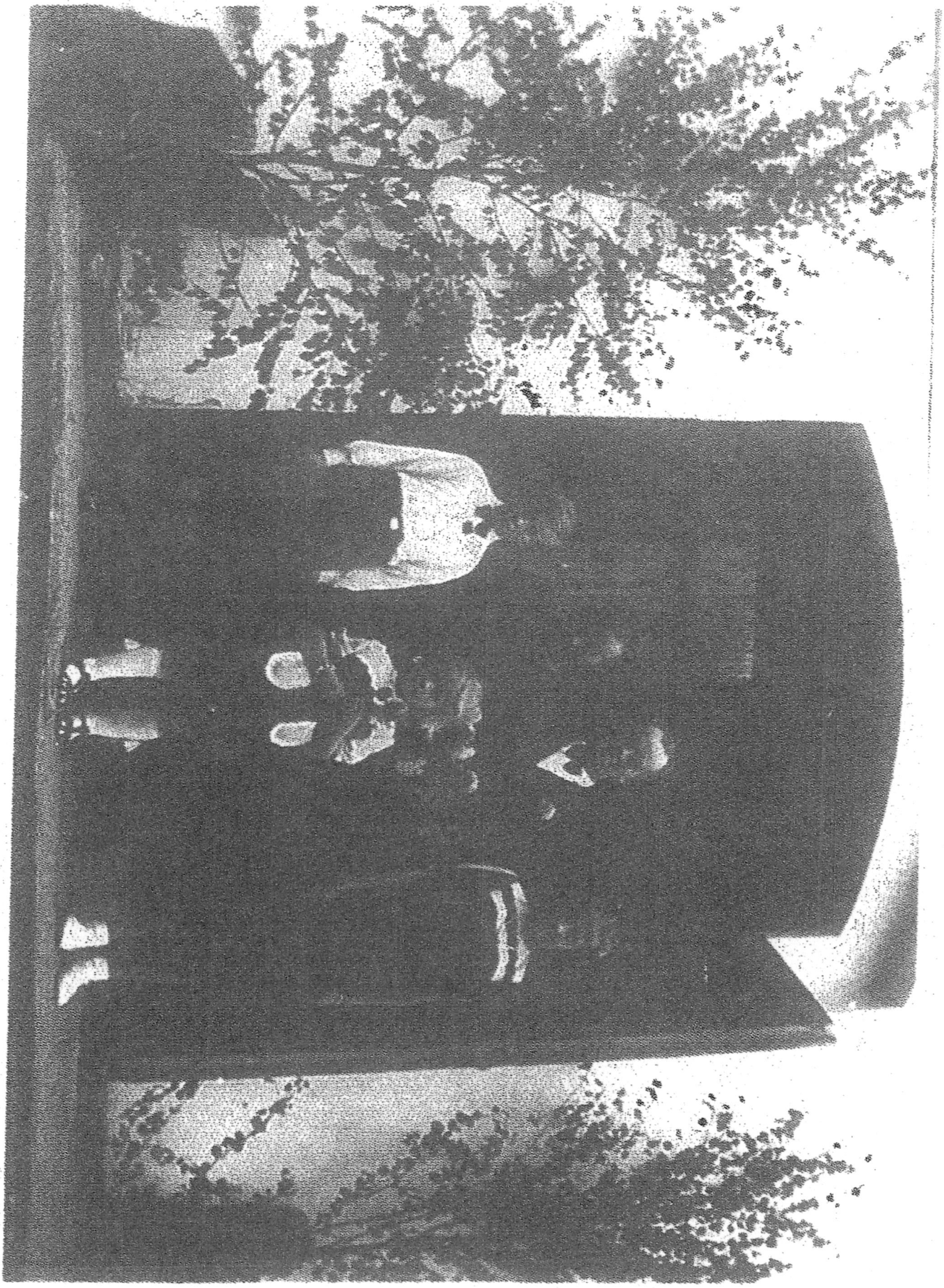

brother, and then Pappa did most of the work building our little house up there in Hållan, he had some help but he made the rooms and put in the stove and such and all that needed to be done.

1949- *Sune was born up there in Hållan in our house Ebba was still the midwife than and helped with his delivery too. She was such a wonderful person she was from (Skåne) and had a great accent. She held Sune up in the window and showed you kids and pappa that we had a brother. You Ruth were born in Strommen and Sune was born up in Hållan and Gunnar was born in Hede and Karin in Sveg. When we were expecting Gunnar it was just in the middle of our seeking to come over to America, and a busy time.* **(1955)** *you kids went over to Grönlandaren hotel and called after Gunnar was born and talked with me, I don't know who took you over there? After he was born was the winter that mamma stayed with us and would rock Gunnar and sing to him. That was the last winter in Hållan and with my dear mother.*

**(TODAY AS I WRITE THIS IT IS THE YEAR 1991 AND 35 WONDERFUL YEARS CELIBRATED IN ALASKA and 50 years of being married to my wonderful husband (make). As I said before, <u>I must say again I chose a wonderful companion. For us in our lives, the clouds have never covered up the sun! We took one another for life and have done the very best with everything each day.</u> Life is a continuation school; those were my mamma's loving words and we have learned every day that we must take of the difficult things and also give the good, for we have learned this through experience! To have raised four healthy kids is something to also be very proud of and (ar ingen fy skam.) that is not a small thing either but something to be proud of.) ☺

1955- The time back then continues to move forward and it took us along also, no matter how it turns out we were on our way. This winter mormor (grandma Tagg) lived with us in our little three room home in Hallan. She really wanted to stay in her own home and do her own thing, and organize at home as long as she was able but we, Göte and I talked to her and convinced her to move in with us, so she could be with me that winter. In this way she would have it a bit better with food preparation, also washing for everything was getting to be a bit hard for her now at 83-84 years old. So in the fall my little mother came and moved in with us. When she moved in she shared the same small bedroom where <u>Karin, Ruth and Sune</u> slept. <u>Gunnar</u> was only a few months old so he slept with pappa and mamma in our living room, we had a sofa bed that I fixed up morning and evening. I can say that it seemed very choosy as I remember, even though the bedrooms and house was very small.

For most of the time our little man (gubben) sat in a very nice (buggy) with wheels that pappa of course bought for us, we felt so important; it was so handy and nice. And when during the day he became a bit cranky it was his luck that we kept that wagon rolling, it became father Gote's job to keep the wagon rolling until Gunnar fell asleep. Sometimes he would crumple up a rug and push the buggy over it. Mormor (grandma) she would rock Gunnar at times in her long skirt between her knees, her skirt became a nice swing, he sat there while she hummed and sang, hum, hum, brrrrrr, brrrrrrr and after a while he fell asleep with that. And it was quite often that both of them fell asleep during that time. I often think about this and it makes me sad now, that these memories that are of such worth for Gunnar, that you Gunnar don't have a memory of these times with your wonderful mormor (grandma) but you were to small then. So you must know that love has been found and imprinted in our generation and to go on forever. These same feelings go with us wherever we go in our lives for all ours. I hope you understand what I am saying and telling you, my hope is that you will inherit this most valuable feeling for your own, one day in your lifetime.

Karin used to go shopping for mormor, so when she came home from school in the afternoon she would wander through the snow down a long small path, down to mormor's house with the goods she had bought for her. And then she would come chewing on a piece of bread, mormor had a special taste to her half thick homemade bread, it was very good. Karin also helped mormor with her baths sometimes and would comb her long hair. Sune you were sweet, you would go out on your skis when the bus was coming with the mailbag and then take it up to Mattias Persson who we paid one half for the mail delivery. That was not a big price then, but pappa Göte did not earn any money just then, so I think we figured that it certainly was enough to pay. Pappa (Far) worked on road crews building and repairing roads and at some times he worked in the woods as a logger. And then Sune you would fill your backpack full of fire starter, some sticks with sap on them for your mormor, these are such fun memories☺ don't you think?

Mormor used to give you karamell (candy) for the good help you were and kindness you showed to her. Sometimes you might get 5 öre instead, then there was a bright sunshine look on your face, but very seldom if ever was money given, for there was not much money to give, you were about 6 years old then. There was too little money but all you children were just as happy and willing help. So there we lived together in Hållan. Very satisfied and happy! Ruth was just as willing to help also as the others. It is hard to remember each episode that happened. But mormor thought that children were a gift from God. She used to call Ruth 'Luta Hanna' and then mormor would say 'Luta Hanna elte mahs' meaning her name and the 11th of March when she was born. Karin the big sister took care of her siblings in a very responsible way. In the spring, May of 1956 Karin became confirmed in the Lutheran Church before we left Sweden, she was 14 years old than was just finishing the 6th grade. And Ruth was 12 and had just finished the 4th grade, and Sune had just one year in school in Funäsdalen.

When I remember how little we had, I look at this generation where all the kids want to be paid for everything they do or help with, such as taking out the garbage or anything that is helpful. I don't think that is right, I think that paying our children for everything they do is wrong. But these are new times for all of us, and we get to learn new customs. But I remember and have respect for my poor childhood days and all the good practical learning I experienced through and from my mother. But now times have moves forward, with new ways and life for all of us, but I have great respect for my very poor parents and those who have gone before me and all the strengths and good that I have inherited from them. Now we have an overflow of everything. I wish mamma and pappa could suddenly come to see me, and see how I have all kinds of comforts and riches in these later years here in our new land of Alaska.

Our way of living back then and how we live now is as different as night and day. But I have learned what is important and that which is of worth. For example, I could never have dreamed about owning several cars in my lifetime, the second bigger than the first. Now it seems as everything we get in life is to make us more comfortable. And that I should come to Alaska, which I never could have dreamed that I would do! But lives paths and the road we travel seem to be decided for us, and our days understanding and the endurance tests we all must go through along the way are a test, for us it has been of the world's highest qualities and made especially for us.

When I think of our lives now, to have the possibilities to fly S.A.S (Scandinavian Airlines) <u>home to the place where pappa and I and our four children received our beginnings and our respect for life, Sweden and Norway we can go almost any time we feel like going.</u> Because that is what we can do now, nothing is holding this pleasure back from us anymore. So times have certainly changed a whole lot from the old days when the immigrants first came to the U.S.A. ----------------------------------

In closing my father and mothers writing for now, mother's paragraph below seems to fit the end of this great saga so deems repeating! She wrote:

*Now that I have receiver this request of my dotter Ruth Cunningham to write all my memories from my childhood to this day, as I sit here in my home in Douglas, Alaska in 1979, it probably won't get written in the exact order of what I remember from my childhood, but those who will get enjoyment out of reading this will at least know that I have tried to start to write a <u>true</u> record of my life, and as I record my time lived, I'm sure it will be enjoyable reading and hopefully you will learn from our stormy and difficult years, this only gives more lessons in life to learn from. ---------------Adjo

** <u>I end this report with this statement</u>: As a reminder to all who read these memories of these great immigrant parents of ours, what was written and recorded herein was completely their own story. I have recorded and translated as perfectly, word for word as they wrote or as I heard them speak. Although not perfect, my hope is that you will enjoy and have a memory also of these our loving parents, who were diligent in providing for us their four children Karin, Ruth, Sune and Gunnar and who did love us very much. May all of those who read this hereafter or get to know them through these pages, learn of them with appreciation and fondness and that you also feel strengthen and loved for having come through their linage, and grow to love and admire them in turn for their patient, positive, wonderful examples!
There is a another chapter of life to learn from after they left Haines on the ferry "The Chilkat" January 1958 as they took the six of us to start their new life in Juneau, Alaska; this will be left for another time.*

Now may God bless us all to learn from their courageous, stalwart and positive lives as they moved forward in very challenging circumstances, and may we be blessed to live up to our potential as they did and would also desire us to do. May we remember their strengths and build upon them, and the wonderful memories of them we have herein received, along with the many other memories we each individually may have had with them! This has been my purpose and remains my hope!   -With love, Ruth-

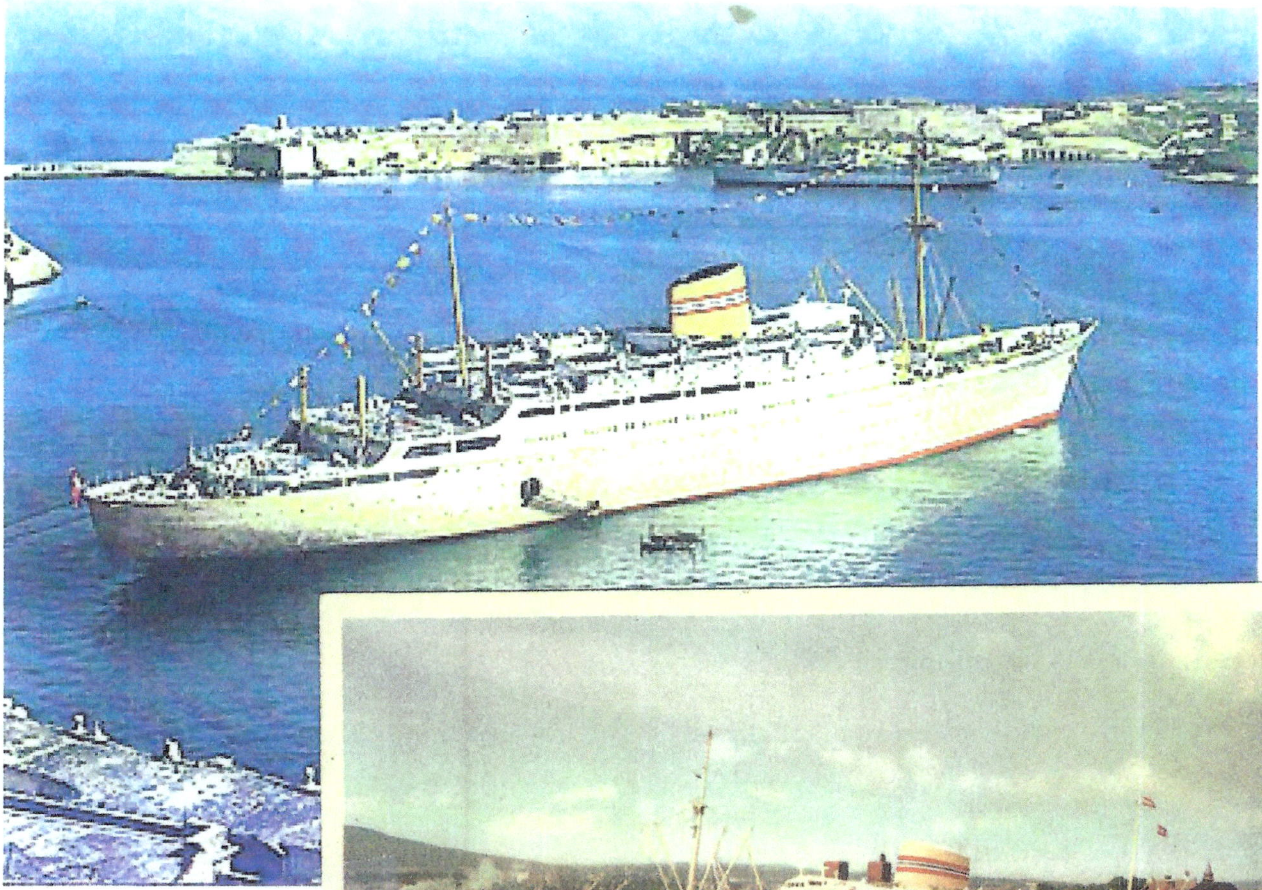

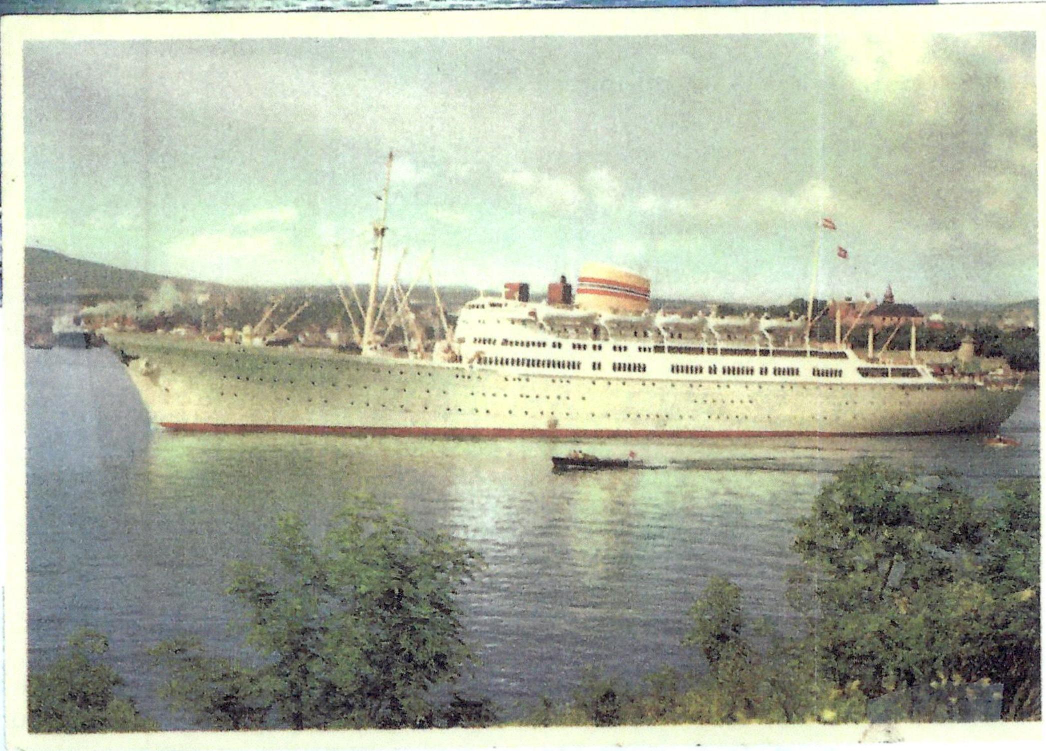

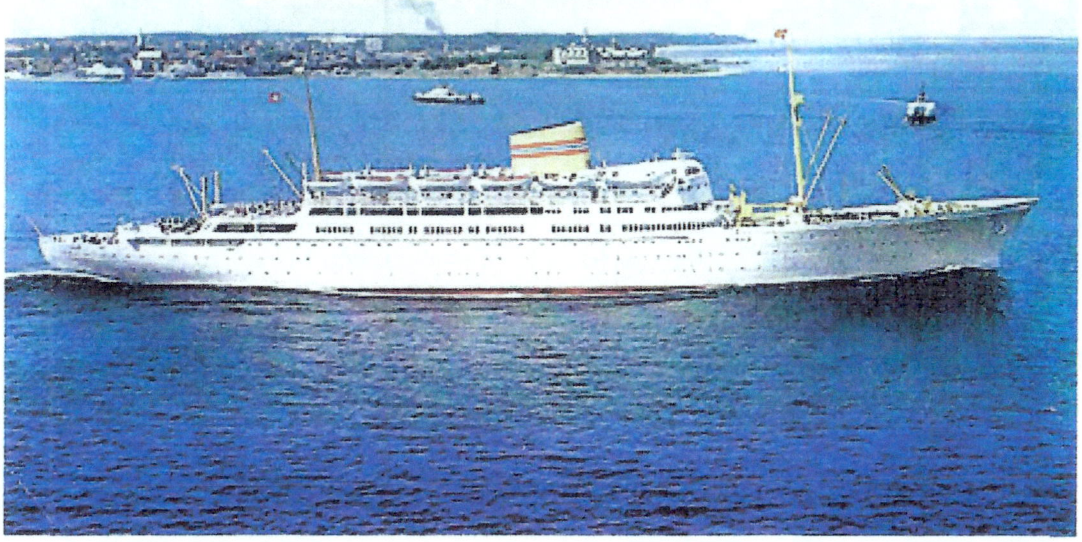

A CELEBRATION OF LIFE
Happy Birthday (90) years old
Ida Maria Tagg Noreen
Born March 3, 1918 in Funasdalen, Sweden
Residing at the Pioneer Home in Juneau, Alaska

- Ida Maria Tagg was born on March 3rd 1918 in Hallan, Funasdalen, Sweden; the snow would still be on the ground at this time of the year up in her mountain village but spring would be just around the corner. This area of Sweden is located in the middle of the country up in the mountains 18 miles from the border of Norway. She is a full-blooded Swede going back many generations. (Ida 5 year's old and pet goat Quilka) (Ida 13 years old) She is very proud of her humble beginnings and she has always had a deep commitment to and love for her father Jonas Jonsson Tagg and her mother Karin Ingeborg Jonsson Tagg. Her father died when she was only 7 years old, but Ida had fond memories of sitting on his lap and she remembered his loving nature. Ida was the youngest of 10 children that her sweet little mamma had given birth to; her siblings were all grown or much older, so she and her mother had lived alone in their very humble circumstances for many years. She remembers how her siblings would sometimes come to visit bringing good food to share. Ida had many responsibilities as a child at home; she helped her mother with many things such as bringing in water and wood for keeping the house warm and for cooking on the wood burning stove. They used lanterns for light and of course the use of the outhouse in all kinds of weather.

(Ida and her mamma Karin Tagg) It was 5 kilometers to school each morning and than 5 more to get home again in the afternoon. Winters sometimes had 2 to 3 meters of snow and the temperature always dipped below freezing as the winter progressed, but there were also beautiful warm sunny summer's days to enjoy. She would walk to school when there was no snow, but as the winter with its harsh weather would set in she would use her skis to travel back and forth. She always said that it was a healthy lifestyle and she believed that hard work built character and this was the way Ida lived her whole life through. Her mother had taught her that life could sometimes be challenging, but with Gods help there would always be a way, she never would shrug away from any labor, nothing has ever been to difficult for Ida.

- It was by example that her mother taught her to trust in the Lord and to always keep Him close by, as He was needed constantly by both in their humble lives. She truly trusted in the divine grace and peace that they felt surrounding them continually.

Her sister Stina was a big help, she sewed all of Ida's clothes until the day she left for Alaska, and Stina also sewed clothing for her children after they were born, as many pictures taken will indicate matching outfits for Karin and Ruth. Ida would spend many summers in Norway at her sister's house in her youth, and then would come home with new clothes, just in time for school.

- Ida met Gote Noren in the year 1937 when he was working on a road crew that was to improve the road from Sweden into Norway; the road came right through the mountain area where Ida lived. She and Gote always felt it was love at first sigh and became engaged in 1939 and were married August 30th 1941. Ida was 21 years old and Gote was 35, he was born Oct. 10th 1903 and there was a 14 year difference in their ages, but it never made a difference because of his youthful nature and their great love for one another.

- Ida used to say that her mother liked him just as much as she did; for he was very kind and helpful to her mother, so he was accepted and loved by her immediately.

-They welcomed their first family member in Dec.1942 with the birth of their first daughter, they named her Karin Sylvia Maria, and the second daughter was born in March 1944 they named her Ruth Inger Johanna. The couple had a good life as they worked together and as they built a home and enjoyed family life. Ida was home with the children while Gote worked many hard hours on road construction and later in forest labor.

-They built their small home close to Ida's mom in Hallan, Funasdalen. They were such a wonderful help for her mom in all ways. Five years passed and another child was born in Sept.1949, he was named Sune Gote, and what fun it was for Ida and Gote to have a little boy along with the girls. The sisters also enjoyed having a brother. The summers were filled with work, getting ready for the long cold winter months ahead. Berries were picked and bottled; the woodshed had to be full of cut wood, in order to last and to stay warm and cook throughout the long winter months that lay ahead. Pappa Gote and Mamma Ida both worked diligently and taught the children to help and do as much as they were capable of. Whether they were ready or not the winter snow soon would blow and it was warm and cozy in their little home that mamma Ida had fixed up as comfortable as she could. Ida did not have running water so there was a lot of work in getting drinking water, cooking, dishes, tub baths and washing clothes. And of course there was the outhouse no matter what the season or weather condition; it was always a cold experience in any weather.

- Mamma Ida would always say that her mother had taught her everything she knew, and she always said the mountain life was hard, but was a good life to live as she remembers they were all healthy for the most part. We had mattresses filled with straw to sleep on with home woven rugs and a blanket on top, but it was wonderful, fresh and healthy. Mamma Ida's home was always orderly and clean and had a wonderful spirit in it as we the children grew up.

- In 1952 Ida's brother, Karl Emanuel Tagg who had immigrated to America approximately 30 years earlier and had ended up in Alaska, came home to Sweden to visit his mother and his siblings. What a wonderful time this was for everyone, all of Ida's siblings came home to spend time together with their mom Karin Tagg, they came from Norway and Sweden and their brother Karl who had been away for such a long time came from Alaska, all children came home to Funasdalen, for this big reunion. What a wonderful fun time this was for all the siblings and words can not explain the happiness their little mother felt at having her children together. To have all living children home and around her for a short time was a thing she had only dreamed of. (Family picture taken 1954) What a joyous time this was for everyone.

-But even as they had this wonderful time together their sweet little mamma dreaded the parting, for this also began a great sadness for her as two more of her children would soon head for Alaska. She could be heard as she sat quietly talking to herself, thinking "Alaska, Alaska it takes my children from me". As would soon become reality to Ida and her mamma, was a pain of sadness and loneliness that would never completely go away.

-As they all sat and listen to their brother Karl, he would tell the stories of the wild and untamed wilderness of Alaska, the fishing of salmon, the eagles soaring overhead and how bears could be seen walking in their yards. At that time something within, a very strong thought seemed to form in both Gote and Ida minds to try this adventure, "the American dream", as Ida's brother Karl put it, for he encouraged all his siblings to come to Alaska, to this untamed wilderness and try the "American dream". He added "you can be a millionaire in America, if you just have the drive" and Gote was a strong minded man and he believed he could make a good attempt.

- Ida's brother Kristian Ingemar Tagg just older than Ida, decided to immigrate in the year of 1954. Ida and Gote with their family were to leave in the summer of 1955, but Ida found that she was expecting another baby so they must postpone their departure date for one more year. Everyone in the family had to be old enough to have all their shots and check up before they were allowed to enter the U.S. It was a very exiting time for the whole family as another baby brother joined the family Sept. 1955; he was given the name Karl Ritz Gunnar, Grandma Tagg loved to hold him and rock him as he lay cradled in her long skirt. We can still hear her humming her sweet songs.

- Now Gote and Ida started in earnest to ready the family for their immigration to Alaska. Getting two sponsors in the new land was first on the list, a trip to Stockholm for health checks and shots and to get the family passport, and the selling of the house. An auctioning had to be held of all the dear things that Mamma Ida had in her little home, booking passage on the streamliner the "Oslo Fjord" from Oslo Norway and airline tickets from New York to little far off Haines Alaska, and much more.

- The route was to take the family from Funasdalen Sweden to Norway via Oslo, then New York, Chicago, Seattle and Juneau in route to Haines Alaska.

- It was a very busy year leading up to the departure date as the 6 Noren's left their little mountain village on that sunny morning of June 17th 1956. For Grandma Tagg the dreaded day had arrived. On that morning Ida's dear little mother stood so old and so crocked, but so very brave, on the porch of Ida's brother Per's home, ready to see her darling daughter whom she loved so much and her entire family finally leave her, to move so very far away yes, Alaska had laid claim to one more of her children.

(This particular picture was taken outside her own home in 1955)

-Ida writes in her memories about her deep feelings and sense of inexpressible sadness and guilt, and the pain her mother must have felt as she bids her sweet little mother who she loved so dearly goodbye, knowing she would probably never see her again, and in reality, she never did.

-The only comfort was that she had a brother there and two sisters, Ingeborg approximately 70 miles away and Stina across the border one days drive into Norway.

-But Ida's thoughts were now that she had never in 38 years left her mother or even been far away from her; she was always there close by, to help her and support her and to receive the same in return. She was the youngest child of her mothers 10 children, and now she would not be there together with her any more at all. "How could we have decided to leave to go so far away?" These are her thoughts as she leaves her home, homeland, mother, and her all, everything she has ever known and worked so hard for and counted on.

- But there seems to be something within both Gote and Ida that pulls them and moves them to want to try this adventure even though the pain, no, it was even more than that, it seems they must try this experience to make this move, they did not fully know why, they simply had to try it, even though it seemed improbable with so much responsibly, not much money, not knowing the language and with 4 young children. However they did give it a lot of thought and prayer. They determined if it simply doesn't work out once we get there, we can come back to Sweden, go to Uppsala, as Gote's brother Karl Theodor has pleaded with them to do and promised them a piece of property there next to the train station, he was hoping they would move there instead of Alaska. But Gote wasn't about to take anything for nothing, so this made Gote even more determined to be successful in his move, in this new venture, in the new land.

- As Ida's brother said "you can be a millionaire in America, if you just have the drive". Gote is 50 years old at this time, maybe they are a little old to start over? But they simply feel they must try this experience, the feeling burns deeply within their whole being, and they are ready for this move.

- So they begin to make plans and preparations and thinking things out, how can we make this dream come true? Little by little the thoughts and plans all came into light and one by one everything was accomplished. They sold their mountain home. They had a huge auction and all personal items accept for a few things that fit into two suitcases and a hat box, and a large wooden box that Gote built, that was all they could bring for their entire family, and everything else had to be sold.

- There were 6 members in their family as they left, Gote 53, Ida 38, Karin 13, Ruth 12, Sune 7 years old and Gunnar 9 months. Grandma Tagg was now in her 83 year, she had lived with Ida and her family the previous winter, It was a wonderful winter being together and the closeness they had this winter was a wonderful experience for all.

- The next winter Ida's mamma would go to an old folk's home close to where her daughter Ingeborg lives. She died 3 years after Ida left for America at age 86. Ida grieved long and hard, over her mother's death and over leaving her dear mother so late in her life. But Ida's mother had told her as she left and these words rang clearly in her ears then and thereafter "the road that God places before you, that is the road that you must travel". This has since then given Ida courage and lifted the pain of guilt and sadness to a degree. Ida always said that her mother had given her by example to never doubt, but to have courage, go forward in faith as she put her trust in God.

-The morning of departure arrives, a taxi cab pulled up, it was to take the Noren family from Sweden to Oslo, Norway. Everything was put into the cab; except for the large wooden box, it was tied firmly to the top of the cab. Well wishes hugs and kisses were given; Ida took a long hair from her mothers head and wrapped it around a button on her coat as she slipped into the taxi cab. Thereby she took the last farewell of her beloved mother and also farewell to her homeland Sweden and all she had known and held dear. (The family passport picture, taken 1956)

- The cab quickly moved out of their sight and we could no longer see Grandma Tagg standing on the porch. We can only imagine the slow lonely walk, down across the field to her home, to the emptiness that awaited her there and would never go away.
- Sweden was soon a past tense as we soon arrived in Roros, Norway in time to have lunch with Ida's brother Johan, who had driven from Trondheim Norway to see us once more, and to wish us well on our adventure. We had a nice lunch together and then back into the taxi cab and on to Oslo, where we overnighter in a hotel that first night.
- Ida and Gote were worried all night long about the big box that was tied to the top of the cab, that someone would disturb it, but morning came and all was well.
- That next day was a big day; we were now going to the harbor where the "Oslo Fjord" was docked, there to check in for our voyage to cross the Atlantic Ocean to the new world, New York, USA. What a festive time it was as we left the dock we looked down on an orchestra playing below and we were given streamers to throw as we pulled away from the dock leaving Scandinavia our home, maybe forever?
- There were some rough waters as we crossed the Atlantic Ocean, many of us were sea sick, but in a few days we were passing the statue of liberty on a stormy night as we came into New York harbor, soon docking at the pier in New York City. The new day brought sunshine, we walked down the long ramp

into a large warehouse and there our big box was waiting for us; our belongings must be opened and looked though by customs agents. Another taxi cab was ordered and it took the Noren family on to the airport for the continuation of their journey. When the family arrived in Juneau, Alaska Dr. Rude meets us, he spoke Norwegian and this was a welcome sound, as no one in our family could understand or speaks English, he helped us to the right plane and later that same day June 29th we arrived in Haines.
- Haines Alaska, where in the world is this from Funasdalen Sweden? If you go completely around to the other side of the world, which our family had just done, you have two locations totally unknown to most people, "where in the world is either of these locations?" for there we were in Sweden, but now here we are in Alaska. Now landing on a dirt runway in an unknown part of the world, we were flying in a sea plane called a "goose" with just enough seats for our family. Ida's brothers Karl and Kristian meets our family at the dirt runway full of old beer bottles and garbage, on a very blustery day. Wow, we are finally here! But where is here? What will we find? What will life be like here? We don't speak English! How ever will we make it? Will we find work and be able to make a living, to care for our children? All these thoughts and questions and many other zooms through Gote and Ida's minds, and become their conversations as they begin their new life, as it spreads before them one day at the time.
- Within a few weeks they have fixed up an old shack in the back yard at Karl and Alice's house as best they could, this would be where their family would stay that first winter. Gote finds some small carpentry jobs through Karl Tagg and brings in enough money to get some food on the shelves. Ida starts doing some odd jobs, cleaning and ironing for people in their homes to help with income. Neither of them speaks any English nor do their children.
- Gote also begins another new adventure, he leases a fishing spot, he builds a 21 ft long skiff and buys an old net from Karl and gets a fishing permit for set nets, he then builds a fishing cabin with several bunks for sleeping and in September he starts set net fishing on the other side of Pyramid Island located on the back road to the cannery from Haines. (Gote's fishing cabin x marks the spot, cannery C, Karl's house O, Port Chilcoot house H)
- Gote fished only for two weeks when the fishing season ends for that year, but he was able to bring in 300 dollars, enough to buy food with after all the expenditures, which took nearly all extra money that they had brought with and now he was ready for next years fishing season. Everything is so new and different, but the challenge is exciting, and they determine that they will endeavor to make this new experience successful. It is a beautiful, exciting place just as Karl told us it would be, and Gote and Ida were not quitters but truly hard workers and they knew now that they would make it.

(In the pictures below (1) Ida is hanging a seal skin up to dry on the cabin wall after skinning the seal (2) Ida is in the fishing boat Gote built, showing the big fish caught)

Gote, he continues working on odd jobs that winter but even so runs out of money and must barrows 1200 dollars from the Lindquist's they were one of the families who sponsored our family in coming to America. This debt was re-paid in full by that next fall; both Ida and Gote were honest, true and steadfast, doing to others as they expected others to do to them, in all their dealings this was their way. This took the Noren family through the first winter in Alaska.

- It was an extremely harsh winter in 1956- 57, and it was so very cold, a wood burning stove had to be bought in order for the family not to freeze and to stay healthy with the very thin walls where they lived. Ida recalls how she and Gote worried greatly about the children's health, they agreed "let it cost whatever it will, we must have a worm place for the kids".

- Because of the extremely cold winter, in an extremely poor living circumstance, our bedding would freeze to the walls during the night, the water froze in the toilet, and the ice was thick on the window. Ida would blow on the window to make a little hole to look out of; the mattresses were set by the wood stove during the day so it would be dried for the next night. Ida recalls "the walls were paper thin in the one room shack that we lived in". They also bought wool army blankets from the canary, this was a big help for warmth. That Sept. the kids started school and our life began to unfold in the new world, so far from everything that was familiar to all of us.

- It was indeed a very difficult first winter in the USA but through endurance and many prayers spring did come. Soon we were able to understand more and we were also able to be understood somewhat ourselves as we spoke. Shopping at the market and learning the names of things and pronouncing them correctly, was surely a challenge.

- But the time the next spring of 1957 came, our family moved over to Port Chilcoot into one of the old Army houses. Gote struck a deal with Carl Heinmiller, he would work on the houses for a place to live for his family. A Swedish family that owned the Halsingland Hotel, which was made into a hotel from the old army housing, gave us old beds and bedding which was a true blessing for our family.

- Gote and Ida continued to work odd jobs and then in the fall Gote started set net fishing again, using the wooden boat that he had built, living during the week in the small cabin he had built on the other side of Pyramid Island. The kids also went along at times and learned how to clean and fix the holes in the nets. The wind was fierce at times and the holes in the nets were big as the seals would rip the fish out of them.

- It was all hard work, Ida also continued in helping with the fishing and doing cleaning jobs on the side. In December of 1957 Karl, Ida's brother died suddenly. Gote and Ida wondered what to do, and decided at that time to move to Juneau for better work opportunities during the winter months. Gote continued to fish during the fishing season. In the 4th year in America he started leasing a gillnet boat from the Haines cannery and did that for some years while the both of them were saving money to buy a fishing boat of their own. A gillnet boat was bought after a few years and the boat was named the "Ida Maria" (Gote on the boat in Douglas harbor) Gote and Ida soon moved into the Cedar Park low-cost housing. They bought old homes and Gote fixed them up and sold them, Ida was by his side all along the way, fixing, holding, sweeping, and she did all the inside painting and some of the outside too. Ida also brought in money by doing house work for many residents in Juneau, including the territorial Governor Steppovich at the mansion, where the girls also babysat on occasion.

- In October of 1964 Ida and Gote decided that their lives were now going to be lived in America, and that this was where they truly wanted to stay. So they went to court and became U.S. citizens, this was indeed a happy day for them, Sune and Gunnar were under 16 years of age so they also became citizens with their parents. Karin and Ruth became citizens a few years later. Pappa Gote changed the spelling of his name at this time to Karl Gothe Noreen, and was thereafter known by the name of Karl.

- All of us continued to work; the children continued their education in our local schools. The girls started dating two wonderful young men and soon got married and moved to their own homes and started families. As the years passed by, the English language started to come a little bit easier for them, and Karl and Ida were always able to care for their own needs and to also help their children. Over the years the boys also married and had families. Karl and Ida always looked ahead, being positive under all circumstances for they really had a great deal of positive energy and the ability for looking at the bright side and never being afraid of a challenge, for there were many of those that proved them as the years continued by, nor were they afraid of long days with hard work but continued faithfully. Karl and Ida loved each another and worked well together, both loved their children with all their souls.

- Some small amounts of money began to be taken from each paycheck and saved away for a rainy day, and there were plenty of them. But that amount grew as the years passed and never did they have to depend on anyone else, to barrow money again, but was able to stand on their own. This was very pleasing for our mother and father, for they were finally truly independent, in their new land. And they had been honest and steadfast their entire lives. They did take out loans over the years to improve their circumstances such as for building. They bought old homes and fixed them up, moved into them and then would sell them; he also built a home from scratch and sold that. As the years passed Ida save enough money to go back to Sweden seven times. There to visit her sisters and relatives, she had only one regret, which was that she was not able to go back while her mother was still alive. This was a constant sadness in her life; she always came back to the thought that she had left her mother when she had needed her the most, but her mother had taught her to follow the road God puts before her, and to also have a perfect love and trust in Him and this would see Ida and her mom both through. This continued to be of great comfort to Ida in her life.

- Karl continued to do gill net fishing on his boat the "Ida Maria" and fixing the nets on his days off along with other odd jobs until his back wore out at about 78 years old. They lived together at 313 'C' street in Douglas Alaska for many years. They both loved working in their home, yard and garden area. Gote loved fixing and making improvements in his home and helping his children with building projects too. He fixed his nets and loved to chop wood outside of their home in Douglas, you could here the wood crackle in the wood stove inside their home as you entered on a cold day.
-The whole family would gather together every Christmas Eve to enjoy the warmth and love that was always present in their home, to sing, laugh and share good conversation, but even more than that, we shared the most wonderful meal of the year. Ida would bake and prepare for weeks, to be ready for the celebration and the get together of all her children and their families; everyone would bring something to add to the table. One could hear Swedish Christmas music playing. We would also exchange gifts. This was a truly joyous time for Gote, Ida and all family members, as all have found memories of these days gone by. (Karl and Ida aprox. 1984)

- Mamma Ida worked for the school district for 14 years as a custodian and retired with a sufficient retirement for their daily needs along with their social security checks and Alaska money that seniors received. With these incomes they were able to live comfortably, while still never touching their savings except to help their children. Ida also had earned health insurance for both Gote and herself which became very important as their bodies started to wear out and both began to experience acute body aches and back pains for the rest of their days.

- Ida continued to do service in her community, volunteering and helping the needy, visiting the old and being a good friend to all. She was an inspiration to everyone she came in contact with her entire life, lifting the downtrodden with laughter and song and good conversation. Ida loved to play the guitar and sing. One could find her singing and playing at holidays and any time friends would come to visit. Ida loved life!

- Karl lived at "St. Ann's nursing home" in Juneau Alaska for the last 4 years of his life. Ida would be found there at the nursing home twice each, every day, helping him with his meals. They celebrated their 50th wedding anniversary together August 30th 1991, with their children and grandchildren surrounding them.

- Karl Gothe Noreen was born October 10th 1903 and died January 7th 1993 in his 89th year. He was a kind, loving, gentle husband, father and grandfather whose love and example we will always feel and remember. They showed their love and example in so many different ways to all of us. They were completely fair in all dealings with all of their children, Karin, Ruth, Sune and Gunnar and of course their in-law children and their grandchildren and great-great grandchildren, we were all recipients of their love, strength of duty and their impeccable integrity, honesty and goodness.

(Son's Gunnar and Sune)

- Ida lived alone for many years. On September 12th 2002 she moved out from her beloved home in Douglas that her husband had built for her, and moved into the "Pioneer Home" in Juneau Alaska where she still resides to this day.
- Thank you to Karin for taking care of mom and dad's financial life along with the paper trail each month for many years. Through the money saved, mom's care was taken care of for over four years, until her savings is now spent.
- Ida has always been a ray of sunshine to everyone she meets. She has never tired of trying to be helpful, thoughtful and kind to her fellow man. She also loved and showed thoughtfulness to the staff and residents of her new home after she moved in.
- Now that her age is great and life has slowed her down and she is not able to move around any more, we still see a ray of sunshine in her smile, when she smiles once in a while. And it gladdens our hearts☺.
- As we in her family have come to her new home twice each day to visit and help her with her meals (following her good example) and more times each day as other family members have also visited as time in their lives has allowed, we all feel that she has the greatest of care at the Pioneer Home.
- All of us in her family have learned to appreciate the watchful, wonderful loving patient and professional care and help that she has received from all her caregivers at her "Waterside home" it truly has become our mothers home, We extend our gratitude, with much love☺.
-The nursing staff has been excellent and professional and the food service wonderful. In her first few years she also enjoyed all the activities. If she herself could speak today she would thank all at the "Pioneer Home" for their thoughtful wonderful care, all of you her new loving family. Thank you from the botto of our hearts☺.

(Sept. 12th 2002 moving day, Karin, Ida, Tony and Ruth)

(Mamma Ida at Christmas 2007)

--To you our dear Mamma and Grandma, we all wish you "A Very Happy Birthday, 90 Years Old"
-                --March 3rd 2008--   -
--" Ja ma du leva, Ja ma du leva ,Ja ma du leva uti hundrade ar, och nar du har levat, ja da skall du leva, ja da skal du leva uti hundrade ar"
----- "Vi alskar dig, var kara mamma"-----

With gratitude to the Pioneer Home and a great love for our mother,
Karin, Ruth, Sune and Gunnar ☺

OBITUARY

Tack för allt far
Du lämnar mig
Bara minnen kvar

- Thank you father for everything you have left me.
- Only memories left.

Ida's note

Karl Gote Noreen

Services for Karl Gote Noreen are set for 2 p.m. Tuesday at the Church of Jesus Christ of Latter-day Saints.

Noreen, 89, died Jan. 7 in Juneau. He was born Oct. 10, 1903, in Islingsby, Borlange, Sweden.

Noreen began working at the age of 12. Later, he served in the Swedish Army during World War II. Noreen worked as a foreman during construction of the East Coast railroad in Sweden and was also a logger and carpenter.

On Aug. 31, 1941, he married Ida Tagg in Funasdalen, Sweden.

In 1956, the couple and their four children immigrated to Haines. Two years later, they moved to Juneau. Noreen built boats and several homes and worked as a commercial fisherman for 20 years.

He was self-educated and an avid reader, his family wrote. In spite of the fact that he was 53 and spoke only Swedish when he came to the United States, Noreen managed to support his family and live comfortably. He used to say, "If I had come to America as a young man I would have been a millionaire."

Noreen was devoted to his family and enjoyed history, politics, sports "and a walk on a beautiful spring day," his family wrote. He was a member of the Pioneers of Alaska and the Moose Lodge.

Noreen leaves his wife of 51 years, Ida, of Douglas; his children, Karin Petaja, Ruth Cunningham and Gunnar Noreen, all of Juneau, and Sune Noreen of Jonesport, Maine; his brother, Karl-Ivar Noreen of Uppsala, Sweden; his grandchildren, Bridget, Brenda, Billy and Brandon Petaja, Troy, Travis, Trent, Tyron and Tony Cunningham, Bernadine Kirkpatrick, Kristine Washburn, Rose, Lisa, Sven and Liv Noreen; his great-grandchildren, Hans Petaja, Savana and Zakary Kirkpatrick, Chance, Kalob and Dylan Cunningham; as well as sons- and daughters-in-law, friends and relatives around the world.

Pallbearers are Gunnar and Sven Noreen; Billy and Brandon Petaja and Troy and Travis Cunningham. Honorary pallbearers are William Petaja, Tyron Cunningham, Kerry Kirkpatrick and Ben Washburn.

The family suggests memorial contributions be sent in Noreen's name to St. Ann's Nursing Home, 415 Sixth St., Juneau 99801, "where he resided in a loving atmosphere for 2½ years."

Obituaries

Ida Maria Noreen

Longtime Douglas resident Ida Maria Noreen died March 15, 2010, in her home at the Juneau Pioneer Home where she ha resided for the past seven-plus years. She was surrounded by her family and the caregivers who have given her loving care during her long decline. She was 92.

Born March 3, 1918, in Funasdalen, Sweden, she and her husband Karl Gothe adn four children, Karin, Ruth, Sune and Gunnar, immigrated to Alaska in June 1956.

They settled in Haines for less than two years where her brother Karl Tagg lived, there she and her husband built a small boat and did set net fishing off the beach for about three seasons as they began to learn the way of life in Alaska and picked up a few new English words each day.

They moved to Juneau for more work opportunities in 1958. She began and continued work in homes and at the Governor's Mansion, cleaning, catering and ironing, the kind of work she was able to do with her limited English. She also worked in a daycare and thereafter worked as a custodian in a couple of the schools, retiring from the Juneau School District.

She was a positive, happy and service-minded person who received certificates for her service, even at the Juneau Pioneers Home.

"She was always visiting and caring for the sick and needy, singing and playing her guitar and gladdening the heart," her family said. "She loved life and always looked forward to the new day, whatever the challenge might be. She loved to be out in her yard, where things were growing, planting and weeding and enjoying God's creations."

She loved to fix up, paint and beautify her small home in Douglas, which she and her husband had strived to build together. She would often stay up after getting off work at midnight to do housework and bake goodies.

"It seemed she never tired," her family said.

Her family remembers happy gatherings at her home, holidays and parties with friends and family, where many home-cooked meals and baked goodies from her days in Sweden were served.

"I learned everything from my Mamma's good example," she always said.

She was preceded in death by her husband of 50 years, Karl Gothe Noreen; and great-grandson, William Jr. Petaja.

She is survived by her daughters, Karin Petaja and husband, Willie, and Ruth Cunningham and husband, Dennis; sons, Sune Noreen and wife, Patricia, and Gunnar Noreen and wife, Mary Kathryn; grandchildren, Bridget, Brenda, Billy and Brandon Petaja, Tyron, Tony, Troy, Travis and Trent Cunningham, Bernadine Kirkpatrick, Kristine Washburn, Rosa and Bragita Noreen, and Sven, Liv, Matthew, Kathryn and Julia Noreen; great-grandchildren, Hans, Kristian and Adele Petaja, Chance, Kalob, Dylan, Levi, Ciarra, Sara, Elana, Hailee, Joshua and Rosanna Cunningham, Savana Barzee, Zakay and Hunter Kirkpatrick, Samantha, Anya, Ammon and Brigham Washburn, and Keelan, Caden, Kajson and Carson, Audrey and Jordan Cunningham.

A memorial service will be held at 2 p.m. Friday, March 19, at the Juneau Pioneers Home.

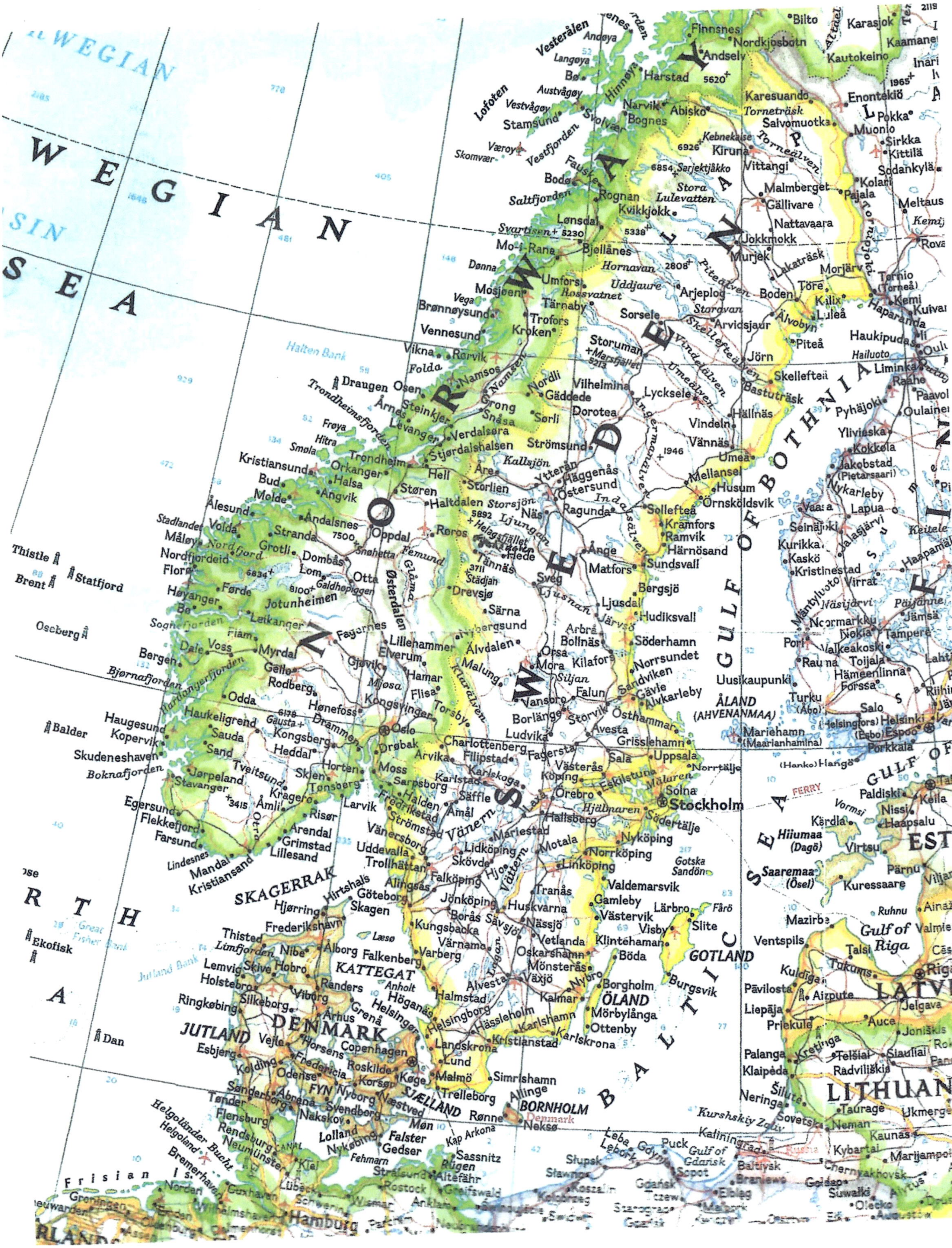

Passasjer Liste

"An incredible journey of remarkable proportion of a courageous couple, from the top of the mountains of Norrland Sweden, to the untamed shores of South East Alaska."

TURIST KLASSE

Norén, Gøte, herr
Norén, Ida, fru
Norén, Karin, frk.
Norén, Ruth, frk.
Norén, Sune, herr
Norén, Karl, herr

Funäsdalen, Sverige

N·A·L Den norske Amerikalinje

Part 1

'An Incredible Journy'

The life of Grand Parents Karl and Ida Noreen

Made in the USA
Columbia, SC
11 September 2024